P9-DXI-005

The Language of Politics in America

NON-RETURNABLE

The Language
of Politics
in America

*Shaping Political Consciousness
from McKinley to Reagan*

David Green

Cornell University Press

Ithaca and London

A good semantic discipline gives the power to separate mental machinery from tangible events; makes us conscious of abstracting; prevents us from peopling the universe with nonexistent things. It does not dispense with poetry, fiction, fantasy, imagination, ideas, intellectual emotions. It checks us from acting *as if* fantasies were real events worth fighting and dying for. It checks a kind of dangerous hypnotism, abnormal reversals of nerve currents, mental states approaching insanity.

STUART CHASE, 1938

Copyright © 1987 by Cornell University

All rights reserved. Except for brief quotations in a review, this book, or parts thereof, must not be reproduced in any form without permission in writing from the publisher. For information, address Cornell University Press, 124 Roberts Place, Ithaca, New York 14850.

First published 1987 by Cornell University Press.
First printing, Cornell Paperbacks, 1992.

International Standard Book Number 0-8014-2029-6 (cloth)
International Standard Book Number 0-8014-8054-x (paper)
Library of Congress Catalog Card Number 91-46982
Printed in the United States of America
Librarians: Library of Congress cataloging information appears on the last page of the book.

⊗ The paper in this book meets the minimum requirements of the American National Standard for Information Sciences—Permanence of Paper for Printed Library Materials, ANSI Z39.48-1984.

For Shoshana
Joy of my life

Contents

Preface

The masquerade is over; it's time to . . . use the dreaded L-word; to say the policies of our opposition . . . are liberal, liberal, liberal."
—Ronald Reagan, 1988

When President Reagan spoke these words to a cheering 1988 Republican national convention, he accomplished two things. First, he set the tone for the entire election campaign, brilliantly focusing attention on the opposition's record rather than his own. Second, he demonstrated the enormous power of language in the political arena. From the moment his speech ended, the most important strategic question of the campaign was how the Democratic nominee, Michael Dukakis, would respond to Reagan's attack.

Many observers have noted the weakness of the Republican position on economic issues that year. George Bush, Reagan's anointed successor and Republican party candidate, carefully avoided discussing such matters as the ballooning national debt, eight years of growing budget deficits, regressive taxation, and the alarming rate at which foreigners were buying up American commercial real estate and manufacturing industries. Faithfully following the strategy set out by Reagan himself, Bush put his energies into tarring Dukakis and the Democrats with the "dreaded L-word."

In the first televised debate between the candidates, Bush went so far as to utter the grammatically baffling sentence, "The liberals don't like it when I talk about liberal." At the same time, Bush brilliantly finessed potentially embarrassing economic issues by focusing instead on the popular theme of holding the line on taxes. "Read my lips," he told a campaign audience, then carefully mouthed the words, "No new taxes."

Unfortunately for the Democrats, Dukakis failed either to spotlight Republican vulnerability on economic matters or to turn back the

rhetorical assault. Apparently believing the "L-word" ploy to be un-
answerable, Dukakis spent most of the campaign running away from
the liberal label, thereby legitimizing and increasing the effectiveness of the Republican attack. Not until the very end of October, and
then only under the prodding of several advisers, did he declare
himself "a liberal in the tradition of Franklin Roosevelt and Harry
Truman and John Kennedy." By that time, the damage had long
since been done.

As Dukakis failed to counter the "L-word" attack, so too did he fail
to respond effectively to Bush's "read my lips" gambit. Analyst Kevin
Phillips has noted the extent to which Republican strategists were
aware of their own vulnerability on economic issues. He has likewise
shown that at least some Democrats recognized the value of attacking
the "pro-rich" policies of the preceding eight years. Dukakis, however, was no more forthcoming in this regard. Fearing to alienate his
own corporate contributors, he was as reluctant to criticize the Reagan-Bush economic record as to take up the "L-word" challenge.

Republican strategists were amazed and delighted at Dukakis' failure. Despite the double-barreled weakness of the Dukakis campaign,
however, Bush's margin of victory was the narrowest of any Republican candidate in a straight two-party contest in eighty years (see
Kevin Phillips, *The Politics of Rich and Poor* [New York: Harper-
Collins Publishers, 1991], pp. 30–31, 215).

The rhetoric of the 1988 campaign raises several issues. First and
most obvious is the question of how important language really is in
determining electoral outcomes. The "L-word" and "read my lips"
ploys were much remarked on at the time, but that does not prove
they made a significant difference. Demographic analysis has shown
that a shift of barely half a million votes in eleven states would have
given Dukakis the victory. Yet one cannot therefore assume that a
change in rhetorical strategy on his part would have done the trick.
Conversely, neither can one assume that the Reagan-Bush approach
was successful in convincing half a million strategically located Democrats and independents to cross the line and vote Republican (Phillips, 215).

No existing research procedures can provide absolute mathemati-
cal certainty in such matters. There is no easy way of quantifying the
effect of words upon voters. But a second and equally important
question arises: If there is no precise way to measure the political

effects of language, why do politicians put so much care and energy into choosing their words?

Here the evidence is abundant. They do so because they *believe* in the power of words. Dukakis' flight from the "L-word" is but one small example. Anyone who has done research in the presidential libraries has likely had the experience of going through eight, ten, a dozen or more drafts of key speeches, looking for both the obvious and subtle differences from one draft to the next. The same basic text may go through all sorts of embellishments, alterations, or deletions, depending on whether it is to be delivered in Peoria, Dallas, or New York. For example, a file in the Harry S. Truman Library in Independence, Missouri, contains two drafts of the same 1948 campaign speech, to be delivered by the president in Los Angeles and Indiana, respectively (Presidential Secretary's File, Harry S. Truman Papers). In the Los Angeles draft the word "liberal" is highlighted; in the Indian draft it is carefully deleted.

This rasies a third question. Is the focus on language merely quadrennial, occurring only in presidential election years, or is it continuous? Here the evidence not only is compelling but also opens a far broader vista. Manuscript libraries from the Hoover Institution in California to the Library of Congress in Washington are replete with carefully drafted and redrafted speeches, press releases, and other documents from the files of presidents, governors, legislators, and journalists. These documents bear as many dates as there are in the calendar and show clearly that the preoccupation with language is ongoing.

Tracing the evolution of political vocabulary through such documents allows a much broader understanding of American politics itself. A key theme of this book is the way in which the evolution of language both reflects and influences the evolution of political institutions. The 1988 campaign provides an excellent example.

Americans who came of age in the 1980s are unlikely to remember a time when the "L-word" was anything *other* than a pejorative. Their grandparents, however, will recall the liberal label as a treasured self-designation of Franklin Roosevelt in the 1930s and even of Herbert Hoover in the 1920s. What significance can we attach to the fact that the preeminent self-designation of the 1920s and 1930s became the preeminent pejorative of the 1980s?

During the latter decade it became fashionable to talk about a "retreat from liberalism." One easy interpretation is that the Reagan-Bush use of the "L-word" simply reflected that "retreat" and turned it into useful political capital. Such an interpretation, however, ignores a key historical fact from the earlier era. Because of the Depression, Hoover's vulnerability as a self-styled liberal was far greater than that of Bush's opposition. Yet Roosevelt did not denigrate Hoover's label; on the contrary, he seized it and appropriated it for his own purposes (see Chapters 4 and 5). Why in 1988 did not Reagan and Bush do the same?

The answer spotlights a major development in American political history. The transformation of the liberal label from self-designation to pejorative reflects nothing less than a shift in American politics from positive to negative self-definition. Whatever the stresses and strains of the Depression, fifty years ago most Americans still defined themselves in terms of what they were *for*. By the 1980s, most had a much clearer sense of what they were *against*. The use of the "L-word" in the 1988 campaign reflected and reinforced this trend toward negative politics. (See Chapter 8 for an analysis of the trend toward negative self-designation in American politics.)

Kevin Phillips, in *The Politics of Rich and Poor* (pp. 32–36, 56–57, 210), and Arthur Schlesinger, Jr., in *The Cycles of American History* (Boston: Houghton Mifflin, 1986), have argued—from different perspectives—for a cyclical view of American history. Each has suggested that the 1990s will bring a reversal of the trends of the 1980s. Viewing politics through the prism of language raises key questions in this regard. Will tomorrow's labels be negative or positive? Will they be new labels or will old ones be updated? Most important, how will they reflect and influence developments in the political arena?

There have already been some early indications of the process in motion. During the summer of 1991, Iowa senator Tom Harkin, an early aspirant to the 1992 Democratic presidential nomination, announced that what America needed was a "populist" and "progressive" leader. Both labels have histories dating back over a hundred years. Both appear to have connotations opposite to the Reagan-Bush policies. Resurrecting such labels is no guarantee of victory, nor is there a necessary correlation between what labels imply and what actions produce. Another key theme of this book is the discordancy between language and behavior.

There is no crystal ball. Historical analysis cannot guarantee accurate prediction. To suggest otherwise is to step beyond the bounds of evidence into the realm of faith. At the same time, the fact remains that politicians continue to put tremendous energy into their choice and use of words. For that reason if for no other, it is important to learn as much as possible about how language and politics have interacted in the past, so that in the future one can analyze events as they occur with greater knowledge and a broader perspective. It is in the hope of contributing to such a perspective that this book is presented.

It is a pleasure to acknowledge several intellectual debts. Once again, my greatest debt is to my teacher, mentor, and friend, Walter LaFeber of Cornell University. He has followed the evolution of the manuscript closely since its inception and has been extraordinarily helpful in reviewing and commenting on several drafts. As always, his suggestions have been insightful and incisive. He has provided constant encouragement and support through the years.

The book had its inception during my year as a Fellow at the Center for Advanced Study in the Behavioral Sciences at Stanford, 1971–1972. For their generous assistance during that year and on subsequent visits to the center, I thank O. Meredith Wilson and Preston Cutler, director emeritus and associate director emeritus, respectively, as well as the present director, Gardner Lindzey. I am also grateful to the entire staff of the center, from kitchen crew to librarians and secretarial support staff. Among the many Fellows from whose company and insight I benefited, I especially thank Lawrence Cremin, David Danelski, Alan Dershowitz, Ray Kesner, and George Lakoff. The center is a truly remarkable place to work, and I shall always have fond memories of my year there.

The Institute for Humane Studies is aptly named. Formerly located in Menlo Park, California, and now at George Mason University in Fairfax, Virginia, the institute provides an extraordinary meeting ground for Fellows of varying academic backgrounds and political pedigrees. My two terms as a Summer Fellow in 1976 and 1978 will always stand out in my mind as among the most stimulating intellectual experiences of my life. To the former executive director of the institute, Kenneth S. Templeton, and his wife, Lois, I express heartfelt thanks for their warm hospitality and good company and for infusing the atmosphere of the institute with a sense of the fun and excitement of intellectual adventure. To the current president of the institute, Leonard Liggio, I am deeply grateful for his generous contribution of time and energy and for his boundless faith in the manuscript through many years of watching, helping, and waiting. He truly embodies all that a humane scholar should. Among the many Fellows and participants in institute seminars who generously shared ideas with me, I especially thank Frank Annunziata, Bart Bernstein, Justus Doenecke, and William Marina.

I also acknowledge three special debts to colleagues over the years: Ronald Radosh of the City University of New York shared ideas and research materials with me and read the entire manuscript with great sensitivity and care. His suggestions have been invaluable. Lloyd Gardner of Rutgers challenged me on several important points and thereby forced me to more than one "agonizing reappraisal" that turned out unusually fruitful. That is the kind of challenge that every historian needs. Unfortunately one acknowledgment must be posthumous. It was always a delight to talk shop with the late William Appleman Williams of Oregon State. From our first conversations about the book more than a decade ago, Bill's genial wit and insight were a source of inspiration. He will be sorely missed.

Among the many library staffs from whose assistance I benefited, I particularly thank those of the National Archives, the Library of Congress, the Herbert Hoover Presidential Library, the Franklin D. Roosevelt Library, the Harry S. Truman Library, the Dwight D. Eisenhower Library, the John F. Kennedy Library, the Lyndon B. Johnson Library, and the libraries of Cornell University, Princeton University, Stanford University, the University of Michigan, the University of Oregon.

The University of Saskatchewan graciously provided me with a sabbatical leave to work on this book during the 1977–1978 academic year, and the Canada Council granted me a supplementary Leave Fellowship during the same period. Scholars in fields other than American history have also been helpful, especially Ivo Lambi and J. Michael Hayden of the University of Saskatchewan, who read several drafts of the manuscript and made many helpful suggestions. Several close friends provided intellectual support and encouragement at critical stages of the manuscript. They include James and Nancy Duncan, Gary Hanson, Richard and Serena Laskin, William and Camille Slights, Mark Hislop, and Richard Mason. My thanks to all of them. I also wish to express my appreciation to Raúl García for editorial assistance and to Peter Agree and Marilyn Sale of Cornell University Press for their skill and care in shepherding the manuscript through the production process.

Finally, my love and appreciation to my wife, Wendy Lynn Green, for her unfailing support and encouragement. In the words of the immortal Groucho Marx, "She makes my life worth living and she understands all my jokes." The dedication is to our daughter, whose love illuminates our lives.

DAVID GREEN

Saskatoon, Saskatchewan

1

Language and the Shaping
of Political Consciousness

Political language and political power

> "When I use a word," Humpty Dumpty said, in rather a scornful tone, "it means just what I choose it to mean—neither more nor less."
>
> "The question is," said Alice, "whether you *can* make words mean so many different things."
>
> "The question is," said Humpty Dumpty, "which is to be master—that's all."
>
> Lewis Carroll, *Through the Looking-Glass*

A hundred years ago Americans did not talk about "liberals" versus "conservatives" or about "communists" versus "anticommunists." They talked about "individualists" versus "paternalists." People generally called themselves "individualists" and their opponents "paternalists." What politicians demanded, they demanded in the name of "individualism." What they opposed, they opposed because it represented "paternalism."

By the mid-1890s, the vocabulary had changed; people now tended to refer to themselves as "conservatives" and their opponents as "radicals." What political leaders demanded, they demanded in the name of "conservatism." What they opposed, they opposed because it represented "radicalism." Within a decade, however, the "good" label was "progressive," the "bad" label "reactionary." What politicians demanded, they now demanded in the name of "progressivism." What they opposed, they opposed because it represented "reaction."

American history is replete with such shifts in labels. These shifts have not always followed neat or precise patterns. Certain labels have lasted longer than others. Some have lost currency, never to regain

1

their previous levels of popularity, whereas others have lapsed for a time, then reappeared with greater popularity than before. Not all political leaders have used the same labels at the same time; conformity and diversity have existed side by side. Nonetheless, the evolution of American political vocabulary has followed a certain logic that has been central to the shaping of political consciousness and thereby the evolution of politics itself.

All language, Benjamin Lee Whorf wrote, "incorporates certain points of view and certain patterned resistances to widely divergent points of view."[1] Political language follows this rule, but does so in a special way. By its very nature, political vocabulary is unusually ambiguous and flexible. Words such as "individualist," "paternalist," "conservative," "radical," and so on serve as organizing concepts and provide people with their basic categories of thought. Yet the words themselves have no fixed, concrete definitions. They are abstractions: broad, general terms that evoke broad, general attitudes. Different people will interpret them in different ways. They may evoke different responses at different times and in different places, or they may simultaneously evoke several, mutually contradictory meanings.[2]

Political labels are image-laden, appealing as much to the emotions as to the intellect. Although they provide basic categories of rational analysis, they may simultaneously evoke responses that are neither analytical nor rational. This broader evocative power, the power to reach both mind and heart, gives the labels a political importance they would not have were their meanings precise and limited.

The abstract nature of political labels not only gives them their evocative power, but causes politicians to fight over them. Because the labels have no fixed meanings, politicians are perpetually attempting to infuse them with politically useful connotations. In so doing, they not only assign specific definitions to abstract concepts; they treat the concepts themselves as if they had actual material existence.

This process of infusing abstractions with material existence is

1. Benjamin Lee Whorf, *Language, Thought, and Reality* (Cambridge: M.I.T. Press, 1956), p. 247.

2. On the "inherent ambiguity" and "cryptic content" of political speech, see J. G. A. Pocock, *Politics, Language, and Time* (New York: Atheneum, 1973), p. 17. On the "contradictory formulas" incorporated in political language, see Murray Edelman, *Political Language: Words That Succeed and Policies That Fail* (New York: Academic Press, 1977), p. 5.

called reification and has a specific function in politics: it accustoms people to think of such abstract concepts as "liberalism" and "conservatism" as things that have real existence and can therefore be defined "correctly." Once the reification process has been set in motion, the matter of who controls the defining of words becomes all-important. Politicians compete to reify labels on their own terms in order to shape the popularly accepted meanings of the labels. Because the labels provide basic categories of political thought, shaping their publicly accepted meanings becomes central to the process of shaping public political consciousness.[3]

The very power of political vocabulary ensures that the reification of specific labels is never permanent. Because politics is an ongoing struggle for power, the competition to define political terms is constantly being renewed. Although the competition may sometimes lead in the direction of intellectual precision, the inherent ambiguity of political vocabulary is such that precision is not always possible. Moreover, given that the purpose of reification is not intellectual precision *per se* but rather the evocation of a political response, there may be situations in which ambiguity is politically desirable. The resulting tension between precision and ambiguity reinforces the ongoing competition over labels, as various practitioners struggle to evoke responses advantageous to themselves. Thus the process of political reification is at once paradoxically self-defeating and self-perpetuating.

The long run effect of the process is that the popularly accepted meanings of political terms constantly change. The words "liberal," "progressive," and "conservative" have in this century undergone major transformations in both meaning and popularity. These transformations have political origins and have resulted from years of intense political struggle. Political language "incorporates certain points of view," but does so in a constantly evolving fashion and in the

3. David Green, "Imagery and Political Language: An Historical Analysis," paper presented to 7th American Imagery Conference, San Francisco, California, October 22, 1983. On reification, see Peter L. Berger and Thomas Luckmann, *The Social Construction of Reality* (New York: Anchor Books, 1967), p. 89.; M. Markovic, "The Problem of Reification and the Verstehen-Erklären Controversy," in *Acta Sociologica* 15, 1 (1972):24–38; Joachim Israel, "Stipulations and Construction in the Social Sciences," in Joachim Israel and Henri Tajfel, eds., *The Context of Social Psychology* (New York: Academic Press, 1972), pp. 161–164; Bertell Ollman, *Alienation*, 2d ed. (Cambridge: Cambridge University Press, 1976), pp. 196–201; and Murray Edelman, *The Symbolic Uses of Politics* (Urbana: University of Illinois Press, 1964), pp. 116–117.

context of an ongoing struggle to shape the language itself to political purposes.

In the evolution of political vocabulary, language and policy are closely related. Reification includes identifying labels not only with general attitudes but with specific policies. To refer to someone as "a liberal" or "a conservative" is to impute to that person certain general attitudes as well as specific policy positions on the issues of the day.

Far from having clear and predictable consequences, however, most governmental policies tend to be as ambiguous and flexible in practice as the labels used to describe them. To attempt to sell a particular policy under a "good" label is not to guarantee a specific outcome but rather to evoke certain positive expectations associated with the label at the time. Similarly, to criticize a policy by branding it with a "bad" label is not to show detailed links between policy and outcome but rather to evoke certain negative attitudes currently in-hering in the label.[4]

Because of the evocative power of political vocabulary, the parallel ambiguity and flexibility of language and policy is of tremendous stra-tegic importance. Employing a persuasively positive vocabulary may earn an untested policy a trial period in which the policy undergoes major changes, is finally rejected, and yet has irreversible conse-quences. By the same token, it is when the unexpected negative consequences of policies emerge that political language may itself begin to undergo a shift. Politicians frequently alter their vocabularies for reasons of political survival. A change in vocabulary therefore need not mean a change in policy direction. As Pocock notes, "a power-structure may survive by successfully transforming its idiom."[5]

Conversely, the retention of an existing vocabulary need not mean fidelity to established policies. A recurring feature of politics is the use of old labels to justify new policies. Politicians initially seek identifica-tion with particular labels because those labels promise increased popularity. A label promises popularity because it has been associated in the past with popular institutions, behavior, and values or appears to embody the dominant values of the moment. Having secured iden-tification with a "good" label, a politician may then attempt to use it to

4. On the evocation of expectations and attitudes, see Edelman, *Symbolic Uses of Politics*, p. 134; Donald J. Foss and David T. Hakes, *Psycholinguistics* (Englewood Cliffs, N.J.: Prentice-Hall, 1978), pp. 99, 155; and William G. Hardy, *Language, Thought, and Experience* (Baltimore: University Park Press, 1978), p. 184.
5. Pocock, *Politics, Language, and Time*, p. 19.

advance new policies with the justification that these policies better express the values embodied in the label or are more "truly liberal" or "truly conservative" than the old policies.

If successful, a politician may alter the publicly accepted meaning of a label to make it coextensive with the new policies. Even more important, should the policies themselves be of sufficient moment, their implementation may alter the entire political scene, the government's relationship to people, people's expectations of government, and possibly even the dominant values of society itself. Political vocabulary thus carries the potential for enormous long-term political impact as the most salient twentieth-century example demonstrates: Americans still live in the shadow of Franklin Roosevelt's use of the liberal label from 1933 to 1945.[6]

This potential for bringing about long-term change is what gives political vocabulary its significance. Gaining identification with a popular label is a source of legitimacy which can in turn result in a massive and possibly long-term delegation of authority and power. Roosevelt sought and received such authority and power in the name of "liberalism." More recently, several presidents have sought and received such authority in the name of "anticommunism" with enormous consequences for American society.

To point out the strategic value of political vocabulary is not to accuse politicians in general of using language cynically or deceitfully. They may seek support with the best of intentions, and for the highest of purposes. In the absence of direct evidence with respect to intent, one can only speculate about an individual politician's intentions in a specific situation. Nor does reification imply conspiracy. Language is itself a public phenomenon and evolves only through consensus.

This has not prevented politicians themselves from accusing each other of using words illegitimately. During the 1920s Herbert Hoover successfully identified himself as both "progressive" and "liberal." Throughout the 1930s he struggled to regain his lost identification with those labels, while accusing Roosevelt and the New Dealers of "perverting" the words for their own purposes.

The power of political language has also caused commentators out-

6. The impact of Roosevelt's use of language upon American society is discussed later in this chapter and in chapters 5–8. On the influence of "labeling" or "naming" upon behavior, see Whorf, *Language, Thought, and Reality*, pp. 134–138; Anselm Strauss, *Mirrors and Masks: The Search for Identity* (n.p.: The Sociology Press, 1969), p. 15; and Edelman, *Political Language*, pp. 26, 45–49, 59–68.

side the political arena to take as active an interest in labels as the candidates and office holders themselves. Some of the most trenchant critiques of usage have come from literary critics, educators, and journalists such as Randolph Bourne, Charles Beard, and John T. Flynn. Although attentive to the language of the moment and to its specific implications, however, they did not explain how political vocabulary had itself evolved and continued to shape public political consciousness. That evolutionary process is central to American history and requires explanation.

The evolution of language in the political process

> Therefore when the kings had regulated names, when they had fixed terms and so distinguished actualities, and when their principles were carried out and their will everywhere known, they were careful to lead the people towards unity. Therefore making unauthorised distinctions between words, and making new words—thus confusing the correct nomenclature, causing the people to be in doubt and bringing about much litigation—was . . . a crime like that of using false credentials or false measures. . . . Hence the people were guileless. Being guileless, they could be easily ordered. Being easily ordered, they achieved results. . . . Should a true king arise, he must certainly follow the ancient terms and make the new ones.
>
> Ancient Chinese text

Although both state and federal governments have at times attempted to use legislation to render certain forms of speech impermissible, in America the "regulation of names" has proceeded less through coercion than through consensus; nevertheless, the powerful have attempted to use their power to influence public understanding of old and new terms. American history reflects the constant and vigorous efforts of government to reify labels, to "fix terms and so distinguish actualities" through nondictatorial means.[7] That old terms have eventually lost their currency suggests that "the people" have not always remained "guileless." At the same time, the very absence of official fiat has contributed to an atmosphere in which the shaping of political consciousness has proceeded by means of a more subtle pro-

7. Quoted in Pocock, *Politics, Language, and Time*, pp. 77–78.

cess. The understanding of that process lies in the relationship between old labels and new.

Since the emergence of the United States as an industrial power
after the Civil War, five sets of labels have dominated political discourse. Roughly from the mid-1860s to the depression of the
mid-1890s, the term "individualist" was the most popular self-designation, with the term "paternalist" as an accompanying pejorative to
be hurled at opponents. In the upheaval and uncertainty that followed, the dominant polarity became that of "conservatives" (good)
versus "radicals" (bad). With brief exceptions, the "progressive" versus "reactionary" polarity predominated from shortly after the turn of
the century until the 1930s, when it was replaced by that of "liberals"
versus "conservatives." Since the end of World War II, the "liberal-
conservative" polarity has remained operative, though it has increasingly been overshadowed by that of "anticommunists" versus
"communists."

This sequence of labels is no accident. Political vocabulary evolves
in response to political need. Each new set of labels reflects the
political needs of its users at the time, while the overall sequence of
labels is part of a larger evolutionary pattern. It is in analyzing the
political significance of this evolution that philology becomes, in Dilthey's words, "not the historian's aid but the basis of his procedure."[8]

Politics is a process of conflict resolution, conflict creation, and
conflict management; and political language at once reflects and con-
tributes to these processes. The use of "good" and "bad" labels indicates an effort on the part of those competing for power to establish
clear polarities between rival personalities and policies. Such usage
reflects and encourages a widespread public need to perceive politics
in terms of such polarities, that is, in terms of identifiable "good guys"
and "bad guys" as well as "good" and "bad" policies. At the same
time, political language is marked not only by polarities between
labels but by a vocabulary in which each separate label has connotations that are internally contradictory. Such internal contradiction also
meets a public political need, but one of a more subtle nature.

Edelman suggests that mass political behavior consists largely of
"social adjustment through contradictory beliefs." That is, people ad-

8. Dilthey is quoted in Jürgen Habermas, *Knowledge and Human Interests*
(Boston: Beacon Press, 1972), p. 216.

just to difficult social conditions by adopting "alternative sets of assumptions" or "contradictory formulas" to explain what they cannot control. The function of these contradictory beliefs is to allow people to move back and forth from one explanation to the other as their emotional needs require. Edelman offers as example two contradictory explanations of poverty, one that the poor are "responsible for their own plight," the other that they are "victims of exploitative institutions." Rich and poor alike "learn to perceive poverty in both ways and to emphasize one or the other view as necessary to justify their roles, to account for developments in the news, and to adjust to changing social situations." Both perspectives are "part of the culture, enabling people to live with themselves and with practices that would otherwise bring guilt and continuous social upheaval."9

Political vocabulary is central to this process of adjustment. By reifying labels in such a way as to evoke contradictory images, people allow themselves not only to construct conflicting interpretations of events but also to remain in a state of conflict without having either to act or to admit powerlessness. Such a state of perpetual yet passive conflict among the masses may be very useful to those in power. In Orwell's *1984*, such passivity was deliberately fostered through the process of "doublethink," which Orwell defined as "the power of holding two contradictory beliefs in one's mind simultaneously, and accepting both of them." Indeed, the language of Newspeak was designed not only to promote "doublethink" but to make it the only possible thought process.10

Although there is horror in Orwell's scenario of total governmental control of thought and behavior, what succeeds in making his depiction credible and even more horrible is the fact that his hypothetical state apparatus drew on and utilized intellectual processes familiar in even relatively free societies such as the United States. Social adjustment through contradictory beliefs is part of the political landscape in America irrespective of any efforts to foster or take advantage of it. Political language reflects the need both to perceive conflict and to rationalize and live with it. The interplay between these two needs is central to the evolution of politics. At the same time, the language

9. Edelman, *Political Language*, p. 5.
10. George Orwell, *1984* (New York: Signet Classics, 1961), pp. 176, 246.

itself is continuously being reshaped by ongoing political and linguistic competition.

The key to understanding the relationship between language and policy lies in correlating their evolution. Within the sequence of five predominant sets of labels, it is the self-designations or "good" labels that indicate the underlying pattern. Correlating those labels with the chief historical developments of their respective eras suggests a remarkable series of historic contradictions: concentration of economic power in the name of "individualism"; innovation in the name of "conservatism"; perpetuation of existing power structures in the name of "progressivism"; coercive authority in the name of "liberalism"; and finally, massive governmental interference with the free market mechanism in the name of "anticommunism."

As the sequence of labels is no accident, neither is the sequence of contradictions. Each "good" label evokes positive yet contradictory expectations regarding policy. So long as both these positive expectations persist, the label works to promote social acceptance or passivity. Because policy cannot perpetually evolve in two contradictory directions, however, one expectation eventually becomes noticeably contrary, under the glare of opposition criticism, to the actual direction of policy. When this happens, expectation gives way to resentment and the label itself is discredited and replaced by a new "good" label that evokes new images appropriate to the situation. The new label thus develops out of the existing situation and in the context of the competitive process.

As "good" labels evolve, so do "bad." The latter complement and reinforce the former. "Bad" labels project onto opponents the very attitudes to which the opponents themselves are attempting to direct critical attention. In so doing, "bad" labels also draw attention away from the contradictory expectations evoked by their corresponding "good" labels.

Anthropologist Clifford Geertz provides insight into how the labels work. He sees ideology as a cultural system, built up through the use of images and other symbols taken from the culture itself. He notes the power of metaphor as a culturally derived symbolic formula: "The power of a metaphor derives precisely from the interplay between the discordant meanings it symbolically coerces into a unitary conceptual framework and from the degree to which that coercion is successful in overcoming the psychic resistance such semantic tension inevitably generates in anyone in a positive to perceive it."

A plausible metaphor can make "discordancy" seem harmonious; that is, it can camouflage contradictions, as in the metaphor, "Life is just a bowl of cherries." Life is not a bowl of cherries; life is a process, and a bowl of cherries is a bunch of fruit. Nonetheless, because the two have something in common—namely a combination of sweet and sour—the metaphor is plausible. The contradiction between a process and a group of objects is camouflaged; "psychic resistance" to the contradiction is overcome, and the metaphor is experienced as a harmonious statement rather than a discordant one.[11]

Similarly, metaphor can also be used to provoke discordancy, to play one metaphor against another, so that while each separate metaphor camouflages its own internal contradiction, the interplay between them creates a discordancy that is projected onto a given target. This projection is part of the interplay between "good" and "bad" labels.

All the major American political labels of the last hundred years, "good" and "bad," have operated as metaphors. Metaphor is central to the reification of political vocabulary and to political competition itself. Within each set of labels, not only are the "good" and "bad" labels politically complementary; they are structurally related in their metaphorical content and interplay. They are built on the same contradictory elements, which they combine differently to produce the desired intellectual and psychological effect.

The "good" label takes up two contradictory elements and attaches positive images to both of them, thereby evoking two positive yet contradictory expectations regarding government policy. Combining these images into a single label, or "unitary conceptual framework," overcomes "psychic resistance" to simultaneous belief in such contradictory expectations, and the resultant "good" label evokes harmony.

The "bad" label utilizes the same elements as its corresponding "good" label, but inverts one element by attaching a negative image to

11. Clifford Geertz, *The Interpretation of Cultures* (New York: Basic Books, 1973), p. 211. On the political uses of contradiction and metaphor, also see Murray Edelman, *Politics as Symbolic Action: Mass Arousal and Quiescence* (Chicago: Markham, 1971), p. 65; Edelman, *Political Language*, pp. 5–8, 16–17; Ollman, *Alienation*, pp. 23, 56–60, and Jürgen Habermas, "On Systematically Distorted Communication," in Paul Connerton, ed., *Critical Sociology* (New York: Penguin Books, 1976), p. 356.

it. The "bad" label utilizes the same metaphorical construction to set up a negative "unitary conceptual framework" against one's political opponents. In so doing, the "bad" label not only camouflages its own internal contradiction; it simultaneously projects onto opponents the very discordancy that might otherwise be apparent in the "good" label. The "bad" label thus evokes discordancy by arousing psychic resistance to an opponent's perspective rather than to the perspective embodied in one's own "good" label.[12]

So long as the gap between positive expectations and policy consequences remains within psychically acceptable limits, psychic resistance is directed against those identified with the "bad" label. It is when such limits are breached that resistance is aroused against those identified with what was hitherto a "good" label. At this point old labels break down and new ones arise to incorporate new metaphors.

In order to be effective, however, new labels must deal with the psychic resistance generated by the breakdown of the old. The new "good" label must redirect political attention toward a new focus by means of a new set of positive images. The corresponding new "bad" label must in turn evoke a new negative image that will again project unacceptable attitudes onto opponents while simultaneously camouflaging the contradiction embedded in the new "good" label. Psychic resistance not only governs whether labels work or cease to work, but also establishes sequential linkages between them. With the acceptance of new sets of labels into the political vocabulary, the renewal of the social adjustment process is complete. A potentially hostile "mass arousal" has been transformed into renewed "mass quiescence," and policy evolution can proceed.[13]

Whorf once remarked that language, "for all its kingly role," was but "a superficial embroidery upon deeper processes of consciousness." He did not mean that language was unimportant in shaping understanding, rather that "the more superficial can mean the more important, in a definite operative sense." Political labels are them-

---

12. Examples of the interplay between "good" and "bad" labels will be found throughout this book, beginning with the "individualist" and "paternalist" labels in Chapter 2.

13. The terms "mass arousal" and "mass quiescence" are from Edelman, *Politics as Symbolic Action;* note especially his discussion of "symbolic reassurance" in *The Symbolic Uses of Politics,* p. 22. Also see George Lakoff and Mark Johnson, *Metaphors We Live By* (Chicago: University of Chicago Press, 1980), esp. chaps. 23–24, 30.

selves superficial but may have profound consequences. Labeling implies judgment, and that stops analysis. To perpetuate social and intellectual passivity through the constant renewal of labels is to keep public analysis of politics, and public political consciousness itself, at a perpetually superficial level. Given the interaction between scholarly and public analyses, what requires attention at this point is the role of scholarship in perpetuating the profound consequences of superficiality.[14]

Custodianship versus critical analysis

Since historians, economists, political scientists, and students of religion are immersed in life, they want to influence it. They subject historical persons, mass movements, and trends to their judgment, which is conditioned by their individuality, the nation to which they belong, and the time in which they live. Does not every analysis of the concepts of a previous generation show these concepts to contain components that originated in the presuppositions of the time? . . . . The first condition of the possibility of historical science is that I myself am a historical being—that he who *studies* history is the same as he who *makes* history.

Wilhelm Dilthey

Dilthey understood the problem very well. Scholars can never be entirely independent of their own historical contexts. To some degree, they are custodians of the concepts and presuppositions of their own time and are themselves in thrall, intellectually limited even by the very vocabulary they inherit and use. In the case of political vocabulary, the problem of custodianship has especially important implications.[15]

In his book *The Structure of Scientific Revolutions*, Thomas Kuhn observes that every investigative discipline has its own paradigms, or central concepts. These paradigms, which are actually categories of thought, are both conceptual and operational. They tell the investiga-

14. Whorf, *Language, Thought, and Reality*, p. 239. On judgment's stopping analysis, see S. I. Hayakawa, *Language in Thought and Action* (New York: Harcourt, Brace, and World, 1964), p. 46.

15. Dilthey is quoted in Habermas, *Knowledge and Human Interests*, pp. 178, 149.

tor how to conceptualize the problem and how to go about solving it. So long as paradigms generate successful solutions, what Kuhn calls "normal science" ensues. When important problems repeatedly resist solution in terms of existing paradigms, however, those paradigms must give way to new ones. It is this replacement of old paradigms by new ones that Kuhn terms "scientific revolution." For him, the history of scientific thought is the history of normal science interspersed with scientific revolution. The historical discipline, like the social sciences generally, is itself subject to this evolution of paradigms.[16]

Applying Kuhn's schema to the study of political thought, Pocock develops an important argument. Any "formalized language" or set of intellectual categories is itself "a political phenomenon in the sense that it serves to constitute an authority structure." Within a scientific discipline, investigative paradigms are at once linguistic, intellectual, and political, "communicating and distributing authority by linguistic means." At the same time, in the actual world of politics, political language has its own built-in authority structure, communicated through its own intellectual categories. Because these categories are also at once conceptual and operational, Pocock likewise refers to them as paradigms. Because the history of political vocabulary is inseparable from the history of politics itself, paradigms of political speech evolve within a political context.[17]

Pocock's use of the term "paradigm" to describe both the intellectual categories of an investigative discipline and those of the political arena as well as his designating both paradigms as political may seem confusing at first, but he has spotlighted a central issue. What happens when a discipline designed to investigate political phenomena takes its intellectual categories, and authority structure, directly from the political arena it is supposed to be investigating? What happens, in short, when the reified political categories used by political actors become the investigative categories of supposedly critical disciplines? Here the problem of custodianship becomes acute.

A basic principle of phenomenological research states that because of the "intersubjectivity" of social reality, social science begins with a recognition of the "intersubjective" nature of social knowledge. So-

16. Thomas S. Kuhn, *The Structure of Scientific Revolutions* (Chicago: University of Chicago Press, 1970), esp. pp. 92–97.
17. Pocock, *Politics, Language, and Time*, pp. 14–15.

ciologists Barney Glaser and Anselm Strauss make a similar point
when they state that theory grounded in the data, or theory that draws
its investigative categories from data accumulated through research, is
more likely to explain reality than "logico-deductive" theory, or theory that begins with logically derived categories and attempts to draw
deductions that fit those categories. Neither the phenomenological
approach nor the grounded theory approach implies the loss of intellectual independence. On the contrary, the conscious recognition of
intersubjectivity reduces the chance of either ignoring the intellectual
frameworks of others or becoming imprisoned within them. Phenomenological analysis and grounded theory lead away from custodianship.[18]

Quite the reverse happens, however, when social scientists ignore
the evolution of language as a political phenomenon and adopt the
labels of the political arena as their own investigative categories. Independent understanding can no longer take place, and what emerges
instead is a reified investigative vocabulary that is necessarily custodial.

A prime example is the interlocking political evolution of the liberal
and conservative labels. It is a commonplace of American history that
"nineteenth-century liberalism" is equivalent to "twentieth-century
conservatism," whereas "twentieth-century liberalism" has little in
common with its nineteenth-century namesake. Similarly, when the
term "liberal" took on its twentieth-century or "modern" meaning in
the 1930s, "nineteenth-century liberalism" somehow *became* "twentieth-century conservatism." So completely have these transitions
been assimilated into the historical vocabulary that they are no longer
recognized as political events.

Both the phenomenological and grounded theory approaches lead,
by way of the data, to the concept of a *struggle* over labels. Available
evidence indicates that Franklin Roosevelt and his opponents struggled for identification with the liberal label, while each side simultaneously attempted to pin the then-negative conservative label, or
other damaging labels, on the other. Although these struggles were
central to the politics of the 1930s, the standard historical vocabulary

18. Alfred Schutz, "Phenomenology and the Social Sciences," in *Collected Papers*,
I: *The Problem of Social Reality* (The Hague: Martinus Nijhoff, 1967), pp. 118–139;
Barney Glaser and Anselm Strauss, *The Discovery of Grounded Theory: Strategies for
Qualitative Research* (Chicago: Aldine, 1967), esp. pp. 3–6, 90. Also see Berger and
Luckmann, *Social Construction of Reality*, p. 20.

reflects only the outcomes of the struggles rather than an awareness of their existence. According to that vocabulary, Roosevelt *was* "a liberal" and his main opponents *were* "conservatives." The winning political paradigm of the era has become the reified investigative paradigm of the historian.

As Pocock's argument suggests, it has also thereby become the basis of an authority structure within the historical discipline. The student wishing to study the history of the 1930s paradigmatically divides combatants into pro–New Deal "liberals" and anti–New Deal "conservatives," and begins from there. Forgotten are the occurrence and significance of the bitter struggles that raged throughout the decade over identification with, and definition of, these political terms. Forgotten, too, are the highly political reasons why Roosevelt wished to be identified with the liberal label and why his opponents wished to deny him that identification. The result is that the relationship between the evolution of language and the evolution of policy remains unexamined.[19]

Although this transformation of a political paradigm into an investigative paradigm has been equally characteristic of pro–New Deal and anti–New Deal historians, the results have not been historically neutral. The dichotomy of pro–New Deal "liberals" versus anti–New Deal "conservatives" was Roosevelt's own, and to adopt it is to adopt his frame of reference and become custodian of his political perspective.

Building on an insight of W. I. Thomas, sociologists of the symbolic interactionist school have stressed the importance of a "definition of the situation." "Power, the control of others," writes Peter Hall, "is accomplished by getting others to accept your view and perspective. This is achieved by controlling, influencing, and sustaining *your* definition of the situation since, if you can get others to share your reality, you can get them to act in the manner you prescribe." Through the process of reification, political vocabularies encapsulate definitions of political situations. Transmitting one's own vocabulary to supporters or to the uncommitted is of course useful. Transmitting it to critics may be even more useful if, as Pocock suggests, that very vocabulary both "summarizes information" and "suppresses the inconvenient" in a manner consonant with the interests of the person being criticized.[20]

19. For documentation regarding the struggle over labels in the 1930s and its historiographical and political implications, see Chapter 5, below.
20. Peter Hall, "A Symbolic Interactionist Analysis of Politics," in Andrew Effrat,

This transmission of vocabulary is especially important when those under attack hold positions of power. The critic may dissent from the goals and values of those in power; yet if the critic's own vocabulary reinforces the information selectively dispensed by the powerful, that criticism itself is effectively undercut. The definition of the situation espoused by those in power becomes concealed within the vocabulary of those in opposition and is no longer recognized as emanating from those being criticized. Not only is the perspective of the powerful thereby reinforced; the critic is inadvertently co-opted by linguistic means.

This co-optation occurs in the case of political combatants as well as historical critics. Intellectual categories, whether political or investigative, are definitions of a situation. The purpose of reification of labels is to embed one's intellectual categories, hence one's definition of the situation, in the labels themselves. Once this embedding has been accomplished, usage of the labels even by critics necessarily transmits those categories and definitions. Roosevelt's contemporary critics understood this process, and for that reason they not only struggled to deny him the liberal label but refused ever to refer to him as a liberal. For the historian to label Roosevelt a liberal, even in a critical context (as for example in discussing the "failures of liberalism"), is to transmit Roosevelt's intellectual categories and his definition of the situation. This his contemporary critics never did.

Nor is the problem solved by reclassifying Roosevelt on the "left-to-right" linear spectrum (possibly the most imprisoning metaphor of all) or by reifying other labels from the political arena. To transform any political categories into investigative categories is still to ignore the historic roles of the categories themselves, and to remain in a custodial position with respect to the political authors of those categories.[21]

Recognizing the danger of custodianship, some scholars have tried

---

ed., *Perspectives in Political Sociology* (New York: Bobbs-Merrill, 1973), pp. 38, 51; Pocock, *Politics, Language, and Time*, p. 18. Also see W. I. Thomas and D. S. Thomas, *The Child in America* (New York: Knopf, 1928), pp. 571–575, and Willard Waller, "The Definition of the Situation," in Gregory P. Stone and Harvey A. Farberman, eds., *Social Psychology Through Symbolic Interaction* (Waltham, Mass.: Xerox College Publishing, 1970), pp. 162–174.

21. For a stimulating history of the "left-right" duality, see J. A. Laponce, *Left and Right: The Topography of Political Perceptions* (Toronto: University of Toronto Press, 1981). Although the author recognizes the "dysfunctional" or "crippling" effects of the duality, he does not specifically discuss the custodial effect. See pp. 206–209.

to meet the danger by stating explicitly the definitions they are assigning to the labels they are using. Although this approach has the merit of frankness, it is still not likely to divest the labels of all the political connotations or implications they have accumulated in the mind of the reader. In addition, any reification of political labels, even by scholars, has the effect of camouflaging the political use of those labels in the political arena.

Other scholars have attempted to avoid custodianship by proposing that their respective disciplines abandon any use of political labels whatsoever. Superficially attractive, such a proposal neglects two aspects of the situation, as Habermas argues tellingly. "Both the pathology of social institutions and that of individual consciousness," he writes, "reside in the medium of language and of communicative action and assume the form of a structural deformation of communication." To neglect the history of political labels would be to neglect the medium through which institutions and consciousness have evolved, and to neglect a vital part of the data.[22]

The critical analysis of language is also indispensable to an understanding of the impact of vocabulary on the intellectual processes of social science. "A state defined by both cognitive performances and fixed attitudes," Habermas argues, "can be overcome only if its genesis is analytically remembered. A past state, if cut off and merely repressed, would retain its power over the present." Intellectual processes are both embedded and reinforced through vocabulary. Simply to throw out a certain vocabulary stops the reinforcement but does not deal with the actual embedding. Habermas is thus proposing the relevance of psychoanalytic method, itself an historical method, for social science. "Psychoanalysis," he writes, "is relevant to us as the only tangible example of a science incorporating methodical self-reflection."[23]

In this context, Habermas makes an important point with respect to Dilthey's argument. For Dilthey, philology was "the basic historical science . . . in the formal sense of the scientific study of languages, in which tradition has been sedimented; the collection of the heritage of earlier men; the elimination of errors contained therein; and the chronological order and combination that put these documents in

22. Habermas, *Knowledge and Human Interests*, p. 288.
23. Ibid., pp. 18–19, 214.

internal relation with each other." Psychoanalysis, Habermas notes, does not "eliminate" so-called errors, but takes them up and "unites linguistic analysis with psychological investigation of causal connections." The point is not to study the history of labels in order to eliminate past "errors" and arrive at "correct" definitions to be used as investigative categories; it is rather to understand the ongoing impact that the evolution of language has had, and continues to have, on the intellectual processes of politicians, societies, and social scientists alike.[24]

There is an irony in all this. Critical analysis suggests the inadequacy of a historiographical paradigm that centers on the transformation of political categories into investigative categories. The inadequacy itself, however, stems from the failure to apply a more basic, antecedent historical methodology to the historian's own discipline, that is, from the failure to take a historical approach to the investigative categories used by historians themselves. What is needed is thus not a new paradigm at all, but the more consistent use of an old one.

If there is irony, there is also paradox. How is that paradigm to be applied? Is there an investigative vocabulary that is critically independent and noncustodial? Not in absolute terms. The logic of language is such that all communicative categories must have their own histories in order to be communicative. All vocabularies, all labels, are therefore to some degree custodial and involve the problem of reification. The historian should aim for a critical analysis of the categories constructed by political actors, yet there is no fully nonreifying vocabulary with which to do this. Moreover, any attempt to establish fixed, unchanging categories runs afoul of both the logic of language and that of self-reflection. What is the historian to do?

The only way to proceed is to admit the paradox, as Stuart Chase did almost fifty years ago. The business of trying to explain words with words, he remarked, is necessarily experimental and, he might have added, limited by the logic of language itself. No answer today can be any more adequate. There is no fully nonreifying, noncustodial vocabulary, no absolute critical independence. There is only what Wittgenstein called "everyday language," historically shaped and historically shaping. Nor is there any retreating from the paradox. If histori-

24. Ibid., pp. 216–217. Also see Hans-Georg Gadamer, *Philosophical Hermeneutics* (Berkeley: University of California Press, 1977), pp. 92–94.

cal writing is to be even relatively critically independent, there is no alternative to critical analysis of existing categories or to self-reflection regarding the custodial role. Despite his comment on the "elimination" of errors, Dilthey was right on the essential point. There is no escape from historical context or from one's own involvement in the historical process itself.[25]

Indeed, it is that very involvement that makes the historical analysis of political language so important. Such analysis necessitates and permits stepping outside the limits of the labels one is analyzing. It allows one to transcend that particular vocabulary and that particular set of intellectual constraints. It provides a relative critical independence, which ought not be dismissed lightly. Given that the constraints incorporated into political vocabulary are the very ones that have shaped historical and political consciousness, it is in fact a necessary task to transcend them, even though the task itself begins with the recognition that the result will eventually require further critical analysis and self-reflection.

To undertake the task, however, is immediately to confront a further question: how does one choose one's research subjects, human as well as linguistic? As the grounded theory approach suggests, only the research process itself can elucidate the choices. Only immersion in the historical data can provide the clues to which labels, phrases, or verbal formulas are politically significant in a given situation; only a sustained analysis of their usage by specific individuals can shed light on who are the primary shapers of political consciousness in a given era.

Here, the historical analysis of language differs from both traditional political history and traditional intellectual history. The former involves choosing subjects in terms of their prominence with respect to specific events and the evolution of specific institutions, whereas the latter centers on those directly involved in the flow of ideas. In contrast to both of these, a linguistically oriented history focuses on people who may or may not have had a direct impact on events, institutions, or even ideas, but who nonetheless had significant long-term

25. Stuart Chase, *The Tyranny of Words* (New York: Harcourt, Brace, 1938), p. v; Ludwig Wittgenstein, *Philosophical Investigations* (Oxford: Basil Blackwell, 1968), pp. 48–49e (#120). Also note Wittenstein's remark, "An expression has meaning only in the stream of life"; quoted in Norman Malcolm, *Ludwig Wittgenstein: A Memoir* (London: Oxford University Press, 1958), p. 93.

effect on the use of language and thereby on political consciousness itself.

What holds for the shapers of political consciousness holds for their critics. Although traditional analysis focuses on those critics most concerned with events, institutions, and ideas, the historical analysis of political vocabulary centers on those whose primary concern was the use of language itself as a political weapon. The latter critics may not in all cases have achieved the same levels of prominence as certain of their contemporaries, but they were nonetheless important because their efforts and indeed their very failures provide vital object lessons for present-day analysts. Again, one's choice of subjects flows from the research process and, like the analysis itself, remains open to further critical examination and self-reflection. In short, one's very choice of material reflects the ongoing issue of custodianship versus critical analysis.

To distinguish between custodianship and critical analysis is to confront once more the issue of intentions. To reiterate, that politicians use language deliberately and with effectiveness is not evidence of cynicism, deceit, or conspiracy. One may well begin by accepting the good intentions of those subject to analysis. To do so is not to overlook or explain away the consequences of political action. Jacques Maritain once observed that a disposition to virtue can be even more dangerous than a disposition to vice because the former trait tends to be unrestrained by conscience. Given the political power of language, a disposition to virtue in the use of political vocabulary may have even more devastating consequences than a similar disposition respecting the use of other tools of power, even military or economic ones. Therein lies the need for an ongoing historical analysis of the role of language in the shaping of political consciousness.

2

The Language of an
Emergent Industrial Power

A once and future insight

> We are individualists mainly. Let that be understood at the start.
> We stand unalterably opposed to the paternal idea in government.
> We believe in fewer laws and juster interpretation thereof. We be-
> lieve in less interference with individual liberty, less protection of the
> rapacious demands of the few, and more freedom of action on the part
> of the many.
>
> Hamlin Garland, 1891

Hamlin Garland was exultant. After years of searching, the well-
known writer believed that he had at last found the answer to America's social ills. It was called the Single Tax, and its author was that
"great teacher," Henry George. Having just attended an enthusiastic
meeting of George's devoted followers, Garland was writing to inform
his readers of an historic "new declaration of rights."

Single Taxers, Garland proudly announced, were "individualists
mainly." As such, they looked forward not to an age of government
"paternalism" but to a new age of liberty: "Liberty, standing high as
Justice, and commanding the whole earth with her peaceful eyes. We
mean by liberty perfect freedom of action so long as the equal rights of
others are maintained." In this, Single Taxers based themselves on
that apostle of "individual rights," Herbert Spencer, and on "the
immortal Declaration of Independence."

The Single Tax, Garland assured readers, was in no way "socialistic." On the contrary, "the whole socialistic theory" was "based
upon a misconception of the tendency of history." The past was "not
individualistic, but socialistic. The age of socialism is not coming on,

21

but departing." The past, "the tribal state, the feudal age, was the age when the individual belonged to the state, and forcible co-operation was at its greatest. The state—it was the people." Citing the authority of Spencer, Garland announced that current problems were but relics of "the surviving and slowly retreating effect of socialism, paternalism, and special privilege." All these relics the Single Tax would sweep away, replacing them with a new age of "liberty and loftier individual development."[1]

Needless to say, things did not turn out as Garland had hoped. The Single Tax never caught on; like all panaceas, it was too simple a solution to complex problems. After a brief fling with the short-lived Populist or People's party, Garland himself withdrew from politics and turned to writing adventure stories.

Despite the inadequacy of Garland's solution, however, something in his diagnosis commands attention. Existing laws, he wrote, restricted the "many" while protecting "the rapacious demands of the few." Through taxation, subsidies, and other devices, government had encouraged a great concentration of wealth, creating "vast corporations and privileged classes." Government itself had created "giant corporations to dominate our legislature," and its intervention had undercut competition and created "the trusts." Corporate power, in short, was based not on the absence of government but on its presence.[2]

In hindsight, Garland's diagnosis is hardly startling. Ever since Charles Beard, historians have documented the links between government and corporate power. Most recently, public demands for the "deregulation" of certain industries have brought those links into sharper focus. Even in his own time, moreover, Garland was not alone in demanding "fewer laws and juster interpretation thereof."[3]

1. Hamlin Garland, "A New Declaration of Rights," in *The Arena* 3 (January 1891):158, 167–168, 184.

2. Ibid.,:165–166, 169.

3. For other, early post-Civil War perspectives similar to that of Garland, see Arthur Ekirch, *The Decline of American Liberalism* (New York: Atheneum, 1967), pp. 147–167. For other historical analyses stressing corporate usage of government intervention, see Charles Beard, *The Myth of Rugged American Individualism* (New York: John Day, 1932); Charles Beard and Mary Beard, *The Rise of American Civilization* (New York: Macmillan, 1944); Vernon L. Parrington, *Main Currents in American Thought:* vol. 3, *The Beginnings of Critical Realism in America* (New York: Harcourt, Brace, and World, 1930); Gabriel Kolko, *The Triumph of Conservatism* (Glencoe: Free

On balance, however, Garland's diagnosis remains contrary to the conventional wisdom of both his era and our own. For the most part, corporate spokesmen and their critics have agreed that corporate power springs from a lack of government intervention. Corporations still attempt to project an image of success through "free market" competition. Accepting the image as accurate, most critics have accordingly sought greater government intervention rather than less.

Bluntly stated, the consequences of that intervention have been disastrous. Americans are over-governed as never before, yet the power of "giant corporations" is greater than ever. Without prejudging the actual extent of corporate dependence on government, one might well wonder why Garland's diagnosis has not been more popular through the years. Part of the answer is undoubtedly that the diagnosis was discredited along with the solution. Even so, there must have been more to it, especially considering how consistently Garland wrapped himself in the mantle of Spencer. The Spencerian arguments were so enormously popular that they should at least have guaranteed a more sympathetic hearing.

Language provides the key. Garland's vocabulary was in no sense mere chance. The label he claimed for himself—"individualist"—was precisely the label corporate spokesmen claimed for themselves. The labels he applied to his opponents—"paternalist" and "socialist"—were the very ones corporate spokesmen applied to their own critics. Garland was competing with the corporations over who would be identified with the good labels and who with the bad. Why the verbal competition? To have accepted the corporate vocabulary would have meant agreeing with the corporate definition of the situation, and this was precisely what Garland was determined to avoid.[4]

Modern American politics begins with this competition over the "individualist," "paternalist," and "socialist" labels. It was during the two decades immediately following the Civil War that large corpora-

---

Press, 1963); Gabriel Kolko, *Railroads and Regulation, 1877–1916* (Princeton: Princeton University Press, 1965); and Joan Hoff Wilson, *American Business and Foreign Policy, 1920–1933* (Lexington: University Press of Kentucky, 1971).

Although influential, the perspectives expressed in these analyses have remained those of a minority. See below. For a contrasting analysis, see Robert Wiebe, *Businessmen and Reform* (Cambridge: Harvard University Press, 1962).

4. Jürgen Habermas, *Knowledge and Human Interests*, (Boston: Beacon Press, 1972) p. 216; J. G. A. Pocock, *Politics, Language, and Time* (New York: Atheneum, 1973), p. 15.

tions first achieved nationwide predominance in such sectors as mining, manufacturing, and transportation, thus creating a concentration of economic power unprecedented in American history.

Garland was not the first to cite the existence, and the danger, of the corporate-government connection. As early as 1873, *Nation* editor E. L. Godkin argued a similar view. Government, he warned, "must get out of the 'protective' business and the 'subsidy' business and the 'improvement' and the 'development' business. It must let trade, and commerce, and manufactures, and steamboats, and railroads, and telegraphs alone. It cannot touch them without breeding corruption."[5]

Godkin's attack shows why corporations chose the "individualist" label. In a culture that valued self-reliance, independent initiative, and widespread opportunity, a growing concentration of power under government auspices could be highly suspect. The term "individualist" was ideal for invoking the dominant values, summarizing corporate techniques as consonant with those values, and suppressing inconvenient indications to the contrary. The question is: how did corporate leaders get the public to perceive their giant organizations as "individuals"?

The term "individualist" is a metaphor taken from the world of nature and the biological individual is a naturally occurring organism. In Darwinian America, what survived "naturally" survived legitimately. Identification with the world of nature, then, helped give the corporations legitimacy. Moreover, the word's derivation from the Latin *corpus* or body fit the metaphor nicely. So did the financial function of the corporation. By means of limited liability, it encouraged disparate individuals to combine their resources to accomplish what few could do singly. Hence the tendency, eventually consecrated in the law itself, to define the corporation as that most exquisite contradiction in terms, an "artificial individual."

This harmonization of "nature" and "artifice" was central to corporate purposes. Once it had been achieved, Darwinian theory could then be invoked in support of the "natural" evolutionary fitness of the corporate "individual." The metaphor nicely harmonized two contradictory expectations: one, that these "artificial" new giants would pro-

5. *The Nation*, January 30, 1873, p. 68.

mote rapid economic growth; and two, that the "natural" order of things would protect widespread opportunity.[6]

A credible metaphor, however, cannot be built merely on an invocation of values. Camouflaging the contradiction between "nature" and "artifice" required a particular summarizing of information. Here, corporate technique is well revealed in the writings of industrialist Andrew Carnegie, a leading claimant to the "individualist" label and, like Garland, a self-proclaimed disciple of Spencer.

Decrying constant "tinkering" by legislators with the "all-wise laws of natural forces," Carnegie insisted that a natural or "individualistic" system had historically spared America the permanent class divisions of Europe. "There are but three generations in America from shirt sleeves to shirt sleeves," he wrote. "Under such conditions an aristocracy of wealth is impossible. . . . Wealth cannot remain permanently in any class if economic laws are allowed free play."[7]

Carnegie's use of the individualist metaphor illustrates what Edelman calls "symbolic reassurance," which is one of the central purposes of political speech. He agreed, indeed insisted, that industrialization created a natural and inevitable trend toward the concentration of capital in large "individual" units, but this did not mean that workers or consumers suffered thereby. On the contrary, increased efficiency benefited consumers through lower prices, and workers through increased production and employment.

Nor did corporate "individualism" mean monopoly. Decrying the "bugaboo of trusts," Carnegie argued that under competitive conditions such supposed monopolies were constantly creating new com-

6. Pocock, Politics, Language, and Time, p. 18; Clifford Geertz, The Interpretation of Cultures (New York: Basic Books, 1973), p. 211; Habermas, Knowledge and Human Interests, pp. 18–19. Also see Cynthia Eagle Russett, Darwin in America: The Intellectual Response, 1865–1912 (San Francisco: W. H. Freeman, 1976), p. 83. Russett correctly notes that relatively few businessmen themselves quoted Darwin or Spencer. Both the Darwinian and the Spencerian vocabularies nonetheless permeated public discussion and thereby reinforced the idea of corporate growth as a "natural" phenomenon. Those entrepreneurs who did use Darwinian and Spencerian vocabulary, such as John D. Rockefeller and Andrew Carnegie, also tended to be among the most influential business leaders of the era. See Chester M. Destler, "Entrepreneurial Leadership among the 'Robber Barons': A Trial Balance," in Journal of Economic History (Supplement), 6 (1946):28–49.

7. Andrew Carnegie, Triumphant Democracy (New York: Scribner's, 1888), pp. 48, 366.

petition for themselves. "The more successful the Trust," he wrote, "the surer these off-shoots are to sprout. Every victory is a defeat."

So long as government did not interfere with nature, corporations posed no threat to individual opportunity. Americans could "smile at [all] efforts to defeat the economic laws by Trusts or combinations, or pools, or 'differentials,' or anything of like character. Only let them hold firmly to the doctrine of free competition. Keep the field open. . . . The only people who have reason to fear Trusts are those foolish enough to enter into them."

In developing his argument for corporate "individualism" Carnegie suppressed anything that might suggest that corporate power required "special privilege" or government interference with free competition. Thus in his book *The Triumph of Democracy,* he never mentioned land grants, subsidies, government contracts, or other aids to corporations. He defended patents as a spur to innovation, but without noting that they amounted to licensed monopoly. He treated tariffs with equal selectivity. Acknowledging the benefits free traders saw in vigorous international competition, he argued that the same benefits could nonetheless be obtained from "vigorous home competition." Left implicit was the assumption that tariffs in no way affected home competition itself.[8]

In its invocation of values, summarizing of information, and selectivity, Carnegie's language contrasted sharply with that of Godkin and Garland. Free competition and individual opportunity did exist in America. The modern corporation was a "natural," legitimate expression of such "individualism." Its size and strength in no way depended on government assistance; nor did its growth threaten individual opportunity.

As Carnegie's use of the individualist metaphor suggests, verbal symbols are highly malleable. The shaping of political perceptions by means of any single symbol nonetheless has its limits. This is why labels come in pairs, "good" and "bad." A well-constructed "bad" label, hurled at opponents, can distract attention from the contradictions contained in one's own "good" label. Historian Louis Hartz notes that escape from the political and social institutions of Europe is

8. Andrew Carnegie, *The Empire of Business* (New York: Doubleday, Page, 1902), pp. 72, 160, 167–168; Carnegie, *Triumphant Democracy,* p. 280. Also see Murray Edelman, *The Symbolic Uses of Politics* (Urbana: University of Illinois Press, 1964), p. 22.

a recurring theme in American history. The theme can be fully understood only when one sees how it became embedded in the pejorative
metaphor of "paternalism." Here one also sees how the contents of
political labels develop historically, and how "good" and "bad" labels
are at once politically and structurally complementary.[9]

The metaphors "individualist" and "paternalist" are both drawn
from the natural world, in which there is no necessary antagonism
between the relationships they symbolize. Individuals can function
independently and still maintain beneficial ties with their fathers. In
the world of politics, however, political meanings develop to serve
political purposes, and in America the paternalist label developed as a
way of implying invidious comparison between "good" American and
"bad" European values. "Individualism" was good, American; "paternalism" was bad, European.

In this ideological and psychological distancing of America from
Europe, the structural complementarity of the two metaphors was
vital. Both built on the elements of "nature" and "artifice," and assigned a positive image to "nature." The individualist or "good" metaphor also assigned a positive image to "artifice," thus harmonizing two
positive yet contradictory expectations about America. By contrast,
the paternalist or "bad" metaphor inverted "artifice," assigning to it a
negative image discordant with that of "nature." The negative image
was the "artificial" or "unnatural" perpetuation of the paternal relationship through the agency of the state, as allegedly took place in
Europe.

It was this inversion of "artifice" and its identification with Europe
that made the paternalist label an ideal pejorative in the American
setting of the time. By projecting onto opponents a discordant, "un-
American" attitude toward "nature" and "artifice," it aroused psychic
resistance to opposition perspectives while simultaneously camouflaging the contradictory expectations inherent in the individualist label.
The paternalist label contained its own internal contradiction in implying that a relationship could be both protective and destructive at
the same time. This contradiction was likewise camouflaged, however, by the identification of the paternal relationship with the state, an
"artificial" or "unnatural" father. As each metaphor camouflaged its

9. Louis Hartz, *The Liberal Tradition in America* (New York: Harcourt, Brace, and
World, 1955), p. 3.

own internal contradiction, the interplay between them created a discordancy that had a powerful psychological impact when projected onto opponents.

This discordancy was especially useful to corporate entrepreneurs. By enabling them to project an "unnatural," "un-American" dependence on government onto their opponents, it helped them camouflage their own reliance on governmental support. It was for this reason that such critics as Garland were as militant in contesting the paternalist label as the individualist label.

There was an irony here, as Michael Paul Rogin has pointed out, for white Americans freely adopted the paternalist metaphor in their efforts to legitimize their control of Indian tribes and nations. For example, Andrew Jackson and others strongly had encouraged Indians to think of white men as their "white fathers."[10]

One can speculate about the deeper psychological motives that led white Americans to use the same metaphor in such diametrically opposing ways. But what is not a matter of speculation is the extent to which the paternalist metaphor was used as a pejorative in debates about political economy. So attractive a weapon also became an object of political struggle. Critics such as Godkin and Garland stressed "paternalistic," European-style government aid to corporations, whereas corporate spokesmen pointed to "paternalistic" laws (also of supposedly European origin) designed to restrict enterprise and to reward "idleness."

The battle was not equal, however, Corporate entrepreneurs had friends in high places. A number of Supreme Court rulings set aside state-level "regulatory" legislation as, in the words of one justice, throwbacks to "seventeenth or eighteenth century ideas of paternal government." Newspapers joined in attacking "paternalistic" laws designed to aid supposed victims of economic inequity. Ironically, the term often used by corporate spokesmen to describe their own views was "laissez-faire," a European term symbolizing a political philosophy of European derivation.[11]

10. Michael Paul Rogin, *Fathers and Children: Andrew Jackson and the Subjugation of the American Indian* (New York: Knopf, 1975).

11. William Appleman Williams, *The Contours of American History* (Chicago: Quadrangle, 1966), p. 329; Arthur Ekirch, *The Decline of American Liberalism* (New York: Atheneum, 1967), pp. 150, 164–165; and Norman Pollack, *The Populist Response to Industrial America* (Cambridge: Harvard University Press, 1962), p. 32. Also see Sidney Fine, *Laissez-Faire and the General-Welfare State* (Ann Arbor: University of Michigan Press, 1956).

Powerful though bad labels can be, there are times when a single pejorative will not suffice. Again the European comparison is central. One of Hartz's main themes is the weakness of the "socialist tradition" in America. Both before and since the Bolsheviks, Americans have feared "socialism" and "communism" as alien, European things (Herbert Hoover called them "European patent medicines"). These fears well illustrate the profound power of superficiality. That the two words have historically been such powerful pejoratives derives not from their precision of meaning, or from any widespread public understanding of Marx, but from their emotional connotations as symbols of an alien culture. Whatever their disagreements, Garland and Carnegie were at one in contrasting individualism with socialism. The European comparison was a powerful one.[12]

A key point now emerges. In politics, real intellectual victory is achieved not by transmitting one's language to supporters but by transmitting it to critics. A person who adopts the usage employed by a particular side, though he remains critical, nonetheless adopts the definition of the situation espoused by that side. Once the critic has been linguistically co-opted, effective opposition is undercut, the more so because the co-optation takes the critic unawares.

Against this background, one can see more clearly why Garland lost. Although he continued to challenge the corporate use of language, most critics did not. What happened was not that a majority of Americans became active supporters of large corporations but that a majority of critics accepted the usage of the corporate spokesmen themselves.

Rejecting the political and economic solutions offered by Carnegie and other entrepreneurs, most critics nonetheless accepted the description of the real world inherent in corporate language. In accepting such phrases as "artificial individual," they accepted the idea that corporate growth was a "natural" and inevitable development, dependent not on government intervention but on the absence of such intervention.

Here the timing of Garland's statement was most important. By 1891 the critical acceptance of corporate language was already well advanced. As early as 1885 the founders of the American Economic

12. Hartz, *Liberal Tradition in America*, pp. 208, 243; for Hoover's use of labels, see Chapters 4-5, below; and Andrew Carnegie, *The Empire of Business* (Garden City, N.Y.: Doubleday, Page, 1913), pp. 235–236, 275, 303, 311.

Association, led by economist Richard Ely, had already adopted that language as part of their critical perspective. "While we recognize the necessity of individual [sic] initiative in industrial life," Ely announced, "we hold that the doctrine of laissez-faire is unsafe in politics and unsound in morals."

If corporations were "individuals" whose growth truly resulted from "laissez-faire," or a lack of government intervention, then the solution lay in greater government intervention. This was indeed Ely's conclusion. The "conflict of labor and capital," he declared, "has brought to the front a vast number of social problems whose solution is impossible without the united efforts of church, state, and science."

Within a year of Garland's attack, the idea of "inevitable" corporate growth would be predominant even within his own People's party. "We have tried to show," declared the party's 1892 presidential candidate, General James Baird Weaver, "that competition is largely a thing of the past. Every force of our industrial life is hurrying on the age of combination. It is useless to try and stop the current. What we must do is in some way make it work for the good of all." Party organizer Ignatius Donnelly put it bluntly: "We have but to expand the power of government to solve the enigma of the world."[13]

What these statements suggest is not that Garland's attack was ill conceived, or badly worded, but that it was anachronistic. By 1891 the fight to define individualism as he wanted it had already been lost. The language of his enemies was triumphant, even among his friends. The corporations had inherited the Spencerian mantle.

Garland's perspective did not disappear entirely. From time to time, it reappeared among some highly articulate, well-placed critics. Nor did the eclipse of his perspective leave large corporations with nothing to fear. Their own vocabulary, their pejorative use of the paternalist and socialist labels, shows that they themselves viewed government intervention as a two-edged sword. Their subsequent energies would go as much into prevention or neutralizing hostile legislation as into continuing to seek friendly legislation.

On balance, however, a fundamental insight into the basis of corporate power was lost in the evolution of language. It would not be

13. Richard Ely, *Ground Under Our Feet* (New York: Macmillan, 1938), p. 136; Weaver is quoted in Ekirch, *Decline of American Liberalism*, p. 164; Donnelly is quoted in Fine, *Laissez-Faire and the General-Welfare State*, p. 303.

generally recaptured until almost a century later, and then only in vastly altered circumstances. In the meantime, the energies of the great majority of critics would be channeled into a sharply different direction. Efforts to control corporate power would be directed not toward removing its governmental underpinnings, but toward balancing it with what came to be called "countervailing" government power. More laws, not fewer, became the predominant approach.

The implications for American society can hardly be overstated. Not surprising, the corporate definition of the situation likewise came to predominate in American historical writing, even among critics of corporate power. This suggests, once again, the appropriateness of Dilthey's remark that the historian is inevitably a "historical being."[14]

All this still leaves an important question unanswered. Why did so many critics accept corporate language, and the perspective contained therein? More specific, how did they come to see as "rugged individualists" and "artificial individuals" people and organizations that accepted land grants, subsidies, lucrative government contracts, patents, tariffs, hard-currency laws, and other forms of government aid?

In an autobiography written half a century later, Ely provided one answer. Until the mid-1880s, he wrote, "little attention was given in this country to systems of political economy." Little "disinterested research" took place. What was taught was a rigid "laissez-faire orthodoxy" as expounded by "influential" people including "Godkin of the New York *Nation*," William Graham Sumner of Yale, and others. Students like Ely were forced to do graduate work in Germany, where they met a far more positive attitude toward government involvement in economic life. They came home determined to break the "crust" of the old orthodoxy, and it was to this end that they established the American Economic Association.[15]

Ely's account reveals much of his own and his colleagues' thought at the time. Their attack was initially directed against an intellectual orthodoxy within their profession. What linked orthodox theoreticians such as Godkin to corporate entrepreneurs was their common reliance on the rhetoric of "laissez-faire." In focusing on this common rhetoric, the new critics missed both Godkin's practical emphasis and his anti-corporate sympathies. They failed to see that he accused corporations

14. Habermas, *Knowledge and Human Interests*, p. 149.
15. Ely, *Ground Under Our Feet*, pp. 121–127.

and government of abandoning "laissez-faire." This suggests that the new critics' view of corporate power as being based on "laissez-faire" sprang more from a general reaction against theoretical orthodoxy than from close attention to the actual corporate-government relationship.

If a preoccupation with professional orthodoxy helps explain the reaction of the younger academic critics, one must look elsewhere for an understanding of party leaders such as Weaver and Donnelly. In their case, the explanation lies in a basic confusion of inevitability, which is a question of fact, and desirability, which is a question of values. Of all the arguments people like Carnegie advanced in support of corporate "individualism," the most important was that large productive units, like biological individuals, were natural and inevitable results of the evolutionary process. From Carnegie's viewpoint, the desirability of such units, hence the temptation to believe in their inevitability, was clear.

Weaver, Donnelly, and other like-minded critics looked at the situation differently. By the mid-1880s, corporate growth had reached a point where it seemed irreversible, so that many critics began to think of harnessing these large units for what seemed socially productive purposes. After all, bigness permitted economies of scale, which meant efficiency, and that, properly harnessed, could be of great social benefit. Once irreversibility had generated a new definition of desirability, the desirable itself easily became confused with the inevitable. As Weaver put it, it was "useless to try and stop the current." The only problem lay in finding a way to "make it work for the good of all."

The solution was obvious. If unharnessed bigness sprang from a lack of government intervention, then, in Donnelly's words, the remedy clearly lay in "expanding the power of government." Moreover, this expanded governmental power would logically have to be in the hands of those critical of corporate behavior, and that argument in turn led straight to political power for these critics themselves. The goal was not power for its own sake but rather to "solve the enigma of the world." Such power, combined with an unyielding disposition to virtue, was inducement indeed to a critical acceptance of corporate language.

The People's party's leaders were not alone in their virtuous pursuit of power. Ely's account suggests that he and his colleagues were moved by similar considerations. As he wrote at the time, a major factor in his decision to move to the University of Wisconsin was its proximity to the state legislature, "upon which," he observed, "we may in time be able to exercise a favorable influence." In short, academic and party-oriented critics alike were so moved by their desire to deal with the consequences of corporate power that they neglected to investigate the actual sources of that power.[16]

Here the consequences of language become paramount. Language may freeze understanding at a superficial level of analysis, depending on the degree to which "psychic resistance" can be overcome. Should there be political or other motives for accepting a particular use of words, such resistance can be reduced or even eliminated, and the acceptance of the superficial is then more likely to occur. The political and professional ambitions of the new critics predisposed them to view corporate growth as an inevitable, if dangerous, consequence of government nonintervention. This predisposition in turn made it easy for them to accept the corporate version of the individualist metaphor.

Once they had accepted corporate language as their own, their use of it reinforced their belief and made them less likely ever to question it. One need only reiterate Whorf's point on the importance of the superficial in an operative sense. In short, the corporate victory in the struggle for the individualist label was the first modern American example of the profound consequences of superficiality. It was not to be the last.

Transforming the terms of the debate

Is there not a golden mean between the too little; namely rigid, obstructive and revolutionary conservatism, . . . and the too much; namely reckless radicalism, which in reaching out for improvement, risks the treasures accumulated during so many ages, treasures so painfully gathered together?

Richard Ely, 1894

Political language evolves within a political context. It was no accident that by 1894 Ely was calling for a golden mean between "conservatism" and "radicalism" rather than for a choice among "indi-

16. Ely, *Ground Under Our Feet*, p. 180.

vidualism," "paternalism," and "socialism." His language was different because the political situation was different. New terms reflected new issues.[17]

Ely's vocabulary illustrates a point once made by linguist Gustav Stern that "change and stability are equally normal phases in the history of language; only the total absence of either would be abnormal." When both change and stability are politically produced, however, the result makes for particularly complex and confusing patterns. Change may appear as stability and vice versa. Old labels may be reworked to promote political innovation, whereas new ones may have the effect of preventing it. Transformation of the terms of the debate may camouflage a sedimenting of existing assumptions which will then shift the focus of attention to new issues, thus calling forth further change. When change and stability are recognized as not only interrelated but as tending to occur simultaneously, the result is what Pocock calls "the complexity of context which the historian needs."[18]

Some especially important changes and stabilizations occurred in the years immediately preceding and following Garland's attack. The retention of such old labels as "individualist," "paternalist," and "socialist" concealed major shifts, while the introduction of a new dominant polarity, "conservative" versus "radical," helped sediment existing assumptions.

Among critics of corporate power, the retention and redefinition of the individualist label heralded one especially important change. Ely's Wisconsin colleague, John R. Commons, summed up the new critical viewpoint: "If governmental control serves to stimulate the self-reliant energies of the people, if it opens up new avenues for private enterprise, if it equalizes and widens the opportunity for employment, if it prevents injustice, oppression, and monopoly, . . . then government is not socialistic but rather is supplementing the highest individualism."

Like Garland, Commons was still competing for the individualist label, but he was doing so in diametrically opposite terms. His focus was not on dismantling the legislative basis of corporate power, but on

---

17. Ely is quoted in Fine, *Laissez-Faire and the General-Welfare State*, p. 230.
18. Gustav Stern, *Meaning and Change of Meaning with Specific Reference to the English Language* (Goteberg: Elanders, 1931), p. 162; Pocock, *Politics, Language, and Time*, p. 15.

constructing a countervailing, governmental power. Henceforth "individualism" was to be linked to "governmental control."

Few changes have been more portentous in American politics. In this context, Commons' retention of the pejorative "socialist" was the other side of the coin. Governmental control was not "socialistic," but rather the best defense against "socialism." Ely retained the pejorative "paternalist" on the same basis. In an article entitled "Fraternalism versus Paternalism," he explicitly denied that the type of intervention he and his colleagues advocated was "paternalistic." In a democracy, he argued, government is the people, and so long as the people use democratic means to advance their interests, they are not submitting to "paternalism" but are engaging in "fraternalism." As in Commons' case, Ely's language indicated a major shift of direction.[19]

Just as the reworking of old labels signaled major changes, so did the introduction of new ones reinforce recently achieved results. Again Ely illustrates the point. His call for a golden mean between "conservatism" and "radicalism" implied a new set of political alternatives. One could attempt to "conserve" an outmoded system in the face of new economic realities. One could seek "radical" or uprooting change through some form of "socialism." Or one could attempt a golden mean based on a "fraternal" approach within a modified free market framework.

Ely's preference was obvious. What was vital was his analysis of the new economic realities. That analysis centered on the "conflict of labor and capital" which resulted from corporate growth and the supposed "laissez-faire" conditions that had made such growth inevitable.

The idea of inevitable corporate growth under "laissez-faire," however, had initially been propagated by corporate entrepreneurs themselves. Like Weaver's argument regarding an inevitable "age of combination," Ely's new terminology tended to reinforce the recently triumphant corporate view of history. This was a crucial development because his usage redirected debate away from the question of *whether* to live with "combination" and toward that of *how* to live with it. The latter question would in turn give rise to other vital developments.

19. John R. Commons, "Progressive Individualism," in *American Magazine of Civics*, June 1895, p. 565; Ely, "Fraternalism *vs.* Paternalism in Government," in *Century*, n.s. March 1898, pp. 781–784.

Of these, none was more important than the political outlook generated by the new critics' own vocabulary. The key lies in the connection between new labels and old. Corporate usage of the individualist
metaphor had been designed to blur the distinction between the
natural and the artificial. That usage had been sufficiently successful to
legitimize the corporation as a "natural" phenomenon, but had also
allowed corporations to reach a size that now aroused widespread
antagonism to corporate power. The antagonism sprang from a fear
that individual opportunity was being eroded.

Critics such as Garland had argued all along that corporate usage of
the individualist metaphor was illegitimate, and corporate growth an
"unnatural" result of artificial governmental stimulation. By the early
1890s, however, this argument had already been generally rejected.
Most critics had accepted in principle the "naturalness" and inevitability of large-scale, "artificial individuals." The task was not to
attack artifice *per se*, but to balance one artifice with another.

In practical terms, this meant balancing corporate and governmental growth to preserve "individuality" and "naturalness" on both large
and small scales. On this basis Ely, Commons, and others initially
undertook to redefine the individualist label rather than throw it
away. Retaining the individualist label was a necessity for the new
critics. Because they were calling for increased government power,
they had to convince the public that they were not "paternalists" and
that they, too, wished to preserve individual opportunity. At the same
time, they had to distinguish clearly between their version of "individualism" and that of the corporations. Building on the same two
elements of "nature" and "artifice," they had to harmonize the old,
still cherished, naturalness with a new and clearly different form of
artifice.

Here one sees how new labels grow directly out of the old. Rebuilding political terms is both a negative and a positive activity. The
negative consists of summarizing in a "bad" label all rival options; the
positive of summarizing in a "good" label one's own option.

Ely's introduction of the conservative-radical polarity was the negative side of his rebuilding of the individualist metaphor. In his usage,
"conservatism," or the retention of an outmoded system of political
economy, was the old artifice of the corporations, hence bad. It was
the very thing that now threatened the survival of individual opportunity. "Radicalism," or the uprooting of the marketplace itself, was a

new and clearly different artifice but did not protect individual opportunity either; hence it was also bad.

Using both labels as pejoratives, however, Ely still needed a positive term to evoke his own position. The phrase "golden mean" was obviously insufficient because it connoted merely a midpoint between two other categories, and did not and could not symbolize an intellectually independent position. Moreover, it could neither be used as a modifier to the individualist label nor be reformulated as an independent "ism."

The label that eventually came to symbolize the new synthesis of nature and artifice was, of course, "progressive." As early as 1895, Commons described his own position as "progressive individualism."[20] Within a decade, the progressive label would stand on its own as the most popular self-designation of American politics. Eventually it, too, would enter the analytical vocabulary of social science, and generations of scholars would debate its "proper" definition.

Looked at historically, however, the progressive label becomes an object of study in a very different sense. It appears not as a value-free analytical tool but as a political weapon developed within a political context. That context was the emergence of a new critical perspective on corporate power.

The progressive label did not at once become a widely used self-identifying symbol. It took time for "progressive individualism" to become an acceptable position, and then to evolve into "progressivism." This was no accident. Political language evolves through political struggle, which tends to take place in stages. The first stage in this particular struggle was the effort of the new critics to discredit the corporations' version of "individualism." Thus the first stage centered on the critics' pejorative use of the conservative-radical polarity.

When Ely talked of a "rigid, obstructive and revolutionary conservatism," he was, as he himself had noted earlier, arguing in both political and moral terms and attempting to put corporate spokesmen on the defensive by whatever means he could. Close examination of the new critics' own vocabulary, however, suggests that they themselves were already on the defensive.

When someone like Garland competed for the individualist label,

20. Commons, "Progressive Individualism," cited n. 19, above. For an extended analysis of the progressive label, see Chapter 3, below.

he could go on the offensive and attack corporate dependence on government. Far from feeling intimidated by corporate countercharges of "paternalism" and "socialism," Garland aggressively turned those labels against the corporations themselves. By contrast, men like Ely and Commons felt constrained to disprove corporate accusations. In calling for the abandonment of "laissez-faire" and its replacement by "governmental control," they had made themselves, in Hartz's words, "peculiarly vulnerable to the waving of the red flag." Hence Ely's denial that "fraternalism" equaled "paternalism," as well as Commons' defensive insistence that "governmental control" was "not socialistic."[21]

This initial defensiveness had two important effects. First, it further validated the corporate argument that corporate growth resulted from "laissez-faire." Second, like most forms of defensiveness, it was self-reinforcing. Denial legitimizes attack, and the more the new critics denied their kinship to "paternalists," "socialists," and "reckless radicals," the more they legitimized a sweeping pejorative use of such terms as a way of dismissing all critics of corporate power. In a contest of insults, the new critics were badly disadvantaged, though one cannot fully understand how badly without considering the struggle over their other chief pejorative label, "conservative."

Herein lies a key issue in the politics of language. What happens when the same label is used negatively by one side and positively by the other? The question spotlights the history of the conservative label in the late 1880s and 90s. Used pejoratively by the new critics, it was nonetheless enthusiastically espoused as a self-designation by leading corporate spokesmen and their supporters. Carnegie not only claimed the label as his own but discoursed gleefully and at length on the "unmistakable conservatism of the American people."[22]

Carnegie's language was not accidental. Like Ely, he defined his categories in both political and moral terms. Indeed, in identifying himself as an "individualist," he had laid claim to the same morality as his critics. Where he differed was in simultaneously claiming the conservative label. The latter claim was extremely powerful. By assuming a label that implied fidelity to established traditions, he was placing corporations squarely in the mainstream of American history.

21. Hartz, *Liberal Tradition in America*, p. 217.
22. Carnegie, *Triumphant Democracy*, pp. 476, 486, and esp. 501.

In his terms, Carnegie's double identification as "individualist" and "conservative" came down to this: corporate success, like all forms of "individual" success, was a "natural," legitimate result of the great American "tradition" of minimal government. As he himself succinctly put it, "The laws are perfect."[23]

Again one sees how political labels are structurally related and how intimately the evolution of language is connected to the social adjustment process. By the late 1880s, there was widespread and growing skepticism concerning the supposed "perfection" of the laws, as the creation of the Interstate Commerce Commission (1887) and the Sherman Anti-Trust Act (1890) demonstrate. Growing skepticism also translated into growing social unrest, as evidenced by the emergence of such groups as the Free Silverites, the People's party, the Socialist Labor party, and others. The gap between the expectations created by corporate language and the actual consequences of corporate growth was coming to stimulate psychic resistance, hence mass arousal, toward the corporate definition of "individualism."

In such circumstances, and notwithstanding the pejorative usage of the new critics, the conservative label emerged as a particularly powerful new self-designation for corporate spokesmen. Among the most salient aspects of corporate growth was its innovative character. The concentration of economic power on this scale was indeed unprecedented and was the very element of "innovation" to which the new critics were attempting to draw public attention. Ely's phrase "revolutionary conservatism" was a semantic effort to spotlight the discordancy between "tradition" and "innovation," to project that discordancy onto corporations, and to reinforce psychic resistance to corporate political perspectives.

Corporate usage of the conservative label turned the strategy against the new critics themselves. There was indeed an inherent contradiction between the elements of "tradition" and "innovation," as in the earlier case of "nature" and "artifice." Used alone as a self-designation and without the discordant modifier "revolutionary," the conservative label worked to camouflage the contradiction and once again created a positive "unitary conceptual framework" that neatly harmonized two new positive yet contradictory expectations. In this case the expectations were that such "innovation" could be accepted

23. Carnegie, *Triumphant Democracy*, p. 471.

and encouraged while the "traditional" social order would be simultaneously preserved.

Complementing this positive usage of the conservative label was the corporations' own pejorative use of the radical label. Like the former label, the latter built on the two elements of "tradition" and "innovation." Whereas the former assigned both elements a positive image, the latter inverted the element of "innovation" and assigned it a negative image that evoked the overthrow rather than preservation of the "traditional" order. In this way, corporate usage paralleled and competed with Ely's pejorative use of the term "revolutionary." Also, by distinguishing the conservative label as a positive one and juxtaposing it to the negative radical label, corporate usage undercut the critics and inverted their strategy. In short, corporate usage of the conservative-radical polarity projected the discordancy between "tradition" and "innovation" onto opponents, discredited critics, and again camouflaged the contradictory expectations embedded in the corporations' own vocabulary.

The success of corporate language during this era is readily explained. The emergence of the conservative label as a leading self-designation of the 1890s suggests the heightened appeal of "tradition" in a time of unrest. Conversely, the pejoratives "revolutionary" and "radical" were far more effective against protest groups than those in power. It was the protestors themselves rather than those they attacked who were seen as threatening "tradition."[24]

Even so, and given the extent of popular resentment against corporate power, corporate success in defusing such resentment requires understanding the combination of linguistic and political factors. When Carnegie simultaneously claimed both the individualist and conservative labels, he was at once reinforcing his position and setting the stage for a subtle shift of emphasis. In part, the elements of "nature" and "artifice" paralleled those of "tradition" and "innovation" respectively. As "nature" was politically and morally coordinate with "tradition," so "artifice" was coordinate with "innovation." In this respect, the new self-designation built on the old.

At the same time, the conservative label allowed corporate spokes-

---

24. See, for example, Thomas J. McCormick, *China Market* (Chicago: Quadrangle, 1967), p. 25, and Stanley Jones, *The Presidential Election of 1896* (Madison: University of Wisconsin Press, 1964), p. 214.

men their own subtle yet highly advantageous transformation of the terms of the debate. Popular resentment against corporate power suggested a widespread belief that however "natural" corporate growth had been, corporations as "artificial individuals" had now reached "unnatural" size and strength, so "nature" and "artifice" were no longer in harmony. For corporate spokesmen to have fought this belief by relying on the individualist label alone would have meant a direct confrontation regarding this contradiction. Such a confrontation would have been most dangerous at this point because the new critics were already challenging corporate identification with the individualist label.

By introducing the conservative label into the debate, corporate spokesmen provided themselves a way, in Pocock's terms, of "preserving a power-structure by transforming its idiom." By focusing on "tradition" and "innovation," these spokesmen directed attention away from problems of "nature" and "artifice," avoided confrontation at the corporations' most vulnerable point (namely, their actual relationship to government), and instead shifted the debate onto the ground where they were strongest (namely, their ability to play on their link with the "tradition" of "laissez-faire" and on the public's fears of innovative "governmental control"). This is not to say that the events of the 1890s had made corporate identification with the individualist label a liability, for the two labels continued to reinforce each other. That they were both now necessary, however, indicates the degree to which events had rendered the former label insufficient.

Here the vocabulary of the new critics in turn reveals the limits of their political sophistication. Challenging corporate identification with the individualist label was both politically logical and potentially effective. But in attempting to use the conservative label as a pejorative, the new critics were actually reinforcing corporate identification with that label. To challenge one corporate self-designation while reinforcing the other was a self-defeating strategy.

The critics' linking corporations with "conservatism" not only helped camouflage corporate innovation; inasmuch as the word "conservative" implied fidelity to a tradition of self-reliance, the linkage also helped camouflage the dependency on government which characterized that innovation. Thus in linking corporations with "conservatism," the critics undercut their own challenge to corporate identification with the individualist label.

In so doing, the critics also revealed their limited understanding of the corporations' use of government. The word "conservative" implied hostility to governmental control, and fit nicely with the critics' own insistence on an increased governmental "regulation" of corporate affairs. But that usage also obscured a growing corporate sophistication in turning such intervention to their advantage, as seen in corporate attorney Richard Olney's sophisticated response to a suggested campaign to abolish the Interstate Commerce Commission.

The Commission [Olney wrote], as its functions have now been limited by the courts is, or can be made, of great use to the railroads. It satisfies the popular clamor for a government supervision of railroads, at the same time that that supervision is almost entirely nominal. Further, the older such a commission gets to be, the more inclined it will be to take the business and railroad view of things. It thus becomes a sort of barrier between the railroad corporations and the people and a sort of protection against hasty and crude legislation hostile to railroad interests. . . . The part of wisdom is not to destroy the Commission, but to utilize it.

Historians have long debated the extent of corporate receptivity to governmental "regulation," and Olney's response cannot be taken as evidence of a universal attitude. Nonetheless, his response indicates the presence on an influential level (Olney became attorney general in 1893, and secretary of state in 1895) of a receptivity that was obscured both then and afterward by the critics' own vocabulary.[25]

In reality, neither corporate nor critical attitudes were uniform. Some critics did challenge corporate identification with the conservative label, and did so specifically to question corporate fidelity to tradition as well as hostility to government. One such critic was William H. "Coin" Harvey, a leading Free Silver publicist. "We are approaching a crisis in the history of the world!" wrote Harvey in 1895. "'Conservative business interests' appeal for quietude." The quotation marks around the phrase "conservative business interests" were deliberate on his part. In Harvey's view, the "goldbug" policies of corporate leaders were both innovative and destructive. Demonetization of silver had "transformed the honest, industrious farmers into tenants" and "transferred forty thousand million dollars of prop-

25. Olney is quoted in Ekirch, *Decline of American Liberalism*, pp. 168–169.

erty from the many to the few." The transfer itself had been secured with government help. "Your property has been confiscated by law!" he told readers. "A law as cunning as the hand of the forger that raises a check!" Those who "committed this crime" had "the courts and machinery of law to enforce their payment."[26]

As in Garland's case, the unpopularity of Harvey's solution obscured his insight. His language was intended to call attention both to corporate reliance on government and to the destructive effects of corporate innovation. His challenge was badly undercut by a majority tendency to affix the conservative label ever more securely to the corporations themselves. Even among critics those who imposed their definition of the situation dominated their side of the debate.

In undercutting Harvey's language, his colleagues succeeded in neutralizing the last semantic challenge to the "laissez-faire" thesis of corporate growth. The result not only cemented the link between corporations and the conservative label but assured the ascendancy of the corporate perspective on government so long as the fear of social upheaval remained the immediate focus of American politics. From this point on, the corporate perspective would be free to run its course. Only its very success would finally lay bare the contradiction between tradition and innovation that language itself had so effectively camouflaged.

In this case, the process would barely take a decade, though that would be long enough to realize one more major innovation in the name of conservatism. That innovation would be presided over, appropriately enough, by a politician whose conservative credential was as solidly established as his disposition to innovate. Again, the consequences would be profound.

The political vocabulary of William McKinley

[Free Silver is] a peril so grave that conservative men everywhere are breaking away from the old party associations and uniting with other patriotic citizens in emphatic protest.

1896

26. W. H. Harvey, *Up to Date: Coin's Financial School Continued* (Chicago: Coin Publishing Co., 1895), pp. 36–41.

> [The] working men of the United States . . . . are the bone and
> sinew of the country and the mighty conservative force which in every
> perilous crisis of our history must be relied upon to preserve National
> honor and the supremacy of law.
>
> 1896

> Strange it would be if the majority of the brainy and progressive
> young men of the Nation did not align themselves with the Re-
> publican Party.
>
> 1896

> [The] events of the past five months . . . . have been so full of
> responsibility, immediate and prospective, as to admonish the so-
> berest judgment and counsel the most conservative action.
>
> 1898

> [The Peace Treaty] now commits the free and enfranchised Phil-
> ipinos to the guiding hand and liberalizing influence . . . not of their
> American masters, but of their American emancipators.
>
> 1899

Conservative, progressive, liberal. Which one represents the "real"
McKinley? Even to ask the question is to mistake the politics of
language. To suggest that a particular label describes the "real" man is
to say the labels themselves have "correct" definitions—that there is
such a thing as a "real conservative," a "real progressive," a "real
liberal." Political labels have no fixed definitions, so it is meaningless
to apply one to McKinley. He used different labels in different ways at
different times for different purposes.[27]

It is quite another matter to say that people *thought* McKinley "a
conservative," identified him with the conservative label, or accorded
him a "conservative credential." What makes the labels important is
that in reifying them people come to believe labels have "real" meaning, so in identifying a politician with a certain label, people think
they understand what his "real" views are. This is not to say that

---

27. All quotations from McKinley are from the microfilms of the McKinley Papers
published by the Library of Congress. They are, in order: "Free Silver," August 26,
1896, Series 4, Reel 81; "Working men," October 7, 1896, ibid.; "Brainy and progressive," undated (1896), ibid.; "Most conservative action," October 19, 1898, Series
4, Reel 82; and "Liberalizing influence," February 16, 1899, ibid.

politicians are necessarily corrupt or dishonest in their use of words, only that language itself has political implications. The question is not what McKinley was "really," but rather how he used language, and how it helped him achieve his goals.

A study of his vocabulary serves two purposes. First, it shows McKinley himself to have been an astute and sensitive politician rather than the stuffy, bumptious fool he is often pictured as. Second, it shows how Americans entered a new era in their history without ever coming to grips with the magnitude or implications of the change.

McKinley used a variety of labels to accomplish his political purposes, most often the conservative label. This was particularly true during such crises as the 1896 election campaign and the Philippine annexation debate of 1898. The political atmosphere in both situations was one of apprehension and uncertainty. McKinley's use of the conservative label provided psychological reassurance that things would not change substantially, and he capitalized effectively on the connotation of respect for tradition.

This is not to accuse him of hypocrisy. He did see himself as a believer in the traditional "American system."[28] Yet he stood ready to make major innovations to preserve that system. Again, what better label under which to innovate than the conservative label? What is crucial is the nature of his innovations. On first glance, McKinley's positive use of the conservative label would seem to have put him in opposition to the new critics, but when one compares his views to theirs, an important parallel emerges.

The core of the new critics' perspective was their claim that modern industrial conditions necessitated greater government intervention on behalf of labor. This sincere sympathy for labor was as essential to McKinley's views as to those of Ely and Commons. Indeed, McKinley's background as a labor lawyer is often forgotten in historical accounts of the era, as is the fact that Mark Hanna, the mining company executive who was his closest political collaborator, had first met McKinley when the latter had been an attorney for the miners' union.

As a labor negotiator, McKinley understood that in an economy dominated by large corporations neither individual job security nor

28. See, for example, his statement in the House of Representatives, May 18, 1888, Series 4, Reel 81.

the escape hatch of small independent entrepreneurship was as readily available to the average worker as in earlier times. He saw trade unions as a natural response to this situation. Combination on the part of capital implied combination on the part of labor, and it was the function of government to maintain a balance between the two.

This attitude is what set McKinley apart from such men as Olney. During the 1894 Pullman strike, when the latter was encouraging President Cleveland to call out federal troops, McKinley, then governor of Ohio, sent his brother to persuade George Pullman to make concessions to the strikers. Hanna strongly supported McKinley. To both men, combination was now a fact of life. Indeed, Hanna would literally tell western farm audiences: "Anybody abusin' you people now? All right, combine and smash 'em!" Unlike Olney, Hanna also understood the political value of labor support. During the 1896 campaign, in which he acted as McKinley's chief organizer and strategist, Hanna made a point of meeting with railway union representatives to assure them of McKinley's solicitude. "I told them," he wrote McKinley, "you were the best friend of the laboring man I knew in public life."[29]

McKinley's verbal strategy is best understood against this background. When he called for "progressive" policies such as the eight-hour day for federal employees, he was establishing himself as a friend of labor. When he simultaneously described workers as a "mighty conservative force," he was insisting that workers themselves wanted their problems solved within the "traditional" system. In short, McKinley presented himself as a reassuring, ecumenical philosopher of class conciliation.

Over and over he made the point explicit. "Labor," he declared during the 1896 campaign, "is indispensable to the creation and profitable use of capital and capital increases the efficiency and value of labor. Whoever arrays one against the other is the enemy of both. That policy is wisest and best which harmonizes the two on the basis of absolute justice." The labels were a shorthand way of saying the same thing. "Class appeals," he added a few days later, "are dishonorable

29. Williams, *Contours*, pp. 361, 345; John A. Garraty, *The American Nation* (New York: Harper & Row, 1966), p. 618; and Hanna to McKinley, January 8, 1896, Series 1, Reel 1, McKinley microfilms.

and dishonest." In an atmosphere of upheaval and fear, it was a brilliantly effective strategy.[30]

McKinley's rhetoric, however, was far more than that. He was proposing to harmonize two related discordancies, one between labor and capital, the other between innovation and tradition. The two were related in that only bold innovation would preserve the labor-capital balance which in turn was the only way to protect the traditional system. McKinley's conservative credential was useful for achieving power, but it would also ultimately be indispensable for implementing his policy approach. That approach consisted of "expanding the power of government" in behalf of labor and capital alike on an unprecedentedly international scale; hence the particular need for a label that would harmonize tradition and innovation.

As early as 1895, McKinley outlined his innovative approach to foreign trade. Labor and capital, he told the National Association of Manufacturers, would both benefit from a combination of traditional protective tariffs and a forward-looking, government-directed reciprocity. Tariffs would protect existing home markets without "degrading our labor" to hold those markets, while reciprocity would provide "foreign markets for our surplus products." In his 1897 inaugural address, McKinley called for "friendly legislation" to accomplish these purposes, and added that the "end in view always [should] be the opening up of new markets." Later that year, he returned to the theme, stressing government's role in the "promotion of trade and commerce at home and abroad."[31]

In stressing reciprocity McKinley was not merely innovative but far ahead of his time, for reciprocity did not become part of American life until the 1930s. In McKinley's day, much of the opposition came from business groups, which did not always support him despite his pro-business reputation. There were limits to his power to innovate. At the same time, McKinley's failure to implement reciprocity throws into sharper relief his success in legitimizing a far more important

30. For McKinley's call for the eight-hour day, see his remarks in the House of Representatives, August 28, 1890, Series 4, Reel 81. For his 1896 references to "labor and capital," see speech at Canton, undated (probably September 17–19, 1896), ibid.; on "class appeals," see speech at Canton, September 26, 1896, ibid.

31. Walter LaFeber, *The New Empire* (Ithaca: Cornell University Press, 1963), pp. 192–193, 329–330, 332.

innovation, namely his use of federal power to conquer, occupy, and govern a people halfway around the world.

It was no accident that in the debate over Philippine annexation, the chief pejorative term that opponents hurled at McKinley was "imperialist." The impact of the label hinged precisely on the implication of innovation. Charles Francis Adams, Jr., one of several vice-presidents of the hastily organized "Anti-Imperialist League," charged that "on every one of the fundamental principles discussed— whether ethnic, economic, or political," McKinley was abandoning "the traditional and distinctively American grounds." To accuse McKinley of abandoning tradition was equivalent to challenging his conservative credential. One could not be "imperialist" and "conservative" at the same time.

Administration spokesmen responded quickly and directly. In a front-page *New York Times* interview, Mark Hanna (now Senator Hanna) replied that "conservative, far-seeing and thinking men" supported the president's position. Shortly thereafter, McKinley himself called for "the most conservative action," which included, however, accepting "the obligations of victory." Duty, he argued, "determines destiny."

Other supporters stressed the theme of tradition. In a major Senate speech, Beveridge of Indiana challenged the opposition as to whether Americans would "proceed along the lines of national development surveyed by the statesmen of our past, or whether, for the first time, the American people . . . [would] prove apostate to the spirit of their race."[32]

McKinley's conservative designation implied both tradition and restraint. Yet Beveridge's flamboyant appeal to tradition was hardly restrained. Against this backdrop one can better appreciate Hanna's emphasis on the cool rationality of "conservative, far-seeing and thinking men." Each man's style was a foil to the other in helping to protect the administration's conservative credential.

Ultimately, it was McKinley himself who most effectively harmo-

32. Adams is quoted in E. Berkeley Tompkins, *Anti-Imperialism in the United States* (Philadelphia: University of Pennsylvania Press, 1970), p. 182; the Hanna interview is in *The New York Times*, October 1, 1898, p. 1; the McKinley quotations are from the McKinley Papers, "Most conservative action," October 19, 1898, ser. 4, Reel 82; and Beveridge is quoted in W. Thorp, M. Curti, et al., eds., *American Issues* (Chicago: Lippincott, 1955), 1:914.

nized the discordancy between restraint and enthusiasm, as he had that between tradition and innovation. In retrospect, his famous "confession" to visiting clergymen about sleepless indecision resolved by prayer may seem corny, but at the time, it was a highly effective way of sounding restrained, enthusiastic, traditional, and innovative all at once. And what could be more reassuring than an invocation of the Deity? Except for a few iconoclasts like Mark Twain, opposition spokesmen had neither the wisdom nor the imagination to take up the challenge on that score. [33]

McKinley recognized that success depended on being able to define annexation not as a foreign policy issue but as a matter of domestic self-image. In the 1890s, the domestic political context was primary for most Americans, the foreign policy context secondary. McKinley's conservative label, a domestic label and therefore of "primary potency," would cancel the imperialist label the opposition was trying to attach to his foreign policy. Indeed, one could *not* be both "conservative" and "imperialist." Accepting the opposition's frame of reference, McKinley neatly turned it against them. [34]

The strategy not only worked but had far-reaching implications. So long as an assertion of governmental power could be credibly defended as "conservative," it could not be effectively attacked as "imperialist," or as innovative at all. In the short run, if the election of 1900 was not a "referendum on imperialism," that was because McKinley's "conservative" image precluded defining the issue in such terms. In the long run, the impact of his triumph can be measured by the fact that not for two generations (and even then only in a minor way) did the word "imperialist" again become a damaging pejorative in American politics. In short, McKinley's neutralization of the word became sedimented in the language. [35]

As McKinley's victory established a continuity between the annexation of the Philippines and the American past, so annexation itself became a portent of the future. The strategic importance of the Philip-

33. For McKinley's "confession," see Foster Rhea Dulles, *America's Rise to World Power* (New York: Harper Torchbooks, 1963), p. 51; for Twain's reaction, see Fred Harvey Harrington, "Literary Aspects of American Anti-Imperialism, 1898–1902," *New England Quarterly* 10, December 1937:661.

34. On "labels of primary potency," see Gordon Allport, *The Nature of Prejudice* (Reading, Mass.: Addison-Wesley, 1954), pp. 179 ff.

35. On the 1900 election and the imperialist label, see Tompkins, *Anti-Imperialism in the United States*, pp. 214–235.

pines in protecting American trade routes and the administration's emphasis on the importance of foreign markets made annexation symbolic of an American self-definition in which domestic stability came to depend on controlling people thousands of miles away.

There was an irony in this. If the annexation of the Philippines symbolized making other people responsible for American well-being, it did so in the very act of asserting American superiority over them. Annexation was thus a simultaneous assertion of vulnerability and strength. Most important, it turned the new American self-definition into an extension of American tradition. The contradictory nature of these assertions underlines the importance of McKinley's language as a harmonizing device.

McKinley's strategy becomes clearer when one examines the vocabulary of the debates more closely. When the administration's supporters felt the need for a foreign policy label to counter the accusations of "imperialism," they chose the word "expansionist," a word that carried the clear implication of fidelity to tradition. The fight, *Outlook* magazine carefully explained, was not between "imperialists" and "anti-imperialists," but between "expansionists" and "continentalists." An expansionist was "one who believes that American ideas and institutions are good for the whole world," as distinct from the continentalist "who thinks they are adapted only to the continent of North America." One could not be both imperialist and conservative, but one could be both expansionist and conservative. Indeed, the implication was that only expansionists were truly conservative in the sense of having unlimited faith in American traditions and institutions.[36]

Like the conservative label, the expansionist label became central to the administration's verbal strategy. Historians have long recognized what McKinley himself stressed; namely, the exceptional nature of the Philippine case. In general, what McKinley wanted was profitable economic relationships without burdensome political control. Only in strategically vital areas was the exception necessary.

Moreover, if the exceptional, extreme case could be justified as "expansionist" rather than "imperialist," who could effectively oppose less extreme cases such as the temporary occupation of Cuba? And

36. *Outlook*, October 22, 1898, pp. 464–466.

who could object at all to the administration's Open Door Policy, which stated the case for economic expansion in explicitly anti-imperialist terms?

The Open Door Policy, enunciated in two stages, was a call to other industrial nations to accept international economic competition without recourse to political domination. If the annexation of the Philippines was not "imperialist," surely the more restrained approach was not.

What the administration's vocabulary established was a hierarchy of foreign interventions ranging from more extreme to less extreme. The justification of the more extreme (annexation) implicitly included the less extreme (Open Door), and by implying continuity with the past, camouflaged the innovative character of both kinds of interventions. The power of this semantic framework is seen in the fact that having successfully defended the annexation of the Philippines as "conservative," the administration's supporters never needed to apply that label to the Open Door Policy itself.

The moment one breaks loose from the framework, however, the Open Door Policy emerges as a major innovation. Americans had long sought foreign markets. The Open Door not only reinforced the new externalization of responsibility for domestic well-being, however. It made domestic prosperity ultimately dependent on government intervention because it implicitly promised such intervention to prevent the closing of crucial foreign markets.

Generations later, historians would develop an analytical category called "Open Door liberalism" which seriously limited historical understanding of the origins and significance of the policy itself. The Open Door was introduced as part of an innovative synthesis that could only be legitimized by getting people to think of it as consonant with tradition. In short, public acceptance of the Open Door Policy reflected the solidity of McKinley's "conservative credential."

In keeping with the broader, "minimal government" connotations of that credential, the stated intent of the Open Door was to minimize government intervention abroad by outlawing all political interference in foreign markets. The policy nonetheless contained the implicit threat of United States action to counter interference by foreign governments (a threat McKinley's successors would ultimately make good). Equally as important, the Open Door implicitly legitimized whatever domestic intervention was necessary to maximize the competitive efficiency of the American productive system.

Far from signaling a reduction in the government's intervention in economic life, then, the Open Door was designed to minimize such intervention where it was weakest (thousands of miles away), and allow for its maximization where it was strongest (in promoting industrial efficiency at home). The assumed connection between efficiency and "combination" also meant a further legitimization in principle of governmental action to promote and protect "combination" itself. McKinley carefully reassured labor that it, too, would benefit from the Open Door.

Not surprisingly, the Open Door Policy received the overwhelming endorsement of business and labor leaders alike, many of whom had vigorously opposed the annexation of the Philippines. The importance of McKinley's triumph, however, lay not merely in the level of support for the Open Door, but in how the policy was generally perceived. That he never had to defend it as "conservative" shows how completely he had neutralized the charge of innovation. Indeed, in combining the annexation of the Philippines and the Open Door Policy, McKinley had succeeded in making innovation itself seem traditional.[37]

Despite its brilliance as a political achievement, McKinley's synthesis was unstable. What he had produced was not a resolution of the underlying labor-capital conflict, but a temporary quiescence on the part of labor. Once the euphoria generated by the events of 1898 had abated, the limitations of his solution would become apparent. Its capacity to harmonize discordancy exhausted, McKinley's conservative label would cease to function as a mechanism for quiescence. Furthermore, the label's identification with the corporate perspective would cause it to lose popularity as a self-designation, and its pejorative usage would at last become general. What was not clear was how the self-identifying symbol of the triumphant critics—namely, the progressive label—would affect such issues as the growth of corporate power, the corporate-government relationship, and the nature of American politics itself.

37. See William Appleman Williams, *The Tragedy of American Diplomacy* (New York: Delta Books, 1972), pp. 50–52; Williams, *Contours*, p. 368; and LaFeber, *New Empire*, pp. 412–416.

Meanwhile, and for the brief remainder of his life, McKinley's definition of the situation was assured. Shortly after his second inauguration, Kansas newspaperman William Allen White summed up the prevailing attitude toward the president and his policies. McKinley, he wrote, was "forcible, wise, conservative, efficient, and truly great."[38]

38. White to H. S. Lewis, May 20, 1901, vol. 2, ser. 2, Letterbooks, William Allen White Papers, Library of Congress, Washington, D.C. (hereafter White MS.).

3

The Struggle for

the Progressive Label

The linguistic transformation of Theodore Roosevelt

I am so far from being against property, when I ask that the question of the trust be taken up, that I am acting, in the most conservative sense, in property's interest.

Theodore Roosevelt, 1902

I say to you that he has been . . . the greatest conservative force for the protection of property and our institutions in the city of Washington.

Elihu Root, 1904

The prime problem of our nation is to get the right type of good citizenship, and, to get it, we must have progress, and our public men must be genuinely progressive.

Theodore Roosevelt, 1910

[The nation must choose between] the tendency to conservatism and the tendency toward progress.

Outlook magazine, 1912

Politicians change labels for many reasons: survival, principle, policy change. As Theodore Roosevelt's career suggests, however, to change labels is not necessarily to change one's basic political outlook. The man described by his closest associate in 1904 as the "greatest conservative force" in Washington was the same man *Outlook* magazine advertised in 1912 as the personification of the "tendency toward progress." Although linguistic transformation did reflect certain specific policy shifts on Roosevelt's part, it did not signal a basic change in

54

his outlook. It did, however, involve matters of both political principle and political survival.[1]

An analysis of Roosevelt's language offers important insights into American history. The chief linguistic events of his presidency were the decline of the conservative label and the rise of the progressive. Unexamined and taken for granted, the change in labels suggests a discontinuity, indeed a major shift in direction, in American politics itself. Whether or not this was actually the case can be determined only by historical investigation. Such an investigation begins with the relationship between old labels and new.[2]

The progressive label is a metaphor built on the discordant yet harmonizable elements of "movement" and "stability." As a political self-designation, the metaphor implies "forward movement" or *progress* without loss of "stability." Historically, the metaphor first emerged as part of a new critical perspective on corporate power. The original formula, "progressive individualism," combined two metaphors implying a "forward-looking" yet "stable" synthesis of "nature" and "artifice." This forward-looking use of "artifice" in the form of "governmental control" or "regulation" was what distinguished the "progressive individualism" of the new critics from the "rigid, obstructive and revolutionary conservatism" of the corporations.

During the 1890s, McKinley had called for both a "progressive" and "conservative" approach to federal intervention. Unlike the new critics, he did not define "conservatism" as rigid, obstructive, or revolutionary. For him, the essence of "conservatism" was a flexibility that allowed for innovation in order to preserve tradition. One could innovate both as a "progressive" and as a "conservative." The two labels were not contradictory but complementary. Indeed, in McKinley's usage, "forward movement" was coordinate with "innovation," just as "stability" was coordinate with "tradition." So innovative was McKinley in his use of power that only his "conservative credential" allowed him to proceed.

McKinley agreed that government intervention was needed to pre-

1. G. Wallace Chessman, *Theodore Roosevelt and the Politics of Power* (Boston: Little, Brown, 1969), p. 86; Gabriel Kolko, *Triumph of Conservatism* (Glencoe: Free Press, 1963), pp. 73–74; Theodore Roosevelt, *The New Nationalism* (Englewood Cliffs, N.J.: Prentice-Hall, 1961), p. 39; and *Outlook*, 101, May 4, 1912:11–12.

2. On how a power-structure survives by transforming its idiom, see J. G. A. Pocock, *Politics, Language, and Time* (New York: Atheneum, 1973), p. 19.

serve the labor-capital balance, yet preferred to rely mainly on promoting business expansion for the benefit of labor and capital alike. To
this end he called for "friendly legislation" to aid in the "promotion of
trade and commerce at home and abroad." To him, "promotion" was
at once forward-looking, stable, innovative, and traditional. In short,
"promotion" was both "progressive" and "conservative."

The new critics differed from McKinley in two respects. First, they
defined conservatism negatively, simply as the political perspective of
the corporations. Second, they preferred "regulation" to "promotion"
as a way of protecting labor. The two differences were related. To the
new critics, "promotion" was "friendly" or nonthreatening to corporate power, hence "conservative," while "regulation" was restrictive
or "forward-looking" in its controls on corporate power, hence "progressive."

So long as McKinley lived, his definition of the situation predominated in American politics. Only in the years after his death did the
language of the new critics emerge triumphant, and the distinction
between "promotion" and "regulation" of corporate power become
synonymous with that between "conservatism" and "progressivism"
respectively.

In this context Roosevelt emerges as the key transitional figure. His
early usage of the conservative label, like McKinley's, indicates that
he believed in using power innovatively to "conserve" both prosperity
and the labor-capital balance. As McKinley had attempted to mediate
the 1894 railroad strike, so Roosevelt intervened to settle the 1902
coal strike. To both men, class conciliation was essential to industrial
society.[3]

Roosevelt also shared McKinley's foreign policy outlook. He was a
self-styled "expansionist," viewed the Open Door approach as basic to
domestic prosperity, and like McKinley, never viewed "expansion" as
a substitute for trade unions. As early as 1899, while still governor of
New York, Roosevelt recorded his belief "that we shall have to pay far
more attention to . . . tremendous problems . . . of the relations of
capital and labor . . . than to any question of expansion for the next
fifty years, and this although I am an expansionist, and believe that we

3. For Roosevelt's views on the labor-capital balance, see Roosevelt to Root, June
2, 1904, Box 163, Special Correspondence, Elihu Root Papers, Library of Congress,
Washington, D.C. (hereafter Root MS.)

can go on and take our place among the nations of the world." On this basis Roosevelt congratulated Congress in December 1903 for acting along "sane and conservative lines" in establishing a cabinet-level Department of Commerce and Labor to "regulate" the activities of both groups.[4]

Roosevelt's vocabulary raises two issues. First, it shows him initially defining the situation differently from the new critics. Where they defined regulation as progressive, he defined it as conservative. This was what he meant when he talked of enforcing antitrust laws for "most conservative" reasons; it was also implicit in his describing the Department of Commerce and Labor as a "conservative" achievement.

Second, Roosevelt's language calls into question the very basis for a hard-and-fast distinction between regulation and promotion. When Roosevelt spoke of enforcing antitrust laws "in property's interest," he was indicating his intention of using those laws as a means of protection, if not precisely promotion. In this, his argument paralleled Olney's earlier defense of the Interstate Commerce Commission. The moment one recognizes an intentionally protective use of what is called "regulation," however, the question immediately arises as to the actual relationship between regulation, protection, and promotion.

In certain cases, protection may be the only promotion required. If so-called regulation furnishes such protection, then it functions as a form of promotion. If it specifically works to protect some firms more than others, then it operates as a form of selective promotion. Conversely, as Garland had argued earlier, what is labeled "promotion" may, through an unequal bestowal of "privileges," alter the competitive balance within a field and make it harder for some firms to survive. So-called promotion then functions as a form of regulation.

Here is an issue central to modern American politics. To question the promotion-regulation dichotomy is not merely to reexamine Theodore Roosevelt but to question the very basis on which some of the most important legislation of his era (and subsequent eras) has been introduced, enacted, labeled, and thereby legitimized. That a law has been labeled "regulatory" is no guarantee against the further growth of "giant corporations"; nor does labeling it "promotional" guarantee

4. Howard K. Beale, *Theodore Roosevelt and the Rise of America to World Power* (Baltimore: Johns Hopkins University Press, 1956), p. 79; and Fred L. Israel, ed., *The State of the Union Messages of the Presidents* (New York: Chelsea House, 1966), 2: 2075.

that it will enhance all interests equally. Labels may at once legitimize intentions and camouflage consequences.

The evolution of American political vocabulary in the first decade of this century suggests that the policy approach Roosevelt inherited from McKinley, an approach Roosevelt himself viewed as regulatory, protective, promotional, *and* conservative, eventually came to be seen as unduly advantageous to large corporations. Because corporate spokesmen had long associated themselves with the conservative label, it became a "bad" word, a pejorative. Yet Roosevelt's subsequent self-transformation from "conservative" to "progressive" does not so much indicate a shift in his actual policy approach as a rhetorical effort to distance himself politically from the corporations.

Roosevelt was not being dishonest. He was sufficiently literate and astute to understand the subjectivity of language. Words like "radical" and "conservative," he told Root in 1906, "are really very loosely used words, and . . . their value depends wholly on the particular circumstances of each case." Roosevelt was not about to let a valid policy approach be crippled by association with unpopular labels. Believing in his policies and recognizing that the impact of words depended on "particular circumstances," he chose his vocabulary very carefully. In shifting from a conservative to a progressive rhetoric, he was acknowledging a gradual yet unmistakable shift in public attitudes.[5]

The sincerity of Roosevelt's intentions is less important than the consequences of his actions. The result of his verbal shift was not only to relabel as "forward motion" a static policy approach but to introduce into an ongoing debate a particular definition of the "forward-looking" label. His shift must therefore be understood not merely as a response to the decline of an old label, but as part of an emerging struggle to embed new political perceptions in a new label. This in turn requires understanding the evolution of the progressive label up to the time that Roosevelt joined in the struggle to define it.

During the first three decades after the Civil War, the courts had disallowed a substantial amount of state-level legislation designed to restrict corporate power. For this reason critics of the corporations had shifted their efforts to the federal level. By the turn of the century, it was clear that federal action alone had not been successful, and a revival of state-level intervention coincided with the emergence of

5. Roosevelt to Root, September 4, 1906, Box 163, Spec. Corr., Root MS.

the progressive label as a term embodying belief in the uniqueness and viability of regulation. As early as January 1901, the connection was made clear by the newly elected governor of Wisconsin, Robert M. La Follette.

To La Follette, vigorous state action was neither unconstitutional nor anachronistic, but was legitimate and indispensable to the "progressive" transfer of power from the "few" to the "many." In his first message to the state legislature on January 10, 1901, La Follette made clear his views on state taxation of corporate capital. It was widely asserted, he remarked, "that the money will be driven out of the State before its owners will consent to pay the tax upon it." Such fears were unwarranted. In "every State in the Union" public opinion was forcing legislative changes that would "make all taxable property, individual and corporate, meet its assessments and pay its taxes." The day was at hand, he declared, "when no State in the Union will offer an asylum of refuge for capital seeking to evade the payment of taxes."

La Follette was equally emphatic about the propriety of state action. "It is of course known," he declared, "that the whole subject of interstate commerce is under our system exclusively a matter of Federal cognizance; but surely the State has some control over the business transactions within its limits, even by foreign corporations." The line between state and federal jurisdictions was "difficult to define, but, the State having some power in the matter, the duty of State government is exactly commensurate with the limits of its powers."6

Because La Follette was a state politician and Roosevelt a federal one, it is understandable that each emphasized action within his own arena, and this difference sharply affected their policy perspectives. The extent of the difference is best understood by comparing La Follette's approach to that advocated by Roosevelt in his first message to Congress eleven months later.

To Roosevelt, the issue was the international basis of American prosperity. Calling for "caution in dealing with corporations," the new president emphasized their importance in international commercial competition: "America has only just begun to assume that commanding position in the international business world which we believe will more and more be hers. It is of the utmost importance that this

6. Robert S. Maxwell, ed., *La Follette* (Englewood Cliffs, N.J.: Prentice-Hall, 1969), pp. 20, 31–32.

position be not jeoparded, especially at a time when the overflowing abundance of our own natural resources and the skill, business energy, and mechanical aptitude of our people make foreign markets essential." In these circumstances, he added, "combination and concentration should be, not prohibited, but supervised and within reasonable limits controlled." Once again, the task was to make combination "work for the good of all."

Here one sees how Roosevelt's approach, which he himself described at the time as "most conservative," was already converging with that of corporate leaders. Testifying before the United States Industrial Commission in 1899, John D. Rockefeller had noted the disruptive effects of nonuniform state incorporation laws. To remedy the situation, he had endorsed federal incorporation statutes, or "in lieu thereof, State legislation as nearly uniform as possible." Financier George Perkins also recommended expanded federal action after reviewing a preliminary draft of Roosevelt's message.

In the final version, Roosevelt took a similar position. "The large corporations," he noted, "though organized in one State, always do business in many States, often doing very little business in the State where they are incorporated. There is utter lack of uniformity in the State laws about them; and as no State has any exclusive interest in or power over their acts, it has in practice proved impossible to get adequate regulation through State action." He called for a federal incorporation law, and for a constitutional amendment if needed as a prerequisite.[7]

On the face of it, Roosevelt's position did not seem controversial. As he had said in proposing expanded federal action, "in the interest of the whole people, the Nation should, without interfering with the power of the States in the matter itself, also assume power of supervision and regulation over all corporations doing an interstate business." In reality, a serious conflict was emerging between Roosevelt's "conservative" federal approach and La Follette's "progressive" state approach. Roosevelt had spoken of federal action as a more "adequate" form of regulation. What corporate spokesmen feared was not the inadequacy but the increasing hostility behind such legislation as La

7. Israel, ed., *State of the Union Messages*, 2:2018–2022; Chessman, *Theodore Roosevelt and the Politics of Power*, p. 83; and Kolko, *Triumph of Conservatism*, pp. 64, 66.

Follette proposed. Rockefeller had indeed called for uniform state legislation, but the Wisconsin model was hardly what he had in mind.

Roosevelt's perspective was not identical to that of the corporations. To him, the problem with state legislation was that it undermined industrial efficiency and reduced America's effectiveness as an international competitor. "America holds its tenure of prosperity," warned presidential adviser Brooks Adams in 1902, "only on condition that she can undersell her rivals, and she cannot do so if her administrative machinery generates friction unduly." To his brother Henry, Brooks wrote privately in 1903: "We must have a new deal, we must have new methods, we must suppress the states, and have a centralized administration, or we shall wobble over."[8]

Even in private, Roosevelt himself did not advocate "suppression" of state governments. He nonetheless shared Brooks's concern for efficiency. He also knew that in taking federal action he was preempting a massive state-level assault on certain corporations. "I think the worst thing that could be done," he remarked at one point, "would be an announcement that for two or three years the Federal Government would keep its hands off [railroads]. It would result in a tidal wave of violent State action against them thruout [sic] three-fourths of this country."

Again, the principle was protection through "regulation," and the purpose of regulation was to preserve an existing system. Equally important, preserving the system was more and more coming to mean, in Brooks's phrase, "centralized administration" in a context of ever-growing "combination." On this point, Roosevelt and corporate leaders stood together.[9]

In his December 1904 annual message, Roosevelt, obviously pleased by his recent reelection, pointed to his "long-continued government policies" as an important factor in the nation's "noteworthy prosperity." The people, he noted, had "emphatically expressed their approval of the principles underlying these policies, and their desire that these principles be kept substantially unchanged, although of course applied in a progressive spirit to meet changing conditions." For the moment, Roosevelt continued to use the progressive and

8. Brooks Adams, *The New Empire* (New York: Macmillan, 1902), pp. xxxiii, 211; Daniel Aaron, "The Unusable Man: An Essay on the Mind of Brooks Adams," *New England Quarterly* 21, March 1948:23.

9. Kolko, *Triumph of Conservatism*, p. 310.

conservative labels conjointly, signifying that, like McKinley, he viewed them as complements rather than as opposites.

As popular resentment toward corporations began to escalate sharply during his second term, however, he began moving away from the conservative label, even linking it with the negative metaphor "reactionary," or "backward movement." Thus in his 1906 message he assailed "reactionary or ultraconservative apologists for the misuse of wealth" who were "themselves most potent in increasing socialistic feeling." The following year he requested further legislation concerning the employment of women and children, arguing that the federal government was "very much behind the legislation of our more progressive States" in this regard.[10]

By early 1908, some self-styled "conservatives" were becoming alienated by Roosevelt's apparently increasing militance. In his January message on trusts, he castigated those who had made "the name 'high finance' a term of scandal" and he called for increased federal "regulation" of railroad rates and stock market speculation. He also criticized the courts for disturbing the delicate labor-management balance by too free a use of antilabor injunctions. After hearing the message, Senator Joseph Foraker of Ohio charged that there was no "substantial difference between what is represented by Mr. Bryan and Mr. Roosevelt." Another critic suggested the formation of a new political organization "which shall comprise the conservative men of both great political parties."

Despite these responses, however, neither Roosevelt's increasingly anticonservative rhetoric nor his new legislative proposals indicated a change in outlook. He had been pursuing the "question of the trust," albeit selectively, and had been warning of the consequences of corporate misbehavior since his early days as a self-styled conservative. He had also been equally consistent in attempting to protect the labor-management balance in the name of conservatism. Most important, since taking office he had been gradually moving to expand federal authority over corporate financial practices. His purpose, as Root publicly explained in 1906, was to "cut out the wrongdoing and save the business."[11]

10. Israel, ed., *State of the Union Messages*, pp. 2105, 2210, 2260.
11. George Mowry, *Theodore Roosevelt and the Progressive Movement* (Madison: University of Wisconsin Press, 1946), p. 28; Philip C. Jessup, *Elihu Root* (New York: Dodd, Mead, 1938), 2:118.

Roosevelt's verbal and tactical policy shift is better explained in other ways. He was responding both to the change in the popular mood and to another major change on the national political scene. During his second term, many of the self-styled "progressives" hitherto active in state politics began moving to Washington. Their move did not indicate an abandonment of state action, but an intent to bring federal policy into line with recent state legislation.

La Follette was the first to take a Senate seat (in January 1906), and he was followed by such men as Borah of Idaho, Cummins of Iowa, and later on, Johnson of California. The early arrivals found the Senate dominated by men who seemed bent on consolidating rather than challenging corporate power. To emphasize the distance between themselves and this dominant "Old Guard," the La Follette group took the label "insurgent." The "insurgents" attempted to challenge the "Old Guard" by amending legislation from the floor and by carrying the fight into the home states of their opponents, hoping to defeat them when they came up for reelection. Initially, the first tactic was futile, except as it created publicity and thereby contributed to the effectiveness of the second. By the summer of 1908, La Follette was receiving national recognition for building a "growing progressive force" within the Senate.[12]

La Follette received little help from Roosevelt in either of the two fights. Beneath their surface cordiality the two men disliked and distrusted each other intensely. Roosevelt privately referred to La Follette as a "shifty self-seeker" and an "entirely worthless Senator." La Follette, in an autobiography published in 1913, scathingly described the former president as "the keenest and ablest living interpreter of what I would call the superficial public sentiment of a given time." Although both men were powerful and commanding personalities, their differences reflected far more than a personality clash.

In actuality, the Roosevelt-La Follette clash marked the beginning of a major struggle within the Republican party over the definition of "progressivism." Roosevelt adhered to the approach he had consistently espoused since 1901 and favored broad discretionary, "regulatory" authority in the hands of federal agencies. Formerly he had labeled this approach "conservative" and thus undercut any semantic

12. Belle Case La Follette and Fola La Follette, *Robert M. La Follette* (New York: Macmillan, 1953), 1:199–261, esp. 261.

correspondence between "conservatism" and "promotion" on the one hand and "progressivism" and "regulation" on the other. He had since shifted to the extent of accepting the progressive label, so that for him, too, "regulation" was now "progressive."

Concurrently, Roosevelt was proposing a definition of "progressivism" which differed sharply from that of La Follette. The latter distrusted both Roosevelt and the principle of discretionary authority and wanted "corrupt practices" clearly spelled out in specific legislation. In addition, La Follette emphatically rejected Roosevelt's de-emphasis of state controls over corporate power.

As the 1908 Republican convention drew near, Roosevelt urged a platform "as free from the Hale type of reactionary policy as from the La Follette type of fool radicalism." Despite La Follette's brief presidential bid, Roosevelt maintained control of the convention and easily engineered the nomination of Secretary of War William Howard Taft. With Taft's victory that fall, the stage was set for a major upheaval that would profoundly affect the evolution of American political language and thought.[13]

The progressive label and the Republican party

[We] now have Progressives, Halting-Progressives, Ultra-Progressives, Progressive Conservatives, Conservative Progressives, and T. R.

Walter Hines Page, 1912

Editor Walter Hines Page could afford to be amused. The fight over labels was not his fight, and it made little personal difference to him who called themselves what. To Roosevelt and his rivals, however, it was deadly serious business. Leadership of the majority party of the nation was at stake and, once again, labels were the key to political allegiances. The fight was not a new one; it had been brewing for years.[14]

13. Kolko, *Triumph of Conservatism*, p. 112; Robert M. La Follette, *LaFollette's Autobiography* (Madison: La Follette, 1918), p. 338; and La Follette and La Follette, *La Follette*, 1:258.

14. Page is quoted in Paolo E. Coletta, *The Presidency of William Howard Taft* (Lawrence: University Press of Kansas, 1973), p. 229.

In one sense, events of the 1909–1912 era can be seen as a kind of personal ordeal for William Howard Taft. Taking office as a self-styled "progressive," Taft eventually lost the support of both Roosevelt and La Follette, and wound up widely condemned as a "conservative." When he subsequently switched labels and attempted to defend himself using the latter label as his self-designation, he only compounded his troubles. By 1912, the conservative label evoked images far more threatening than reassuring. Taft's use of it reflected his lack of political acumen as much as his differences with his self-styled progressive critics.

The Taft era is best understood in the context of the developing battle within the Republican party over the progressive label. Again language provides a vital clue. In the traditional view, the chief intraparty struggle of 1912 was between the "progressive" Roosevelt and the "conservative" Taft. This struggle split the Republican party and made for the triumph of Woodrow Wilson. Such a view accurately reflects the fact that by 1912 Roosevelt and Taft were calling themselves "progressive" and "conservative" respectively.

A close look at the language of the era provides a different perspective. Taft's political eclipse, though poignant, serves as background to the larger struggle between Roosevelt and La Follette over the definition of "progressivism." Only in this context can one understand the linguistic transformations of both Roosevelt and Taft as well as the rival efforts of all three Republican leaders to shape the publicly accepted meaning of the progressive label.

Every so often a book appears that not only has a great impact on its times but emerges in retrospect as a "classic" statement of an era. Such a book was Herbert Croly's *The Promise of American Life*, published in 1909, at the outset of Taft's presidency. As many critics have suggested, the book did not contain any important ideas Roosevelt himself had not previously expressed publicly or privately. In bringing together the major themes of Rooseveltian thought, Croly nonetheless helped delineate the battle lines within which Roosevelt and others would struggle over the progressive label and thereby control of the Republican party.

It is significant that Croly rarely used the progressive label itself, and on those occasions when he did, he used it in a noncontroversial context. When dealing in controversy, he preferred the surrogate, "reformer." Rather than compete directly for the progressive label,

Croly chose to compete indirectly by using a less controversial, more ecumenical word. Hence he pitted "reformers" against "conservatives," while also distinguishing between "reformers" of forward-looking and anachronistic type. Context, however, clearly reflects his use of the one label as surrogate for the other.

Croly began his analysis with a capsule history of critical attitudes toward corporate power. Harking back to the old Godkin-Garland critique, he agreed that imbalances of wealth were the result of "legal support [for] . . . certain economic privileges." Although he accepted the diagnosis of the earlier critics, Croly nonetheless rejected their prescription. It was not true, he argued, that "individual and public interest will, on the whole, coincide, provided no individuals are allowed to have special privileges." It was unjustifiable and dangerous to expect that "the familiar benefits will continue to accumulate automatically." For this reason, reform in the shape of "effective regulation" was needed.

Even in espousing the perspective of the newer critics, however, Croly was already using words differently. "The Promise of American Life," he warned, "is to be fulfilled not merely by a maximum amount of economic freedom, but by a certain measure of discipline; not merely by the abundant satisfaction of individual desires, but by a large measure of individual subordination and denial." Critics such as Commons had originally introduced the progressive label in conjunction with the individualist label; in Croly's usage, the individual as the "natural" political unit was itself under attack.

Concentration of power, he went on, was not "wholly an undesirable thing," nor could its abuses be remedied by reconstructing a Jeffersonian "extreme individualism." The "policy announced in Jefferson's first inaugural was in all important respects merely a policy of conservatism," and Croly had little respect for latter-day Jeffersonians "who believe reform to be a species of higher conservatism." In short, "progressivism" and "conservatism" were not complementary.

Here a key term enters Croly's discussion. As an admirer of Jefferson's arch-rival Hamilton, Croly saw "true reform" as the "attempt to unite the Hamiltonian principle of *national* political responsibility and efficiency with a frank democratic purpose." Primary responsibility for the existing situation lay with Congress and the state legislatures, which necessarily represented a variety of selfish local interests. The remedy thus lay in strengthening the federal executive, which represented the national interest. Forthright use of executive power to merge the "national idea" with the "reform idea" had been Roosevelt's greatest contribution. Roosevelt, wrote Croly, was "even more of a nationalist than . . . a reformer."[15]

In stressing "the nation" as his "natural" political unit, Croly was attempting to alter the publicly accepted meanings of both the terms "reform" and "progressive." The progressive label implied a forward-looking synthesis of nature and artifice as well as of tradition and innovation. But where the old natural unit had been the individual, and the old tradition that of protecting individual opportunity, Croly's new unit was the nation, and the new tradition that of "national responsibility." Nation was replacing individual in the name of "reform" and "progress."

At first glance, Croly's argument seems calculated to promote arousal, for he literally wrote that the "mass of mankind must be *aroused* to still greater activity" through an "increase of their aggressive discontent." A closer look at his language indicates that his real purpose was to restore quiescence.

Again timing is vital. All of Croly's major proposals had already been advanced by Roosevelt under the conservative label. Indeed, the rise of the progressive label, as used by La Follette and other state-level politicians, indicated a growing discontent with Roosevelt's perspective. The real arousal had already been accomplished by La Follette and others as Roosevelt's belated shift to progressive rhetoric demonstrates. Croly's book was intended to help re-establish Rooseveltian quiescence by aiding the former president in snatching away La Follette's chief weapon, namely, his preeminent identification with the progressive label.[16]

Croly was particularly emphatic in supporting Roosevelt against La Follette on the vital issue of corporate "combination." Before coming to Washington, La Follette had made vigorous efforts to strengthen state controls over corporate activities, and he had come to Washington to harmonize federal policy with those controls. By contrast, Croly accepted the position of Roosevelt and corporate leaders that the "control of the central government over commerce and the corpo-

15. Herbert Croly, *The Promise of American Life* (New York: Dutton, 1963), pp. 23, 12, 17, 22, 47, 153–154, 168 (italics added).

16. Ibid., p. 15 (italics added).

rations" should "be substituted for the control of the states rather than added thereto."

Accepting the "national idea" meant looking to Washington as the chief "regulatory" authority—a view previously advanced in the name of conservatism but now in the name of progressivism. Indeed, Croly was going beyond Roosevelt in arguing that federal control be "substituted" for state control. "True reform" meant that state action on this crucial issue should cease.[17]

As quiescence was Croly's object in domestic policy, so was it in foreign policy. In an important chapter often overlooked by historians, he set forth his views on the relationship between the two. Again his vocabulary centered on the terms "national" and "responsibility." A "national foreign policy," he wrote, would stimulate "better realization of the Promise of our domestic life," whereas a negative attitude toward international affairs might undermine that promise. As an emerging world power, the United States had inescapable "responsibilities" such as the guaranteeing of Latin American independence, defending the Philippines, and protecting the Open Door in China. Croly warned Americans to recognize the "responsibilities created by Chinese political development and by Japanese ambition."

Rebuking those who wished to evade such "responsibilities," Croly remarked: "The irresponsible attitude of Americans in respect to their national domestic problems may in part be traced to freedom from equally grave international responsibilities." Internal reconstruction, "so far from being opposed to . . . vigorous assertion of a valid foreign policy," was "really correlative and supplementary thereto." Indeed, the United States might eventually "be forced into the adoption of a really national domestic policy because of the dangers and duties incurred through her relations with foreign countries." Like Roosevelt, Croly used foreign policy to bolster his domestic arguments, but in this case with explicit reference to "the nation" as the natural focus of all "true reformers."

Again Croly's language shows the difference between superficial and deeper messages. On the surface, the word "responsibility" was another call to arousal. As is often the case in foreign policy, however, what Croly was really demanding was the subordination of critical

17. Ibid., pp. 356–357.

judgment to military enthusiasm. In Latin America, for example, the guaranteeing of independence might require "forcible pacification of one or more . . . centers of disorder." Defense of the Open Door in China might require "quite as considerable a concentration of naval strength in the Pacific as is required by the defense of the Philippines."

Accepting such commitments in turn meant adopting the "Hamiltonian principle" of national economic efficiency, which was yet another reason to desist from disruptive state-level action. In short, "responsibility" with respect to foreign policy meant restoring, in the name of "progress," the Rooseveltian perspective at home and abroad.[18]

Having redefined the situation, Croly ended with a revealing peroration on "individualism." He had substituted nation for individual as his natural political unit and denigrated as "extreme" any perspective that put "individual desires" ahead of "national responsibility." He now offered his own definition of "constructive individualism." Stressing "individual self-assertion," he linked this to emulation of the "exceptionally able individual." Reminding readers of the vital role of leadership in fulfilling the national promise, he wrote: "The common citizen can become something of a saint and something of a hero, not by growing to heroic proportions in his own person, but by the sincere and enthusiastic imitation of heroes and saints, and whether or not he will ever come to such imitation will depend on the ability of his exceptional fellow-countrymen to offer him acceptable examples of heroism and saintliness."

Not since McKinley had the harmonization of discordancy been so thorough. As McKinley had made innovation itself seem traditional, so Croly made self-denial seem assertive and negation of the natural unit seem natural. Not even Carnegie had harmonized nature and artifice so completely.[19]

Croly's importance lies not merely in his redefinition of terms but in his contribution to the political struggle raging around those terms. His immediate objective is evident in his pejorative usage of the term "conservative." By linking it to Jefferson's "extreme individualism," and then implying that anticorporate activity on the state level was neo-Jeffersonian, Croly was in effect labeling the La Follette group

18. Ibid., pp. 289, 301–302, 309–310.
19. Ibid., pp. 449, 454.

"conservative." This attack neatly complemented his effort to deprive
La Follette of the progressive label. Croly's strategy shows the struggle over the progressive label to have been the central one of the era,
and Roosevelt and La Follette to have been the main antagonists.

This is not to discount Taft entirely. He had created problems for
himself through lack of political acumen, but nonetheless had his own
definition of "progressivism," and many of his difficulties with both
Roosevelt and La Follette flowed from this difference in definitions.
Ultimately, it was the combination of political ineptitude and defini-
tional divergence that brought matters to a head.

Part of Taft's concern was about the issue of executive power. As a
self-styled "progressive," he was willing to seek additional "regulatory" legislation, yet he worried far more than Croly about executive
usurpation. As secretary of war, he had criticized Roosevelt's use of
executive prerogative in the Dominican customs takeover. As president, Taft found that many of his troubles in the celebrated Ballinger-
Pinchot controversy arose from his insistence on legitimizing through
legislation Roosevelt's executive incursions in the field of conservation.

To Taft, the conservation controversy was a microcosm of the problem of ends and means. He regarded Gifford Pinchot not as a "progressive" but as "a good deal of a radical and a good deal of a crank."
Pinchot represented the new "impressionistic school of reformers who
regard laws as obstacles and only the higher moral tenets of a real
reformer as limitations to be paid attention to." To Pinchot and his
supporters, Theodore Roosevelt's executive achievements in the field
of conservation were the epitome of "progress." To Taft, it was "a very
dangerous method of upholding reform to violate the law in so doing,
even on the ground of high moral principle, or saving the public."
Where Croly had lauded the "sincere and enthusiastic imitation of
heroes and saints," Taft saw the "impressionistic reformers" as influenced not by saints but by demagogues.[20]

Ultimately, issues of executive power and moral principle came
under the larger heading of respect for law. As a self-styled progressive, Taft, too, saw "regulation" as the new "saving" artifice, but
there was nothing "saving" about an approach that simply replaced

20. Donald F. Anderson, *William Howard Taft* (Ithaca: Cornell University Press,
1973), pp. 20–21, 73–75; Coletta, *Presidency of Taft*, pp. 82–100.

the arbitrary power of corporate entrepreneurs with that of well-meaning politicians and bureaucrats. Were it truly to protect both individual rights and national traditions, "regulatory" authority had to be carefully circumscribed by legislation. In this, Taft stood closer to La Follette than to Roosevelt or Croly.

However, there was one issue of discretionary authority on which Taft diverged sharply from La Follette. A once and future jurist, Taft insisted on "judicial independence," by which he meant the untrammeled power of judges to make constitutional interpretations. He viewed any attack on the judiciary as an attack on the constitution itself. By contrast, La Follette saw "judicial independence" rapidly being transformed into "judicial legislation." Along with other "progressive reforms," he supported a broadly defined power of popular recall that included judges as well as judicial decisions.

For Croly and Roosevelt, the issue of judicial power was initially not of high priority. Croly had said nothing in his book about judicial recall; indeed he distrusted much of La Follette's "popular government" approach. By early 1912, however, Roosevelt was supporting the recall of judicial decisions involving constitutional interpretations on the state level. In a bitter, three-way struggle such as this, no issue of importance could be safely ignored.[21]

As an ideological competition, the 1912 campaign actually began in the summer of 1910 with Roosevelt's return to national politics. His Osawatomie address at the end of August was a bold attempt to unite a torn party under his leadership, and provides an excellent example of "ambiguous and cryptic speech" designed to "invoke values, summarize information, and suppress the inconvenient." The address contained all the major labels of the day: individual, national, conservative, progressive, reform, regulation, efficiency, and combination. All were used positively. In lieu of Croly's term "responsibility," Roosevelt spoke of "tasks" and "duties."

In general, the address reflected a combination of Croly's influence and Roosevelt's independent judgment regarding verbal strategy. Because Roosevelt's objectives were to unite the party and assert his leadership, he was careful to be as ecumenical as possible while distinguishing himself from his rivals. Where Croly had used the conser-

21. Anderson, *Taft*, pp. 230–233; Coletta, *Presidency of Taft*, pp. 67, 156–163; La Follette and La Follette, *La Follette*, 1:336–337.

vative label as a pejorative, Roosevelt harked back to his own earlier harmonizing of "progressivism" and "conservatism." "The true friend of property, the true conservative," he declared, "is he who insists that property shall be the servant and not the master of the commonwealth." True conservatives were also true progressives.

In introducing his famous phrase "The New Nationalism," Roosevelt closely followed Croly's method of setting himself apart from La Follette. The New Nationalism, he declared, was "impatient of the utter confusion that results from local legislatures attempting to treat national issues as local issues," and "regard[ed] the executive power as the steward of the public welfare." This second innovative phrase served the dual purpose of setting Roosevelt off from La Follette while conveniently suppressing the fact that one of Roosevelt's main policy proposals—the physical valuation of railroad properties—was one La Follette had supported since 1906. As president, Roosevelt had given short shrift to the proposal. Now it was his.[22]

Like Croly, Roosevelt used rousing language to make a subtle call for quiescence. For all the rhetorical flourishes, his position on "combination" and "control" had not changed since 1901. "Combinations in industry," he declared, "are the result of an imperative economic law which cannot be repealed by political legislation." The remedy lay "not in attempting to prevent such combinations, but in completely controlling them in the interest of the public welfare." In conjunction with his abrupt dismissal of local efforts, this amounted to a reiteration of Croly's demands for quiescence on the state level.

Roosevelt closed with a restatement of Croly's doctrine of "constructive individualism." Referring to Grand Army victories in the Civil War, he told his audience, "You could not have won simply as a disorderly and disorganized mob. You needed generals." Granted, it was "even more vitally necessary that the average soldier should have the fighting edge, the right character." But good leaders would produce good followers, and in this context Roosevelt made his claim to "progressive" leadership. "The prime problem of our nation," he declared, "is to get the right type of good citizenship, and, to get it, we must have progress, and our public men must be genuinely progressive."[23]

22. Roosevelt, *New Nationalism*, pp. 21–39; La Follette and La Follette, *La Follette*, 1:206.
23. Roosevelt, *New Nationalism*, pp. 29, 38–39.

The Osawatomie speech shows how ambiguous and cryptic political language can be, for even friends and colleagues as close as Taft and Root responded to it in diametrically opposite ways. To Taft, the speech was a call to "revolution"; its doctrines were "utterly impracticable, because they could never be gotten through without a revolution or revisions of the Constitution, either of which is impossible." By contrast, Root saw nothing in the New Nationalism "that was not taught in my class at the law school forty odd years ago." Taft's reaction may have partly reflected the fact that Roosevelt had directly criticized him in the speech, but even so, the disparity of the two responses suggests the depth of the perceived ambiguity.

Of course, ambiguity was central to Roosevelt's purpose, for the speech marked the start of his concerted effort to regain a commanding position within the Republican party. Ambiguity enabled him to appeal to a wide audience, and thus provided an excellent base from which to broaden his support. He was nonetheless careful to maintain his verbal distance from La Follette, and "pointedly" insisted, when described as "insurgent through and through," on being called a "progressive."[24]

By 1911 the battle was joined. In January, the La Follette group formed the National Progressive Republican League to press for "popular government and progressive legislation." The name indicated La Follette's intent to secure pre-eminent identification with the progressive label within the party. By June, he was officially launched as the League's candidate to oppose Taft for the 1912 Republican nomination. When invited to join the League, Roosevelt refused. At first unconvinced that Taft could be denied renomination, he was also determined not to be subordinated to La Follette, particularly in an organization that bore the progressive label.[25]

Most analyses of Roosevelt's entry into the 1912 campaign focus on his split with Taft. La Follette is regarded as never really having had a chance, even before his disastrous Philadelphia speech of February 2.

24. Anderson, *Taft*, p. 178; Jessup, *Elihu Root*, 2:169; for Roosevelt's reaction to being called an "insurgent," see William Leuchtenburg's introduction to Roosevelt, *New Nationalism*, p. 8.

25. La Follette, *Autobiography*, pp. 494–495; Coletta, *Presidency of Taft*, p. 220. For Roosevelt's attitude toward the League, see Elting E. Morison, ed., *The Letters of Theodore Roosevelt* (Cambridge: Harvard University Press, 1954), 7:194–195, 201–202, 213–215.

That may well be true, but what is more important is Roosevelt's perception of La Follette's chances, particularly because Roosevelt's own attitude and behavior undoubtedly influenced those chances.

Roosevelt took the La Follette candidacy seriously. In a "Private & Confidential" letter written in December 1911, he indicated his "present impression . . . that either Mr. Taft or Mr. La Follette will be nominated." Roosevelt's consistent refusals to rule himself out in La Follette's favor suggest that he did not want to endow the latter's candidacy with any more support than it already had.

Roosevelt clearly considered La Follette far more dangerous than Taft, as he revealed in a letter written in late March 1912. Taft was a "flabby" leader "who means well, but means well feebly"; whereas La Follette was "half zealot and half self-seeking demagogue." By mid-April, with his own campaign in full swing, Roosevelt had taken over another of La Follette's key phrases, and now referred to himself as a champion of "popular government."[26]

The outlines of the 1912 campaign are well known. Unable to wrest the Republican nomination from Taft, Roosevelt turned to financier George Perkins and publisher Frank Munsey for financial support to form the new Progressive party. The move irretrievably split the Republican vote and paved the way for the triumph of the Democratic candidate, Woodrow Wilson.

From a dramatic standpoint, the formation of the new party was the highlight of the campaign, but it was ideologically anticlimatic. Within the Republican ranks, the real ideological battle had ended months earlier with the elimination of La Follette's candidacy. Taft's hold on the party machinery enabled him to retain the nomination, but his ideological appeal was extremely limited. Relabeling himself a "constitutional conservative" was a principled attempt to remind voters of the dangers of "impressionistic reform," but the label only weakened him further, and he ran a poor third.[27]

26. Ibid., pp. 452, 532, 533. For contemporary as well as retrospective assessments of La Follette's chances, see James Holt, *Congressional Insurgents and the Party System, 1909–1916* (Cambridge: Harvard University Press, 1967), pp. 50–55, and Coletta, *Presidency of Taft*, pp. 220–221. For Roosevelt's activities prior to the La Follette speech of February 2, 1912, see George Mowry, *The California Progressives* (Berkeley: University of California Press, 1951), pp. 158–179; Richard Lowitt, *George W. Norris: The Making of a Progressive, 1861–1912* (Syracuse: Syracuse University Press, 1963), pp. 235–237; and Morison, ed., *Letters*, 7:451–493.

27. For Taft's 1912 conservative rhetoric, see Coletta, *Presidency of Taft*, p. 239, and Anderson, *Taft*, pp. 185–193.

Meanwhile, Wilson's linguistic campaign strategy was impeccable. Although he was weak on specific policy proposals, he claimed the progressive label for himself and lambasted the Republicans as the party of "big business." The phrase "progressive Republicanism," he noted, was "but another way of spelling Democrat." Relying on the evocative power of metaphor, Wilson refrained from spelling out a political definition of the word "progressive" and instead reminded his listeners that "progressiveness" meant "not getting caught standing still when everything else is moving." He distinguished between three contemporary political types; namely, "Socialists, standpatters, and progressives." The standpatter was like "a great dam holding back accumulated waters from the valleys below," whereas the socialist "would break the dam and let the waters run riot and spread ruin and death in their course." The progressive, by contrast, "would bore through the dam and with sluices and valves would control and govern the waters and make their force turn the whole of industry."

By the time the Democratic convention opened in late June, Wilson had largely succeeded in making his name synonymous with the progressive label within his own party. Nominated on the forty-sixth ballot, he continued throughout the campaign to substitute evocative language for concrete policy. The Democrats were the only true "progressives," whereas the Republicans, among whom he pointedly included the Roosevelt "third party," were but "conservative" defenders of "special privilege." Roosevelt's own judgment had been "captured" by big industrialists, whereas the Democratic platform was "the only platform which says that private monopoly is indefensible and intolerable." With Taft and Roosevelt splitting the Republican vote and La Follette tacitly supporting the Democrats, Wilson scored a narrow victory on election day.[28]

If La Follette could take grim satisfaction from the outcome of the election itself, Roosevelt could do the same from events earlier in the year. Although he had failed to recapture the presidency, he had succeeded in turning back the one major challenge to the ideological direction that he and his predecessor had set for the Republican party.

Still, for all his political acumen, Roosevelt had failed to match McKinley's achievement of an image sufficiently ecumenical to absorb

28. Arthur S. Link, ed., *The Papers of Woodrow Wilson* (Princeton: Princeton University Press, 1977–78), 24:56, 127, 186, 314, 346, 501–502, 526; and 25:234–235, 350–353.

all challenges. He had not only had to switch labels, but been forced to compete for a label which in its implication of "forward motion" indicated dissatisfaction with his own established policy framework. Again, Roosevelt's adoption of the label is no proof of hypocrisy. His success with it merely indicates his ability to convince himself and others of his own dynamism. That very success, however, would once more have profound implications for American politics.

Woodrow Wilson and the limits of linguistic flexibility

I am a progressive. I do not spell it with a capital P, but I think my pace is just as fast as those who do.

1916

May I not add that I hope and believe that I am in effect speaking for liberals and friends of humanity in every nation and of every programme of liberty?

1917

Progressive in 1916, liberal in 1917. Coincidence, perhaps, then again, perhaps not. What, if anything, one can learn about Wilson, American history, or our own era from such verbal artifacts depends on one's view of the political relationship between the two labels. If one takes the history of the language itself as a frame of reference, then a good starting point is Wilson's preoccupation with "capital P" and "small p."[29]

People often tend to be preoccupied with what they *feel* they do not have, and politicians are no exception. If in his reelection campaign in 1916 Wilson was preoccupied with being identified with the progressive label, this concern suggests that he was not sure that that identification was secure in the public mind. There was good reason for this. He had come to the presidency not in advance of, but in the wake of the great intra-Republican struggle to establish the predomi-

29. Arthur Link, *Wilson: Campaigns for Progressivism and Peace, 1916–1917* (Princeton: Princeton University Press, 1965), pp. 105–106; and Albert Shaw, ed., *The Messages and Papers of Woodrow Wilson* (New York: Review of Reviews, 1924), 1:355.

nant definition of the label, and he had not made any independent contribution to that definition.

Wilson in 1912 was no more an ideological match for Roosevelt than was Taft. He did have some trenchant criticisms of Roosevelt's program, for example, that Roosevelt's call for "regulated monopoly" (the phrase was Wilson's) would have resulted in "an avowed partnership between the government and the trusts." But Wilson himself had neither a consistent policy framework nor a clearly articulated ideological approach, and his slogan, "The New Freedom," had little specific content. His own attitude on the "monopoly" issue was summed up in his ambiguous statement, "I am for big business, and I am against the trusts." He won only as a result of the Republican split.[30]

Even after taking office, Wilson made no significant contribution to the public debate on the "meaning" of "progressivism." He provides a classic example of a politician who comes along after a label achieves popularity, then seeks to share in its legitimacy by attempting to identify himself with it.

Some of Wilson's contemporaries were aware of this. Shortly after the 1914 midterm elections a thoroughly disgusted Roosevelt dashed off a letter to his old friend William Allen White. The results, Roosevelt noted, had been a disaster for the Progressive party: the country was "sick and tired of reform," while within the party itself there had been disturbing signs of defection to the Democrats. It was "exceedingly unfortunate," Roosevelt wrote White, "that so many of our people kept talking as if Wilson and Bryan were themselves progressives" because Wilson had no "constructive ability from the standpoint of reform." The new president was "a wonderful dialectician, with a remarkable command of language. But his language [was] admirably and intentionally designed not to reveal the truth but either to conceal his real purpose or else to conceal the fact that he has no definite purpose at all."[31]

Estimates by rival politicians are rarely disinterested, and Roosevelt's is no exception. Nonetheless, he was substantially correct in at least one respect. Wilson clearly had no detailed plan for implementing his New Freedom rhetoric. Indeed, historians have long been

30. David M. Kennedy, ed., *Progressivism: The Critical Issues* (Boston: Little, Brown, 1971), p. 56; Kolko, *Triumph of Conservatism*, p. 209.

31. Roosevelt to White, November 7, 1914, White MS.

aware that once in office, Wilson quickly took over the Rooseveltian program. Arthur Link observes that "in the end Wilson accepted almost entirely the New Nationalism's solution for the regulation of business by a powerful trade commission." And Wilson himself agreed after having campaigned on a militant antitrust platform that the Clayton Act of 1914 emerged from committee so weakened that "you cannot tell it from water." This was so, Link notes, "because the administration had put all faith in the trade commission plan and had given up its efforts to prohibit restraints of trade by statutory action."

Accepting Roosevelt's approach to domestic "regulation," Wilson likewise accepted his position on economic foreign policy. This latter adoption was relatively easy in view of Wilson's long-standing belief in the connection between domestic prosperity and foreign markets. Like Roosevelt, he believed that competition for markets abroad required efficiency at home. He had never intended to cripple large corporations but rather hoped to make them more efficient and competitive. With this in mind he assured members of the newly formed National Foreign Trade Council that he would assist them in their "righteous conquest of foreign markets."[32]

The derivative nature of Wilson's program accounts for his being derided by contemporary critics for his claim to originality. La Follette was particularly disappointed by Wilson's early performance and charged that the Federal Reserve bill of 1913 was a "big bankers bill" that placed control of industry "in the hands of a few men." It "just breaks ones [sic] heart," La Follette wrote of Wilson, "to see him throw away chances for good things and swallow bad things with good labels."[33]

Wilson himself well understood that he could not count on another Republican split in 1916, and saw as essential his picking up both "capital P" and "small p" support as quickly as possible. Despite the flurry of activity during his first two years in office, he did not initially meet with unqualified success. When he publicly declared in the fall of 1914 that the basic program of the New Freedom was complete, no less an authority than Herbert Croly berated him for making "extravagant claims . . . on behalf of the Democratic legislative achieve-

32. Arthur Link, *Woodrow Wilson and the Progressive Era* (New York: Harper, 1954), pp. 70–73; Williams, *Tragedy*, pp. 58, 82–85.
33. La Follette and La Follette, *La Follette*, 1:487, 500.

ment." In a stinging *New Republic* editorial titled "Presidential Complacency," Croly charged that Wilson could not have made his claims "unless he had utterly misconceived the meaning and the task of American progressivism."

In the face of such a challenge to his identification with the label, Wilson redoubled his efforts during the next two years. For much of the period, he was heavily preoccupied with maintaining American neutrality during World War I. Nonetheless, by early 1916 he was adopting more and more Progressive party planks from 1912, such as child labor legislation, workmen's compensation, and rural credits, all of which he had previously failed to support.

In his renomination speech that summer, he stated his case bluntly. "We have in four years," he declared, "come very near to carrying out the platform of the Progressive party, as well as our own; for we are also progressives." Wilson's efforts were rewarded in late October, when eleven of the original nineteen members of the 1912 Progressive party platform committee issued a statement endorsing him on the grounds that he had signed into law all or part of twenty-two of the thirty-three planks of the 1912 platform.[34]

Wilson's rhetoric candidly revealed his strategy. Unable to escape the struggle for the progressive label, he did what was necessary to strengthen his position in the struggle. Yet the very intensity of his efforts inevitably raises the question why he switched so abruptly to the liberal label the following year.

Historians often use the terms interchangeably, and this is understandable because many leading figures have espoused the two labels simultaneously. Even so, such usage should not be permitted to obscure the possibility that Wilson's shift from one to the other carried political significance. Once again, historical analysis of language provides clues.

The word "liberal," from the Latin *libertas*—"freedom"—was central to nineteenth-century English politics but was not used much in early post–Civil War America. Americans of that era were preoc-

---

34. Herbert Croly, "Presidential Complacency," in *New Republic*, November 21, 1914, p. 7. On Wilson's 1916 legislative program, see Arthur Link, *Wilson: Confusions and Crises, 1915–1916* (Princeton: Princeton University Press, 1964), pp. 321–327. For his renomination speech and his endorsement by members of the 1912 Progressive party platform committee, see Link, *Wilson: Campaigns for Progressivism and Peace*, pp. 94, 125–126.

cupied more with concrete social units and processes than with abstract principles. For them, the idea of "freedom" was embodied in
the individualist label which referred to a social unit and the social
process by which it functioned ("atomistic social freedom," in Hartz's
terms). There were exceptions, as when McKinley spoke of the "liberalizing" influence of Americans upon Filipinos. By and large, however, American political vocabulary in the half-century after the Civil
War centered on concrete units and processes rather than abstractions; hence the individualist, conservative, and progressive labels.
Even McKinley's use of the term "liberalizing" was process-oriented.

In introducing the word "liberal" as an expression of an abstract
principle, Wilson was effecting a major change in emphasis while
giving himself greater latitude in affecting social units and social processes. In nineteenth-century English thought, the word "liberal" was
used primarily to refer to the individual's relationship to the soverign
state, and described a national rather than an international relationship. Wilson introduced the label in an international context in
"speaking for liberals and friends of humanity" during his "Peace
without Victory" address in January 1917. He not only introduced the
liberal label as an abstraction, but did so in the context of war.

In the summer and fall of 1916, Wilson had campaigned both as a
"progressive" and as a "peace" candidate. Apart from his domestic
achievements, much of his appeal rested on the fact that he had "kept
the country out of war." To many people, the two achievements were
complementary. As Link points out, the "great majority of [self-
styled] progressives" felt that America's "unique mission" was to set
an example of social justice and peaceful behavior. A minority, led by
Roosevelt, linked "progress" at home to a crusading humanitarian
approach abroad. In the main, however, antiwar sentiments prevailed
among those who identified themselves as "progressives." The label
thus had predominantly antiwar implications.[35]

This is not to suggest that Wilson switched labels because he wanted war. Like McKinley in 1898, he hoped to avoid war; and like
McKinley, he succeeded until he reluctantly concluded that his larger
policy aims could not be achieved without military participation. Indeed, the "Peace without Victory" address was an antiwar address,
and La Follette himself led the applause. Wilson's language nonethe-

35. Link, *Wilson: Confusions and Crises*, pp. 23–30.

less suggests that the rhetoric of liberalism gave him a maneuverability in the situation that progressive rhetoric could not. It would have been extremely dangerous to have argued foreign policy in the language of progressivism, especially as he moved closer to war.

As Roosevelt had shown, the progressive label was a flexible one that could be stretched to cover a variety of situations. There are limits to linguistic flexibility, however, and Wilson apparently sensed that he had reached those limits with the progressive label. So long as America was at peace, it would be difficult if not impossible to advertise war as an agency of "progress." Dropping the progressive label avoided a confrontation on this crucial issue.

The liberal label was far more appropriate to the situation. It was relatively untainted at the time by domestic political controversy and could be used as a fresh means of refocusing public attention on international affairs. And because it was a label with an international, specifically European history, it could be a means of opening up a direct dialogue with a popular European constituency. Wilson realized in 1917 that he was speaking to an international audience and that this enhanced his prestige at home.

Most important of all was the political content of the liberal label. Again one sees the power of words to "coerce discordant meanings into a unitary conceptual framework." There is probably no more fundamental semantic discordancy in political vocabulary than that between "liberty" and "authority." As the threat of war drew closer, the effect of Wilson's rhetoric was to spotlight this discordancy by casting the United States in the role of defender of "liberty" against the "authoritarianism" of Imperial Germany. At the same time, this rhetoric helped prepare Americans themselves for an unprecedented assertion of governmental authority in the name of liberty. There could be no better label under which to demand the extraordinary authority of wartime controls than one that implied defense of liberty. Here one sees Wilson the "dialectician" at work.

There was an irony in all this. Because the political implications of the progressive and liberal labels were opposed with respect to the war issue, the substitution could not have worked unless the two labels could have been taken to have some common connotation, however superficial. Indeed that is what happened, for on a general level both appeared to connote sympathy for the underprivileged or oppressed. "Forward motion" could be interpreted as "liberation" from oppression. By resolutely confining his public statements to this general level Wilson was able to effect a smooth, virtually unnoticed substitution.

Again, this is not to imply hypocrisy. In shifting from progressive to liberal rhetoric Wilson was no more conspiratorial and no less sincere than Roosevelt had been in moving from conservative to progressive rhetoric. Like Roosevelt, Wilson believed in his policies and formulated his rhetoric to be most effective in pursuing them. The climax came in the war message on April 2, when Wilson asked the American people to fight for the "peace of the world and for the liberation of its peoples." There was no mention of progressivism.

Wilson's use of the liberal label raises a central issue in the relationship between historical writing and political understanding. Historians frequently use the phrase "Wilsonian liberalism." The phrase is itself a reification, for it suggests that there is a concrete phenomenon known as "liberalism" with a specifically Wilsonian version. Like its author, that version is generally described as "nineteenth-century" in outlook.

But the phrase fails to analyze Wilson's usage of the word at the time, and so does more than reify the word "liberal." It inhibits understanding of language as political strategy, obscures both the nature and significance of Wilson's shift from progressive to liberal rhetoric, and thereby fails to locate Wilson as a distinctly twentieth-century strategist. Most important, the phrase makes historian and reader alike custodians of Wilson's definition of the situation: the war was a "liberal" enterprise, and to disapprove of it is to disapprove of "liberalism."

Because hindsight is deceptively easy, it is always important to know if there was any challenge to a particular use of language at the time. The existence of a contemporary challenger serves both to underline the political nature of language and to aid in the recovery of lost insights.

In Wilson's case, the most trenchant attack came from the young literary critic Randolph Bourne. In a series of articles written during the war, Bourne systematically dissected the justifications for what he skeptically called "war-liberalism." His attack was not reserved for Wilson alone, but was also directed at self-styled "liberal intellectuals" who provided Wilson with his most effective public support. Bourne's principal target within this group was his own former mentor, philosopher John Dewey, who saw in the war not an "end to reform" but rather an "immense impetus to reorganization."

Once America was in the war, administration supporters such as Dewey immediately began doing what they could not do in peacetime: they began advertising the war as an agency of social betterment. Bourne contemptuously dismissed the idea that government could be counted on even in wartime to advance the "liberating" aims of well-meaning crusaders. "If the war is too strong for you to prevent," he wrote, "how is it going to be weak enough for you to control and mold to your liberal purposes?" Apart from the physical destructiveness of the war itself, this was the most "inconvenient" problem Wilson's language had suppressed.

In his war message, Wilson had talked of "making the world safe for democracy." Dewey and others had picked up the phrase, and were quoting it widely to drum up support for the war. Bourne scornfully noted that philosophers were supposed to be experts in the precise use of language, yet Dewey's use of the word "democracy" was anything but precise. "I search Professor Dewey's articles in vain," wrote Bourne, "for clews as to the specific working-out of our democratic desires, either nationally or internationally, either in the present or in the reconstruction after the war." For Dewey and his supporters, Bourne noted, "democracy remains an unanalyzed term, useful as a call to battle, but not an intellectual tool, turning up fresh sod for the changing future."

It was in connection with the war's domestic effects that Bourne took issue most directly with administration rhetoric. On the apparent concern of self-styled liberals over wartime intolerance of dissent, he pointedly remarked: "It is only 'liberal' naivete that is shocked at arbitrary coercion and suppression. Willing war means willing all the evils that are organically bound up with it." By placing the word "liberal" in quotation marks, Bourne underscored the incongruity of talking about "liberty" and supporting a policy that rested on massive coercive authority. What was at fault, he concluded, was the very idea that a coercive process such as war could be used to "liberate" society. Of this idea he wrote: "Its flowering appears in the technical organization of the war by an earnest group of young liberals, who direct their course by an opportunistic program of State-socialism at home and a league of benevolently imperialistic nations abroad. At their best they can give us a government by prudent, enlightened college men instead of by politicians. At their best, they can abolish war by making everybody a partner in the booty of exploitation." Shortly before his death in 1918, Bourne summed up his own view of what Wilson was accomplishing in the name of liberation. "War," he wrote, "is the health of the State." Pushing this thought to its logical conclusion, he added: "We cannot crusade against war without crusading implicitly against the State."[36]

Had Bourne's critique found widespread support at the time, American history might have taken a very different turn after 1918. Given their faith in the ameliorative powers of government, however, most Americans were reluctant to accept his conclusions; as he himself noted, "In a time of faith skepticism is the most intolerable of all insults."[37] The excitement of the moment was not conducive to a detached analysis of the interplay of language and politics in the years since McKinley's death.

During a period of barely a decade and a half, there had been two major shifts in American political vocabulary. The decline of the conservative label reflected a loss of public confidence in McKinley's synthesis. Roosevelt's consequent shift to progressive rhetoric, ably supported by Croly, was a classic example of a "power-structure surviving by successfully transforming its idiom." In the face of threatened hostile action at the state level, Roosevelt's shift protected the continuity of the more "friendly" relationship between large corporations and the federal government while his progressive rhetoric indicated sympathy for what Olney had called the "popular clamor for government supervision." Roosevelt's linguistic transformation thus helped restore the underlying quiescence of the McKinley years, and Wilson's adoption of Roosevelt's rhetoric and policies reinforced this result.

Had the war not intervened, this era in American politics might have lasted longer. But the approach of war added a crucial item to the agenda. Although quiescence in the face of growing corporate and federal power had been restored, there was still widespread opposition to involvement in war. Wilson was forced to stand for reelection on an antiwar platform and an antiwar label, then to jettison the label abruptly as he moved closer to intervention in the war.

36. Randolph Bourne, *Untimely Papers* (New York: Huebsch, 1919), pp. 93, 122–124, 101, 135, 145, 167.
37. Ibid., p. 26.

At this point, for the second time in barely a decade, a linguistic shift preserved a power-structure intact. Wilson could not possibly have used the progressive label for war and so chose a label that brilliantly combined an appeal to liberty with a demand for massive coercive authority. The call to battle was a demand for subjugation to federal power. Not even Croly had more effectively harmonized the discordancy between self-assertion and self-negation. This time, however, it was being done in the name of liberation.

What it all added up to was a power-structure surviving by twice transforming its idiom. Entry into war accelerated both America's emergence as an industrial power and the centralization of political power under discretionary administrative authority. Wilson's shift to liberal rhetoric stood in partial contrast to previous patterns of linguistic evolution in that the new verbal symbol did not emerge through a breakdown of the old, which remained intact but useless. What was needed in this case was an "ignoring" of the old symbol and a substituting of "fundamental new categories" of Wilson's own. Even so, the substitution worked only because the progressive and liberal labels could be understood as having something in common.

Wilson's use of the liberal label again spotlights two fundamental discordancies in American politics, one between nature and artifice, the other between tradition and innovation. His artifice was by now a traditional one; namely, the use of federal power to "control" or "regulate" human conduct. But his natural unit was now the world. Once the substitution had been effected, it was much easier to redefine the relationship between tradition and innovation. The tradition was still that of protecting "freedom," or what Wilson called "self-determination." The innovative method was participation in international war.

"God helping her," America could "do no other."[38]

38. "God helping her, she can do no other," is the final sentence of Wilson's war message. See Shaw, ed., *Messages and Papers*, 1:383. On ignoring the categories of one's opponents and substituting "new fundamental categories" of one's own, see Louis Hartz, *The Liberal Tradition in America* (New York: Harcourt, Brace, and World, 1955), p. 28.

4

The Linguistic Synthesis
of Herbert Hoover

Disaster as a lost opportunity

This country is no country for radicalism. I think it is really the most
conservative country in the world.

William Howard Taft, 1924

As a matter of fact, all the political parties are progressive. I can't
conceive of a party existing for any length of time that wasn't progressive, or of leadership being effective that wasn't progressive.

Calvin Coolidge, 1924

Images of a decade. The idea of Coolidge calling himself a progressive may seem odd. His statement was of course campaign rhetoric. To explain it as such, however, is not to explain it away. That he
deemed it in his interest to claim a "progressive credential" is striking
commentary on his evaluation of the prevailing mood, and suggests
the inappropriateness of simply accepting Taft's view as "correct." To
examine the 1920s through the prism of language is to encounter a
"complexity of context" indeed.[1]

One of the most difficult aspects of studying history is recapturing
the emotional intensity with which people experienced events. Yet if
anything fairly leaps from the contemporary written record of the
postwar years, it is a profound and widespread disillusionment with
lofty rhetoric. Critic Harold Stearns observed that Wilson had pro-

---

1. Taft is quoted in Arthur Schleslinger, Jr., *The Crisis of the Old Order* (Boston:
Houghton, Mifflin, 1957), p. 60; Coolidge's statement is in Robert Ferrell and Howard
Quint, eds., *The Talkative President* (Amherst: University of Massachusetts Press,
1964), p. 9.

vided a merely "verbal" idealism: "It is the cheapest on the market, this century just as the previous centuries of organized mankind. And as dangerous." John Dewey warned, "It may be that the words idealism and ideals will have to go—that they are hopelessly discredited. It may be that they will become synonyms for romanticism, for blind sentimentalism, for faith in mere good intentions, or that they will come to be regarded as decorative verbal screens behind which to conduct sinister plans."[2]

With the disillusionment came a wave of fear. The Red Scare of 1919–1920 was a product of many things—long-standing fear of "socialism," a climate of labor unrest, and most important, the Bolshevik Revolution. Nor should one overlook Wilson's contribution. He had built an image of a world more manageable than it turned out to be, and its collapse was frightening. He had also strongly encouraged anti-Bolshevik feeling.

Randolph Bourne caught the latter contribution quite early. "Which do our rulers really fear more," he asked, "the menace of Imperial Germany, or the liberating influence of a socialist Russia?" As the rhetoric of 1898 had made imperialism and conservatism mutually exclusive, so Wilson made Bolshevism and liberalism mutually exclusive. Military intervention in Russia, the jailing of antiwar "socialists" and "radicals" at home, and the denial of mailing privileges to "subversive" newspapers all followed logically from his definition of the situation. If the situation itself ultimately got out of hand, it was more a culmination than a betrayal of what Bourne had called Wilson's "war-liberalism."[3]

During the war few had anticipated such outcomes. Bourne did warn against letting the war "pass . . . into popular mythology as a holy crusade," and wrote that there "must still be opposition to any contemplated 'liberal' world-order founded on military coalitions." Again, the quotation marks around the word "liberal" were meant to call attention to the contradiction between freedom and coercion. For most Americans, however, the contradiction remained camouflaged.[4]

2. Harold Stearns, *Liberalism in America* (New York: Boni and Liveright, 1919), p. 144; John Dewey, "The Discrediting of Idealism," *New Republic*, October 8, 1919, p. 287.

3. Randolph Bourne, *Untimely Papers* (New York: Huebsch, 1919), pp. 123–124. Also see David M. Kennedy, *Over Here: The First World War and American Society* (New York: Oxford University Press, 1980), pp. 77–88.

4. Bourne, *Untimely Papers*, pp. 45–46.

Given the gap between Wilson's lofty rhetoric and the peace treaty he helped produce, the postwar disillusionment is understandable. Yet as important as the disillusionment itself was the profound intellectual confusion that accompanied it. What emerges clearly from the debates of 1919–1920 is an agonizing among self-styled liberals concerning the "true" meaning of their label.

Here one encounters a poignant and tragic moment in American history. Learning from disaster does not begin with finding the "right" answers, but with a search for the appropriate questions. Even to ardent supporters of the war, it was clear that postwar developments at home and abroad had been disastrous. For those who had opposed the war all along, such disasters were the inevitable result of American involvement itself. In searching out the lessons of the experience these two groups of critics inevitably devised different answers. The tragedy is that neither group really articulated the pertinent questions.

In this respect the failure of the antiwar critics is most poignant. In their view, Wilson's rhetoric had played a major role in the disaster. He had used language to camouflage a most dangerous contradiction between freedom and coercion. It was for this reason that the critics focused on his use of the liberal label. The way in which they attacked his rhetoric, however, was self-defeating.

Because they believed in the value of freedom, they sought analytical categories that would be neither manipulative nor coercive. To them, the liberal label contained such categories. Wilson's "misuse" of the word made its rescue from his clutches all the more important politically. In an atmosphere of disillusionment and fear their efforts had a certain heroic intent, for they were desperately attempting to salvage the liberal label as a weapon with which to promote freedom. Therein, however, lies their failure.

In their effort to use the label as a weapon the critics chose to give it concrete form, to reify it. Yet reification is itself a type of manipulation, even coercion; it posits one "true" meaning and demands acceptance of it. This attempt to reify the liberal label in a nonmanipulative, noncoercive way was not merely self-contradictory, but at once ironic and tragic: ironic, in that the critics undercut their own purpose; tragic, because in pursuing this line of attack, they prevented themselves from asking the more searching question. Instead of "What is the true meaning of liberalism?" they should have asked, "How can we prevent the further use of political labels for manipulative purposes?" This ongoing postwar reification of "liberalism" suggests a major opportunity lost. The critics failed to construct a politics of de-reification, that is, a sustained, cumulative analysis of how linguistic manipulation works.

Stearns provides a case in point. Often seen as a spiritual successor to Bourne, he differed in one major respect. Whereas Bourne focused his energy on a comprehensive indictment of wartime language and policy, Stearns felt it necessary to advance an alternative "liberal" vision. Where Bourne's purpose had been to de-reify, to expose the liberal label as a manipulative abstraction, Stearns fell into the trap of counter-reification, or competition over labels.

His book *Liberalism in America* contains telling insights into the process of self-delusion through language. He attacked Wilson for embodying the "technique of liberal failure," which consisted of allowing one's lofty or "liberating" aims to free one from any concern over mundane realities. "Perhaps the most evil consequence of the amiable habit of enunciating noble platitudes," Stearns wrote, "is that it soon gets one into the habit of ignoring details." At the same time, his own analysis rested on an entire opening chapter entitled, "What Liberalism Is."

Like Bourne, Stearns laid bare the contradiction between freedom and coercion that Wilson's language had camouflaged. "What the liberal ever seeks," he wrote, "is voluntary allegiance, not enforced allegiance." His insistence on a consistency of ends and means led him to a definition one might easily and sympathetically view as "correct"; yet in setting up his own archetypal "liberal" he was merely reifying in another direction.

Such counter-reification not only missed the point about political manipulation through language; it undercut Stearns's specific argument as well. By entering into a competition over the definition of the "true liberal," he laid himself open to the rejoinder that "liberal" goals sometimes required coercive means. This was precisely Dewey's position. Even when lamenting the "defeat of idealistic aims" Dewey had argued that it was a defeat "which will always come to idealism that is not backed up by intelligence and by force—or, better, by an intelligent use of force." To "go on opposing ideals and force to each other" was to deny the distinction between "materialism" and "idealism."

Coercion and freedom could legitimately be harmonized if coercion were used "intelligently."[5]

In their opposing views Stearns and Dewey marked out the boundaries of what quickly became yet another struggle over a label. In November 1920, *Nation* editor Oswald Garrison Villard charged that the "temporary knell of American liberalism was sounded the minute its false leader put it into the war." To Villard, the lesson was clear: "For war and liberalism to lie down together anywhere, at any time, with any excuse, means only one thing—disaster to liberalism." More pacifistic than Stearns, who had explicitly allowed for defensive war, Villard nonetheless reinforced Stearns's counter-reification of "liberalism" by reading Wilson out as the "false" leader of a "genuine" tradition.

As Villard built on Stearns, so Herbert Croly built on Dewey. Writing in the *New Republic*, Croly took Villard directly to task for making war and liberalism "absolutely incompatible." The "endorsement of any war [did] not sound the 'knell' of any and all liberalism." That depended, he noted, "upon the specific meanings we attach to the words 'war' and 'liberalism.'"[6]

This renewed struggle over the liberal label was short-lived, partly because the public disaffection with Wilson and his preeminent identification with the label made it a much devalued prize. Moreover, the spectacle of some of America's leading publicists debating the very meaning of a word that until recently had dominated political discourse may have contributed to its further, if temporary, devaluation. The debate nonetheless had major consequences.

First, the renewed competition over labels reinforced the process of reification itself and further camouflaged the central problem of political manipulation through language. Second, by reinforcing a positive or favorable reification of the liberal label, the debate ensured that despite current disillusionment, the impulse toward the manipulative or even coercive "liberation" of others would still be seen as positive. In fact, throughout the 1920 election campaign, no Republican contender used the liberal label as a pejorative. Third, the debate added

    5. Stearns, *Liberalism in America*, pp. 124, 135, 3–31, 66; Dewey, "Discrediting of Idealism," pp. 285–287.
    6. Villard, *The Nation*, November 3, 1920, p. 489; Croly, "Liberalism vs. War," *New Republic*, December 8, 1920, p. 35.

other connotations to the competing definitions of liberalism, of which one particularly bears mentioning.

Although the tendency was not universal, combatants on both sides used the progressive and liberal labels interchangeably. Not all went so far as Croly, who began one sentence with the words: "Progressivism or liberalism is fundamentally. . . ." However, the fact that no critic appears to have called attention to earlier distinctions in their usage suggests an ongoing insensitivity to Wilson's prewar linguistic shift and its implications.[7]

Such insensitivity would have important effects when the focus of attention shifted back to domestic matters. In the short run, in a curious reversal of the events of 1917, the progressive label, untainted by war, would regain much of its former popularity as a self-designation. Once this reversal occurred, and the Wilsonian shift receded into the background, the possibility diminished that future critics would ever be able to refer to that shift for insights into the linguistic strategies that were to follow. Again, the evolution of language would result in a lost opportunity.

In the long run, the effect of the debate was not only to incorporate the liberal label more firmly into domestic political vocabulary but to incorporate into the label itself categories long associated with the progressive label, including the promotion-regulation dichotomy. Eventually, belief in the uniqueness and viability of regulation would be as much the hallmark of the self-styled liberal as the self-styled progressive, and the liberal label would become a multidimensional vehicle of coercion and self-deception. No "fundamental new categories" would issue from the war; rather it is the reemergence of the progressive label that holds vital clues to a much misunderstood decade.

The 1920s are often classified as "conservative," and that label did regain popularity as a self-designation in the context of postwar disillusionment and fear, particularly among those fearful of "labor radicalism" and excessive "regulation" of business. Still, the revival of the conservative label should not be permitted to obscure the equally significant revival of the progressive label. Revival of the latter suggests not only an ongoing faith in "regulatory" solutions, but a wide-

7. Croly, "The Eclipse of Progressivism," *New Republic*, October 27, 1920, p. 210.

spread sense of "unfinished business" with respect to the prewar era. Taft's assessment of America as the "most conservative country in the world" was undoubtedly shared by many; yet it is Coolidge who ultimately emerges as the more astute political analyst.

Like McKinley, Coolidge could and did boast an unchallengable conservative credential. His record as governor of Massachusetts during the 1919 labor unrest, his serene confidence in the "business of America," and his apparent attachment to "minimal government" all marked him as a believer in the "traditionalist" connotations that still attached to the label. That such an identification was once again something to boast of indicates the extent of the popular reaction to immediate postwar events. It is therefore all the more significant that Coolidge also chose to claim a progressive credential.

His immediate aim was to neutralize as much as possible the impact of the La Follette third-party candidacy. Although La Follette had even less chance of victory in 1924 than in 1912, there was always the possibility that a strong third-party showing could throw the election into the House of Representatives. During the campaign Republican spokesmen frequently concentrated their fire on La Follette rather than on the Democrats.

As was usually the case, Coolidge's assessment of the temper of the times proved accurate. Although La Follette carried only his home state of Wisconsin, he polled almost five million votes, one-sixth of the total, and ran ahead of the Democrats in eleven other states including California. Had it not been for party regularity and poor financing, he might have done considerably better. Coolidge's assessment, however, reflected far more than the strength of the La Follette candidacy. It reflected the ongoing popular belief in "regulatory" solutions, a faith in the constructive uses of coercion that not even the war had undermined, and ongoing popular blindness to the possibility that corporate ascendancy could be advanced under the label of "progressivism."

Coolidge's verbal strategy extended beyond the election campaign. It was to be expected that when someone like La Follette criticized particular legislation, he used the familiar language of regulation versus promotion. Laws such as the Esch-Cummins Act and the Fordney-McCumber tariff, he charged, were not regulatory or "control" measures at all but rather promotional "great charters of special privilege." Yet when Coolidge vetoed the McNary-Haugen farm price supports bill of 1927 (his first of two such vetoes), he used precisely the same kind of language. The bill, he charged, was advertised as regulatory but was in fact unfairly promotional in that it singled out "a few products, chiefly sectional," and proposed to "raise the prices of those regardless of the fact that thousands of other farmers would be directly penalized." The language of the charge was the same: "special privilege."[8]

Throughout the decade representatives of both major parties continued the struggle for the progressive label. Debates over legislation passed or defeated were carried on in the rhetoric of progressivism. This was true of the successful Capper-Volstead Cooperative Marketing Act of 1922 as of the variously unsuccessful McNary-Haugen bills. As in prewar years, the issue was still how to respond to "inevitable combination."

To the former chairman of the War Industries Board, Bernard Baruch, cooperative marketing was an "attempt to put the six millions of scattered and competitively selling farmers on an equal footing with the largely consolidated buyers of their products, and with industry generally." New York banker Otto Kahn agreed. "I am inclined to think we have gone too far," he wrote, ". . . in attempting to enforce competition in all circumstances and to prevent natural and legitimate cooperation."

Hopes, demands, and fears were all equally expressed in the rhetoric of progress, cooperation, and consolidation. Mr. Justice Brandeis noted his apprehension at the continued growth of federal power in the name of progress. "The extremes of concentration," he wrote, "are proving its failure to the common man. . . . The new Progressivism requires local development—quality not quantity."[9]

Closely related to the competition for domestic labels was the struggle to define foreign policy options. Here the issue is further complicated by yet another contentious term. For many years after World War II, historians routinely described American foreign policy in the

---

8. Maxwell, ed., *La Follette*, pp. 73–74; Coolidge is quoted in Dexter Perkins and Glyndon Van Deusen, *The United States of America: A History* (New York: Macmillan, 1968), 2:446.

9. Baruch to Senator Arthur Capper of Kansas, May 29, 1922, Selected Correspondence, Bernard Baruch Papers, Princeton University Library, Princeton, N.J. (hereafter Baruch MS.); Kahn to Baruch, September 20, 1922, ibid.; Arthur Ekirch, *The Decline of American Liberalism* (New York: Atheneum, 1967), p. 263.

1920s as "isolationist." Absorption of this label into the historical literature reflects its use in the political arena during the 1930s and 1940s.
More recently, historians have partly succeeded in exploding the
"legend of isolationism" with respect to the 1920s. That they have
only partly done so is indicated by continued use of the label when
describing administration policy or the views of certain critics. In
particular, critics are so labeled if they opposed not only Wilson's
League of Nations but the economic foreign policies of his successors.

Neither Coolidge nor La Follette called himself "isolationist." La
Follette's self-designation was "antiimperialist," and only in terms of
his own vocabulary can his views on foreign policy be understood. For
him, being "progressive" and "antiimperialist" were complementary.
The war, he charged, had "openly enthroned Big Business in mastery
of government," advanced the cause of "financial imperialism" while
betraying "progressive" principles, and promoted the interests of capital while viciously regulating those of labor. Corporate enthusiasm for
military conscription, he argued, was proof of this.

Nor was La Follette impressed with Wilson's peace settlement. The
Versailles Treaty, he declared, was "a treaty of financial imperialists,
of exploiters, of bankers, of all monopolists, who sought through man-
dates to sanctify and make permanent a redistribution of the spoils of
the world and to cement forever the stranglehold of the power of gold
on the defenseless peoples of the earth." Far from thinking of himself
as "isolationist," La Follette feared isolating the United States ideologically from such peoples. The Harding-Coolidge policies, he
charged, were but an extension of Wilson's policies without the
League. A truly "progressive" foreign policy would allow for "nonag-
gression" and "cooperation."[10]

No more than La Follette did Coolidge identify as an "isolationist."
Benefiting from McKinley's neutralization of the imperialist label, he
simply ignored La Follette's charge and substituted categories of his
own. They were categories that both Roosevelt and Croly would have
found congenial. The "one great duty that stands out," Coolidge declared, "requires us to use our enormous powers to trim the balance of
the world." Stressing the domestic connection, he added, "Our investments and trade relations are such that it is almost impossible to

10. Maxwell, ed., *La Follette*, pp. 75–80. Also see David P. Thelen, *Robert La
Follette and the Insurgent Spirit* (Boston: Little, Brown, 1976).

conceive of any conflict anywhere on earth which would not affect us injuriously."[11]

The point is not to reclassify Coolidge or La Follette but to analyze their rhetoric in context. Both spoke the language of the time. In foreign policy Coolidge could afford to ignore La Follette's terms, but in domestic matters, he felt impelled to compete. That he did so at all suggests the continued strength of prewar categories of thought. That he competed successfully suggests the ineffectiveness of those categories in deepening public understanding of politics. Coolidge's success again suggests a lost opportunity for reconsideration.

The crux of the matter was still the promotion-regulation dichotomy. So long as Americans assumed both inevitable combination and the uniqueness and viability of regulation, they would be unable to recapture lost insights into the sources and supports of corporate power at home and abroad. Shortly before his death in 1929, historian Vernon Louis Parrington summed up the dilemma that self-styled progressives of all descriptions had failed to resolve. "Have you been able to convince yourself," he wrote a friend, "that the corporative wealth of America will permit the centralized political state to pass out of its control and become an agent to regulate or thwart its plans? . . . We must have a political state powerful enough to deal with corporative wealth, but how are we going to keep that state with its augmenting power from being captured by the force we want it to control?"[12]

In short, how could anyone prevent regulation from being perpetually transformed into promotion?

Bringing it all together

America has been steadily developing the ideals that constitute progressive individualism. . . . Regulation to prevent domination and unfair practices, yet preserving rightful initiative, are in keeping with our social foundations. Nationalization of industry or business is their negation.

Herbert Hoover, 1922

11. Williams, *Tragedy*, pp. 130. 127.
12. Parrington is quoted in Ekirch, *Decline of American Liberalism*, pp. 264–265.

The Republican Party has ever been a party of true progressivism.

Herbert Hoover, 1928

Liberalism should be found not striving to spread bureaucracy but striving to set bounds to it. True liberalism seeks all legitimate freedom first in the confident belief that without such freedom the pursuit of all other blessings and benefits is vain.

Herbert Hoover, 1928

Of all the prominent figures who wrestled with Parrington's dilemma during the 1920s, none met with a less deserved fate than Hoover. Intelligent, sensitive, deeply analytical, he has only recently begun to receive his due from historians. To speak of Hoover's linguistic synthesis is to indulge in deliberate *double entendre*. In synthesizing into one framework the emotional and political messages inherent in three labels, he was at the same time synthesizing his own political image. This is not to say the image was dishonest. Hoover was as sincere a man as ever walked the American political stage. He was also the finest public relations expert of his time. Therein lies the tragedy.[13]

It was appropriate to the 1920s that Hoover was a professional engineer, a man who presumably understood systems. Belief in the uniqueness and viability of regulation fit nicely with the illusion that human social systems could be understood and manipulated with the same efficiency as mechanical systems. His vocabulary also fit the times. The apparent care with which he defined his terms enhanced his image as a systematizer. "We shall use words," he announced in accepting nomination, "to convey our meaning, not to hide it."

One's vocabulary is one's method of both understanding and participating in politics, and Hoover's reflected not only his own choices but those of the great majority of his contemporaries. Far more than that of Coolidge, Hoover's vocabulary reflects the outer limits of the conventional wisdom of the decade.[14]

In this connection, an essential starting point is that the one major label with which Hoover did *not* identify in the 1920s was the conser-

13. Herbert Hoover, *American Individualism* (Washington: Herbert Hoover Presidential Library Association, n.d.), pp. 4, 25; Herbert Hoover, *The New Day: Campaign Speeches of Herbert Hoover, 1928* (Stanford: Stanford University Press, 1928), pp. 182, 163. The best biography of Hoover is Joan Hoff Wilson, *Herbert Hoover: Forgotten Progressive* (Boston: Little, Brown, 1975).

14. Hoover, *The New Day*, p. 11. Also see Wilson, *Hoover*, p. 31.

vative label. Ironically, it was the one that would later be thrust upon him, and which, after years of struggle, he would reluctantly accept. During his period of ascendancy, he chose a synthesis of the three labels that in his view embodied the most important and constructive wisdom of American political experience: "individualist," "progressive," and "liberal."

It was not accidental that Hoover revived the old phrase "progressive individualism." Like the new critics of the 1880s and 1890s, he defined his categories in both political and moral terms. His primary commitment, like theirs, was to "individualism" as he defined it. The individual was both a political and a moral unit. "Progressive" was a modifier; an important one, but still a modifier. Even when Hoover talked of "progressivism" as a social philosophy, it was within this context. As the title of his 1922 book indicates, his chief goal was to protect *American Individualism.*

Hoover is often compared to Croly, yet an analysis of his vocabulary shows him to have been far more sensitive and less manipulative. His natural political unit was always the human being, the biological individual, never the "nation," or as in Wilson's case, the "world." Hoover never defined self-assertion in terms of self-negation. For him, "constructive individualism" was not emulation but personal development. This was a basic "spiritual" principle.

Although Hoover could be extremely sensitive, he was still profoundly limited by conventional wisdom. If, despite Croly and Wilson, the individual human being was still the natural unit, Hoover still had no trouble harmonizing the discordancy between nature and artifice. He accepted without question the idea of the "artificial individual" and its concomitant thesis of inevitable combination. He pointedly utilized the individualist label in connection with corporate activities abroad, and explicitly defended the Open Door Policy as a stimulant to natural, worldwide economic growth. As he put it in 1921: "I am thus making a plea for individualism in international economic life just as strongly as I would make a plea for individualism in the life of our own people."[15]

Like McKinley and Roosevelt, Hoover understood inevitable com-

15. Address to National Association of Manufacturers, May 18, 1921, Public Statement #154, Public Statements File, Herbert Hoover Presidential Library, West Branch, Iowa (hereafter HHPL).

bination to be as applicable to labor as to capital. Collective bargaining in a spirit of "cooperation" was essential to modern industrial society. "If we could secure this cooperation throughout all our economic groups," he declared in 1920, "we should have provided a new economic system, based neither on the capitalism of Adam Smith nor upon the socialism of Karl Marx; we should have provided a third alternative that preserves individual initiative, that stimulates it through protection from domination, we should have given a priceless gift to the Twentieth Century."

Although he revived prewar categories of thought, Hoover was very much a man of his times. In his view, categories remained valid so long as they evolved with experience. For example, "individual initiative" in the 1920s involved far more than mere bargaining over wage scales and working hours. Because he was acutely aware of the major technological developments of recent years, Hoover understood far better than most politicians the problem of the dehumanization of work in a machine-ridden, bureaucratized society.

He hoped, however, to make technology the servant rather than the master of the American worker and advocated adapting production methods to allow workers "a chance to give expression to their own ability, to their own knowledge as to improvements which can be made in their work." He also favored giving them "some interest in the results of their increased efficiency and production" and argued that "the greatest field for organized labor lies in bringing about its side of this relationship and the greatest field for employers lies in meeting such efforts two-thirds of the way."[16]

Since the 1890s, Hoover noted, there had occurred "an extraordinary growth of organizations" in American life. America was "passing from a period of extremely individualistic action into a period of associational activities." Following the "great depression of the early nineties," he observed, there had been a "flood of combinations and consolidations by the combining of capital." This was part of a "natural" process and represented "a groping for something that would serve as a basis for stability." Combinations of capital had been matched by combinations of labor.

16. Address to Federated American Engineering Societies, November 19, 1920, PS#102; and "Self-Expression Is Need of Today," November 1920, PS#100A, both in HHPL.

What was natural and voluntary was also valuable. The "legitimately formed associations," he wrote, had improved "business morals and practices," cheapened production and distribution processes, improved working conditions, and "enabled our whole commercial public to form safer judgments as to their future policies." Such services, he added, "should be preserved and even better organized."[17]

To label something "natural," however, was not to put it beyond criticism or legislative interference. Herein Hoover's definition of "progressivism" came into play, and one sees both how conventional he was in reifying categories, yet how different in his emphasis from La Follette.

Both men viewed promotion and regulation as real and distinct categories. Whereas La Follette was skeptical of most forms of promotion, Hoover saw both activities as explicitly and equally contributory to "progress." Government, he declared in 1928, could be of "invaluable aid in the promotion of business." By using appropriate measures it could "promote financial stability," protect workers, farmers, and manufacturers, help eliminate waste, and through "promotion of foreign trade . . . contribute greatly to stability and employment."

Regulation had a similarly constructive role. Existing antitrust and public utilities legislation were "proof that we have gone a long way toward the abandonment of the 'capitalism' of Adam Smith." A "progressive" approach meant maintaining a proper balance between promotion and regulation. Anything else was "reaction," either directly through abandonment of "forward motion," or indirectly through the destructive effects of "radicalism."[18]

Hoover's use of the promotion-regulation dichotomy, sharply different from that of La Follette, helps explain his broader appeal. What made him politically attractive was that within the limits of conventional wisdom he seemed far more attentive to balance and complexity. The "dreamy social ferment" of the war era, he wrote, had given "much stimulation to two schools of thought: one that all human ills can be cured by governmental regulation, and the other that all regulation is a sin." The test of any form of government intervention was whether it safeguarded equality of opportunity and maintained indi-

17. Address to Cleveland Chamber of Commerce, May 7, 1924, PS#378; "Trade Associations Should Stabilize Business," in *Co-operative Competition*, March 18, 1922, reprinted as PS#214, ibid.
18. Hoover, *The New Day*, pp. 33–34; Hoover, *American Individualism*, pp. 24, 30.

vidual initiative. The "period of regulation" had been "highly beneficial," but had also "developed weaknesses in the throttling of proper
initiative that require some revision."

It was in this context that Hoover indicated his awareness of the
potential interchangeability of promotion and regulation. In an oft-
quoted passage, he cited the danger of private groups competing for
control of government. If such groups were to "develop into warring
interests, if they dominate legislators and intimidate public officials, if
they are to be a new setting of tyranny, then they will destroy the
foundation of individualism. Our Government will then drift into the
hands of timorous mediocrities dominated by groups until we shall
become a syndicalist nation on a gigantic scale." Regulation would
then become promotion and vice versa, thus perverting the purpose
of both activities.

Hoover quickly balanced apprehension with optimism. The same
forces that permeated the nation as a whole, he wrote, eventually
permeated these groups. "The sense of service, a growing sense of
responsibility, and the sense of constructive opposition to domination,
constantly recall in them their responsibilities as well as their privileges."[19]

The danger was nonetheless real, and the only way out was to refuse
to build a political state capable of exercising full economic control.
This was as close as Hoover ever came to offering a direct answer to
Parrington's dilemma. The nation would have to rely on limited promotion, limited regulation, and the constructive potential of voluntary
action. Although this approach was not particularly dramatic, it had
the merit of being "the only safe avenue to further human progress."
In any case, Hoover insisted, the most effective and constructive
governmental technique was not coercion but inducement. "While I
am no believer in extending the bureaucratic functions of the Government," he wrote, "I am a strong believer in the Government intervening to induce active cooperation in the community itself."[20]

These two elements, the opposition to "bureaucracy" and a preference for inducement over coercion, indicate more than anything else
the distance between Hoover and so many other self-styled pro-

19. Hoover, *American Individualism.* pp. 22, 25, 19–20.
20. Ibid., p. 6; letter to John Dunlap, Editor, *Industrial Management*, November
18, 1920, reprinted as PS#106, HHPL.

gressives of the 1920s. They form the core of his definition of his third label, the liberal label. Again one sees unusual sensitivity within the bounds of conventional wisdom, for if Hoover, like so many of his contemporaries, was a reifier at heart, he was careful not to use the progressive and liberal labels interchangeably (another difference between him and Croly). His definitions of liberalism and progressivism were complementary; the two were not equivalent.

Indeed, in his use of the liberal label Hoover was closer to Stearns than to Croly or Wilson: for Hoover, voluntary activity was the spiritual essence of "liberalism." Whereas Wilson had supported peacetime conscription in the postwar period, Hoover stood with Stearns in opposing it as a "stimulation to militarism." The United States, Hoover proudly announced in 1924, was the "only important nation today whose standing army is less than the policemen on its street corners."[21]

If faith in voluntary activity was the spiritual core of Hoover's definition of liberalism, opposition to "bureaucracy" was its political core. For him, the term "bureaucracy" was a pejorative comparable in significance to "socialism," though not interchangeable. "Socialism," in the sense of governmental "production and distribution of commodities and services," was a social philosophy which sprang from a mistaken understanding of human nature. "The will-o'-the-wisp of all breeds of socialism," wrote Hoover in 1922, "is that they contemplate a motivation of human animals by altruism alone." Because of this misunderstanding of individual motivation, socialism stood opposed to individualism. Similarly, because "bureaucracy" was a governmental technique that consisted of delegating arbitrary coercive authority to elected or appointed officials, it was incompatible with liberalism.

Hoover's political lexicon thus centered on three dichotomies: individualism versus socialism, progressivism versus reaction, and liberalism versus bureaucracy. As the "good" labels intersected and reinforced each other, so did the "bad." Socialism necessitated "a bureaucracy of the entire population" which was the road away from progress and toward reaction. That Hoover maintained these semantic distinctions is an important clue to his thinking. Croly notwithstanding, liberalism was not progressivism. One did not confuse categories of action with categories of restraint. Progressivism involved both

21. "Militarism and Defense," speech on Defense Day, September 12, 1924, PS#398, ibid.

promotion and regulation; liberalism involved neither. On the contrary, liberalism set the limits of both promotion and regulation.
Again, the labels and the categories they embodied were not interchangeable but complementary.[22]

One cannot fully understand Hoover's vocabulary, however, without understanding his use of three other words: "opportunity," "responsibility," and "cooperation." Again one sees his tendency to define categories in both political and moral terms, though here one also
moves from the realm of theory to that of action. What made American individualism "progressive," what distinguished it from "individualism run riot" was that the American version was "tempered
with that firm and fixed ideal . . . *equality of opportunity.*" The purpose of American individualism was not to guarantee success or security, but equal opportunity for all. The individual, in turn, had to
"stand up to the emery wheel of competition."

Far from being a moral limitation of the system, this reliance on
competition was its greatest strength. Opportunity was a necessary
stimulus, indeed "the sole source of progress." However, maintaining
a true equality of opportunity involved far more than mere "legalistic
justice based upon contracts, property, and political equality": it
meant legislation to guarantee "social and economic justice," and particularly "certain restrictions on the strong and the dominant."

This was where "responsibility" became a central theme. Because
equality of opportunity was a moral issue, its maintenance was a moral
responsibility. This was the justification for both promotion and regulation. The responsibility lay not only with government but with
individuals and groups as well. The limit of government action was the
point at which government usurped or denied private responsibility.
Conversely, individuals and groups had a responsibility not to demand that government do for them what they should be doing for
themselves. This also held true as between the various levels of government. "I want to live in a community," Hoover declared in 1925,
"that governs itself, that neither wishes its responsibilities onto a
centralized bureaucracy nor allows centralized bureaucracy to dictate
to that local government." The responsibility for maintaining equality
of opportunity was a shared one.[23]

22. Hoover, *American Individualism*, pp. 25, 8; Hoover, *The New Day*, p. 162.
23. Hoover, *American Individualism*, pp. 4–5 (italics in original); Address to 37th
Annual Convention of National Association of Railroad and Utilities Commissioners,
October 14, 1925, PS#513, HHPL.

The sharing of responsibility in turn made "cooperation" vital. To Hoover, the essence of cooperation was its voluntary character: people "operating together." True cooperation could never be imposed, only induced. Regulation became necessary where cooperation was impossible or so unlikely as not to be worth the risk. Because regulation was coercive, however, it was the responsibility of government and citizenry, respectively, not to impose or demand it unnecessarily. For this same reason, when given a choice between regulation and promotion, Hoover preferred promotion. In his view, this did not make him any less "progressive." On the contrary, promotion, properly conceived, was an inducement to cooperation, and any victory for cooperation was a victory for "progress" and a move away from bureaucracy toward liberty.

Against this background, one can more easily understand Hoover's policies as secretary of commerce. As a cabinet official, Hoover was never happier than when "intervening to induce active cooperation in the community itself." His most widely publicized interventions concerned trade associations; in seven and a half years, he helped organize over two thousand of them.

To Hoover, trade associations represented the best of individualism, progressivism, and liberalism in action. They stimulated the economy and thereby increased opportunity for all; they were voluntary and thus cooperative; and they required no heavy-handed, governmental bureaucracy. That Hoover vastly increased the size and operations of his own Commerce Department in connection with his trade association work was not an increase in bureaucracy so far as he was concerned; the activities of the department were advisory and promotional rather than coercively administrative, and represented not the "imposition of government in business, but the cooperation of government with business to bring about common action not otherwise possible."

Trade associations did enhance a kind of regulation, but it was of the most positive kind; namely, the self-regulation of industry that was not only a victory for freedom over coercion but a powerful spur to efficiency and the reduction of waste. For Hoover, waste was more than a technical issue. In a country where living standards were high but still not universally so, the reduction of waste was a moral issue because each reduction freed both capital and labor for the further production of needed goods and services. The argument for trade associations was at once economic, moral, and political. Hoover's 1928 campaign speeches were replete with references to his trade association work, efficiency and the reduction of waste, and the utility of trade associations as an alternative to governmental regulation.[24]

What made sense domestically made sense internationally. The Open Door was an expression of "individualism in international economic life" not merely because it enhanced the international activities of "artificial individuals," but because it was "a part of the pledge of our democracy—an equality of opportunity to all our people." During his years at the Commerce Department, Hoover complemented his domestic activities with a vigorous promotion of trade and investment abroad. Frequently the two overlapped: a number of trade associations were primarily export promotion agencies, and the department published a considerable pamphlet literature detailing foreign sales opportunities for American exporters.

Among Hoover's more celebrated efforts in the international field were those directed toward incorporating the Open Door principle into Russian-American relations. Although he refused to accept the permanence of the Bolsheviks, he favored American penetration of the Russian economy through trade, loans, investments, and branch plant manufacturing to assure American "leadership in the reconstruction of Russia when the proper moment arrives."[25]

As trade associations embodied Hoover's three ideological labels, so did the Open Door approach. Because of the tendency among historians to reify something called "Open Door liberalism," a critical analysis of Hoover's vocabulary becomes especially vital. When McKinley introduced the Open Door policy, he did not explicitly link it to any ideological label. Nonetheless, the policy was part of an innovative synthesis he legitimized as traditional and presented as consonant with the principle of "minimal government." In the context of the 1890s, the policy was easily accepted as compatible with McKinley's conservative credential.

Hoover's explication of the policy a generation later reflects

24. "No Imposition of Government in Business," reprinted from *Factory Magazine*, October 1925, as PS#412, ibid.; interview in *Success Magazine*, January 1926, reprinted as PS#538A, ibid.; Address to Chamber of Commerce, May 12, 1926, PS#579, ibid.; and Hoover, *The New Day*, passim.

25. Address to National Association of Manufacturers, cited n. 15, above; William Appleman Williams, ed., *The Shaping of American Diplomacy* (Chicago: Rand McNally, 1970), 2:145–146.

McKinley's success. In addressing the National Association of Manufacturers in 1921, Hoover began with the by-now innocuous statement: "This country has long been pledged to the open door in the world's trade." The innovation had become a tradition.

Hoover's vocabulary nonetheless indicates an important change in the terms in which the policy was to be justified. For him, the Open Door was not merely a defense of individualism; it was a defense of "human progress." As a progressive policy, it depended upon a balance between legitimate promotion and legitimate regulation. Recent legislation was designed "to prevent the growth of economic groups where the few could dominate the many." This "national aspiration" applied "with equal force to our relationships abroad and enters into every avenue of our foreign trade."

The problem was that not all countries shared this aspiration. Some were allowing or even encouraging within their borders "the creation of great trusts whose activities can dominate the efforts of individual merchants of other nationalities in foreign trade." Not all governments were as progressive as the United States government. Fortunately, America was fulfilling its responsibilities with respect to "human progress": promotion and regulation were in balance. America contained "no combinations of capital that can, by unfair competition, crush the energies of other nationals." Americans wanted "only that share of the world's commerce that our citizens can secure without special privilege."

The Open Door was more than individualist and progressive; it was also liberal. Its abandonment, Hoover warned, would mean a massive growth of coercive bureaucracies and military establishments. This in turn meant renunciation of equal opportunity at home. "This system can not be preserved in domestic life," Hoover declared, "if it must be abandoned in international life." Should the day ever come when the United States, "with her gigantic resources and the intelligence of her people," were forced to emulate the objectionable practices of others, it would be "a day of infinite losses to real progress and real liberalism."[26]

In terms of policy, Hoover's version of the Open Door was much the same as McKinley's. For both men, the policy was designed to maximize foreign trade while minimizing political interference in for-

26. Address to National Association of Manufacturers, passim.

eign markets; it was at once an assertion of American economic strength and a declaration of dependence on external factors; it was "friendly" to domestic corporate interests within the context of an assumed balance between capital and labor. Yet Hoover's rhetorical justification was markedly different from that of McKinley. Again one is faced with choosing the appropriate questions. One might ask: was the Open Door Policy "really" individualist, conservative, progressive, or liberal? A better question, however, would be why the policy had to be explicated so differently in the 1920s.

Here the political significance of Hoover's language becomes clear. Despite the postwar revival of the conservative label, it was simply no longer possible for a rising politician with national ambitions to defend a procorporate policy using the old conservative rhetoric; it was now not only possible but mandatory to justify "friendly" government intervention in the language of progressivism and liberalism. By the same token, Hoover could use such language before an audience composed of some of the most powerful corporate leaders in the country, and be warmly applauded. Having learned from experience that their interests could be harmonized with what Olney had called "the popular clamor for a government supervision," they no longer found such language threatening.

Again, this is not to accuse Hoover of hypocrisy. Like McKinley, Roosevelt, and Wilson, he believed in his policies, and chose a rhetoric that explicated them most effectively in the situation. The result was nonetheless familiar. Once more, a linguistic change helped reinforce policy stability. In terms of Hoover's personal ambitions, he had not only synthesized existing political wisdom, but synthesized an acceptable idiom in which to express it and associated himself with that idiom. The result was indeed a synthesis by and of Hoover himself.

Like many synthesizers, Hoover did not add any new ingredients to the mixture; he simply combined them differently. Whereas others used certain categories of thought interchangeably, Hoover defined and harmonized them to make them complementary. He did envision society in systemic terms, and his language reflected a sincere effort to make its parts fit together. Artifice complemented nature, promotion complemented regulation, coercion (where it was unavoidable) complemented freedom. Complementarity and balance were constructive. If categories became interchangeable, a distortion of their intended meanings would result. To discard constructive categories altogether or to let them become unbalanced was likewise a betrayal of principle.

In building his synthesis Hoover never attempted to question "firm and fixed ideals" or alter the fundamental direction of American political and economic development. The synthesis itself was but another innovation to bolster legitimate tradition, and for this reason later commentators have found it easy to label him "conservative." Such reification misses the point. The 1920s were not "a conservative decade," and Hoover was not "a conservative." The decade was one in which Americans generally defined their system as a synthesis of individualism, progressivism, and liberalism, and in which they associated Hoover, as he associated himself, with the most positive values embodied in all three labels.

As some commentators have labeled Hoover conservative, so have others labeled him a "corporate liberal." The latter term, popularized in the 1960s, was of course not Hoover's; nor does it reflect his actual usage of the liberal label in the 1920s. The term "corporate liberal" draws on a later notion of "liberalism" as governmental "liberality" or generosity, a usage popularized only after Hoover left office.

The term "corporate liberal" also reflects a skeptical or sardonic attitude toward the possibility of using a corporate-government partnership as a foundation of economic generosity. Although Hoover did view properly regulated corporate enterprise as an agent of economic growth, efficiency, and progress, he would never have defined himself as "a corporate liberal" in the 1960s sense of the term any more than he would have called himself "a conservative" in the 1920s. For Hoover, liberalism meant the restraint of governmental power rather than the aggressively overbearing exercise thereof.

Because of the extent of his triumph, it is important to note that in Hoover's case, as in Wilson's, there were contemporary critics who challenged him on his own terms. To attorney Samuel Untermyer of New York, Hoover's professed enthusiasm for "voluntary cooperation" masked a willingness to help construct ever more coercive combinations. Many of Hoover's trade associations, Untermyer charged, were no more than informal cartels promoting corporate monopoly rather than competitive enterprise. He accused Hoover of being the "most plausible of all our apologists for and the most sympathetic friend of the many criminal combinations posing as trade associations."

Untermyer's was a serious challenge to Hoover's sincerity. Whatever Hoover was saying about making promotion and regulation complementary, his actions were making them interchangeable. To promote combinations of the size and power of the larger trade associations led inevitably to giant organizations that had at least informal power to coerce and regulate entire industries. Moreover, promoting such giant organizations in the industrial sector inevitably meant allowing the responsive growth of similar organizations elsewhere in the economy. The ultimate result could only be what Hoover claimed to fear most; namely, a "syndicalist" system controlled by a bureaucratic tyranny. In sum, even on his own terms, Hoover was neither truly progressive nor truly liberal.

Nor was Untermyer's the only such challenge. Although *American Individualism* received a generally favorable press, it got a scathing review from Stanton Coblenz in the New York *Herald*. Accusing Hoover of inconsistency, Coblenz charged that he looked at American institutions with a "comprehensive social vision" that took "no thought of individuals" and that he judged the American system "not by the minority of the unfortunate but by the majority of the fortunate." Hoover, Coblenz insisted, was "satisfied because at heart he is *not* an individualist, because in his mind the social machine as a unit is more important than the effects of that machine upon individual men and women." Despite Hoover's sincerity, he was the "victim of a self-delusion."[27]

As serious as Untermyer's challenge was, that of Coblenz was even more so, for he challenged Hoover's most fundamental political identity—that of "individualist." It was as serious as the "antiimperialist" challenge of McKinley's conservative credential in 1898 or Bourne's challenge of Wilson's liberal credential during the war. The complaint in 1898 had been that one could not legitimately harmonize innovation and tradition in that particular way; in 1917 the complaint centered on Wilson's harmonization of coercion and freedom.

Coblenz was now raising the same kind of objection with respect to Hoover's harmonization of nature and artifice. The social "machine" or "system" was as artificial a construct as the "artificial individual."

27. Untermyer's public telegram to Senator Capper of Kansas, dated March 19, 1924, is reprinted in the *Washington Post*, March 21, 1924. Hoover's reply, in the form of a letter to Capper, is dated March 21, 1924, and can be found in Commerce File–Personal, Untermyer, Samuel, HHPL. Coblenz' review is in the *New York Herald*, January 14, 1923.

The moment one began thinking of the machine itself as a unit, one undercut the possibility of treating the individual human being as a unit; one's units of social organization could not be both artificial and natural at the same time. Hoover's systemic thinking, in short, was not an asset at all, but an overwhelming liability to his individualist credential.

Coblenz' critique was itself subject to the rejoinder that he was implicitly offering a competing definition of a label. Even so, exposing the contradictions within Hoover's usage was a powerful challenge, couched as it was in Hoover's own terms of reference. That the challenge was not more widespread at the time is an indication of the short-term success of Hoover's synthesis. Years later, reviewing his performance as president, a majority of voters would register their conclusion that, however attractive the synthesis looked in theory, it had not worked in practice. Many also came to accept Coblenz' view that Hoover was a man of small sympathy for individual human beings. For that reason, it is important to emphasize that such was not the general verdict in the 1920s. Far more typical was the reaction expressed in the *New York Times's* review of *American Individualism*. "His liberalism, his progressivism," it stated, "is a thing of the heart no less than of the head."[28]

In reflecting on Hoover's overwhelming victory in 1928, several historians have suggested that the prosperity of the times, so useful in his campaign, was unstable and in part illusory. Although this is undoubtedly true, the instability and illusion were not the results of any wholesale abandonment of prewar patterns of thought or action. The 1920s had been a complex decade of reflection and reevaluation, but on balance the prewar categories had held, and Hoover's synthesis reflected that continuity. The synthesis would ultimately prove inadequate. While this inadequacy indicated the limits of Hoover's personal vision, it also reflected those of conventional wisdom. For those limits Hoover and millions of others would pay a heavy price.

Economic collapse and political labels

True liberalism is found not in striving to spread bureaucracy, but in striving to set bounds to it. True liberalism seeks all legitimate free-

28. *New York Times,* December 7, 1922.

> dom first in the confident belief that without such freedom the pursuit
> of other blessings is in vain.
>
>   Herbert Hoover, 1932

In the face of overwhelming disaster, what could an honest man do but repeat himself? Standing one's ground is not necessarily a mark of either integrity or intelligence. Baffled though one may be, however, when one sees others proclaiming solutions of no greater apparent value, and possibly even greater danger, one stands on basic principles and takes the consequences. This Hoover did.[29]

Needless to say, this time the language did not work. There are some catastrophes that even the most carefully chosen words cannot smooth over. What is noteworthy is not that Hoover's political ascendancy came to an end, but that his vocabulary did not entirely go down with him. During the depression, Hoover's primary self-identifying label, the individualist label, did fade into general disuse. The phrase "rugged individualism," which he had actually used in the 1928 campaign, became a particularly bitter anachronism. Hoover's other two labels, the progressive and liberal, were not effaced. He lost his public identification with them, and they were transferred to the very people he attacked in 1932 as "reactionaries." Ultimately, Hoover himself was saddled with both the reactionary and the conservative labels. The former he contemptuously rejected; the latter he reluctantly accepted, though only after a prolonged and significant struggle.

Because of the obviously pejorative content of the reactionary label, historians have avoided it in discussing Hoover's policies during the depression. However, they have frequently described him as "conservative." In doing so they have mirrored but failed to analyze one of the most important twentieth-century developments in the use of political language. The relabeling of Herbert Hoover helped set the stage for a massive expansion of federal power. Ironically, that relabeling no more reflected a purposeful change in public attitudes toward government than it reflected a change in Hoover's own perspective. On the contrary, the public relabeling of Hoover was the result of two parallel desires—one on the part of Hoover himself, the other on the part of

---

29. Campaign speech at Madison Square Garden, New York City, October 31, 1932, in William Starr Myers, ed., *The State Papers and Other Public Writings of Herbert Hoover* (Garden City, N.Y.: Doubleday, Doran, 1934), 2:425.

the majority of American voters—to see the problems of the depression solved within the existing "system," within the limits of conventional wisdom.

A standard criticism of Hoover is that he "developed a streak of doctrinaire conservatism," and "put his faith in voluntary cooperation when the times called for active government intervention." The charge itself spotlights the main issue. For Hoover, "voluntary cooperation" and "active government intervention" had never been conflicting alternatives. The very purpose of government intervention was to "induce active cooperation in the community itself." Maintaining complementarity and balance between intervention and cooperation was in fact integral to his definitions of progressivism and liberalism. Intervention came in two forms, promotion and regulation. "Responsible" promotion helped maximize cooperation and thereby progress. "Responsible" regulation was necessary where cooperation was not forthcoming, and this, too, ensured progress. Because regulation was coercive, however, it was important not to let it get out of hand or it would spread bureaucracy and "poison the very roots of liberalism."

In Hoover's view, to treat intervention and cooperation as conflicting alternatives, to refuse to recognize their complementarity, was to define intervention in purely coercive terms. This not only undercut progress, but opened the way to imbalance in favor of coercion and thereby undercut "true liberalism" as well. It was precisely because his opponents defined the 1932 situation in such terms that Hoover insisted they were "not liberals," but "reactionaries of the United States." Far from becoming a "doctrinaire conservative," he was, in his own mind, defending progressivism and liberalism against particularly dangerous enemies.[30]

From Hoover's perspective, it was a matter of applying principles consistently in time of adversity. Actively interventionist (by his own definition of the term) during his years in the commerce department, he remained so throughout his presidency. He explicitly rejected the advice of such "leave-it-alone liquidationists" as Treasury Secretary Andrew Mellon, and utilized both legislative and executive action in

30. On "doctrinaire conservatism" and shunning "active government intervention," see Perkins and Van Deusen, *The United States: A History*, 2:487. The references to "poisoning the very roots of liberalism" and "reactionaries of the United States" are from the 1932 Madison Square Garden address, cited n. 29, above (p. 425).

an ongoing effort to reverse the downward trend. Hoping to maintain stable agricultural prices, he poured millions of dollars into his newly created Federal Farm Board. He increased public expenditures and, in 1932, sponsored the creation of the Reconstruction Finance Corporation. Because he was anxious that the brunt of the collapse not fall primarily on labor, he called numerous White House conferences to persuade business leaders to maintain production and wage levels and induced labor leaders to respond with a no-strike pledge. In all these actions, Hoover sought to maintain complementarity and balance with respect to intervention and cooperation.

Recognizing the link between domestic prosperity and foreign trade, Hoover also did his best to maintain foreign trade levels. Although he was frequently criticized for signing the 1930 Hawley-Smoot Tariff, he never intended that it should isolate the American economy. As he pointed out at the time, under the new schedules some 62 percent of imports remained on the free list as compared to 66.3 percent under Wilson's 1913 tariff. For Hoover, the most important part of the new law was that it increased flexibility by allowing the Federal Tariff Commission to raise or lower rates according to its analysis of economic trends.

As with so many of Hoover's interventions, the 1930 tariff backfired both economically and politically. His sponsorship of it did not thereby constitute an abandonment of progressive principles as he defined them. Indeed, from his perspective, enlarging the powers of the Tariff Commission followed an approach initiated by Wilson under the banner of progressivism. Meanwhile, Hoover also took the lead in promoting the 1931 international debt moratorium and in planning for the 1933 London Economic Conference, thus demonstrating his belief in the complementarity of "active government intervention" and "voluntary cooperation" on the international level.[31]

In short, Hoover neither relabeled himself nor redefined his self-identifying labels. His electoral defeat is hardly surprising, considering the results of his interventions both domestic and international. What still requires explanation is his relabeling by others, for the question remains why the progressive and liberal labels did not disap-

31. Herbert Hoover, *The Memoirs of Herbert Hoover: The Cabinet and the Presidency* (New York: Macmillan, 1952), pp. 291–299; Myers, ed., *State Papers and Public Writings of Hoover*. 2:passim.

pear with him, why they did not become pejoratives or at least lose popularity as self-designations (as did the individualist label).

One possible answer is that the progressive and liberal labels had never really been his to the same degree as the individualist label. During the 1932 campaign, columnist John T. Flynn expressed a widespread judgment when he referred to Hoover as a "bogus liberal." But that only indicates that by this time Hoover had lost his identification with the label, not that he had never had it.[32]

Survival of the progressive and liberal labels as self-designations indicates faith in the existing system: voters wanted the system retained, just more effectively operated. This continuing faith, however, must be considered in the context of the simultaneous eclipse of the individualist label.

For Hoover, a system based on individualism, progressivism, and liberalism meant the complementarity and balance of nature and artifice, promotion and regulation, and coercion and freedom, respectively. It also meant defining the individual human being as the natural political unit. Other self-styled progressives and liberals had posited different natural units. For Croly, the natural unit had been the nation; for Wilson, the world community. The eclipse of Hoover's individualist label suggests the revival of belief in these other units, especially Croly's national unit; the depression seemed to demand far greater national (and to some extent international) organization. Artificial units were again becoming natural, and categories interchangeable.

Hoover's loss of the progressive and liberal labels also suggests the revival of interchangeable categories: regulation as a form of economic stimulation or promotion, coercion as the only practical route to freedom. This was what Hoover had feared most. Yet one can also interpret the survival of the labels as indicative of an ongoing faith in complementarity and balance as well. Unlimited regulation was not unlimited promotion, nor was unlimited coercion the same as unlimited freedom. Usage had not yet become Orwellian. Circumstances merely required a temporary recombination of categories, a rebalancing or even a temporary unbalancing with respect to artifice, regulation, and coercion.

32. Flynn to Senator Hiram Johnson of California, October 15, 1932, in John T. Flynn Papers, University of Oregon Library, Eugene, Oregon (hereafter Flynn MS.).

From Hoover's point of view, the key term in the situation was "responsibility." Two of his public statements in February 1931 confirm its centrality. The first, a White House press release (February 3), bore the title "The Importance of the Preservation of Self-help and of the Responsibility of Individual Generosity as Opposed to Deteriorating Effects of Government Appropriations." The second, Hoover's radio address on Lincoln's Birthday, was titled "Dangers from Centralization and Bureaucracy to Liberty and Individual Initiative if National Government Assumes Responsibility for Local Relief."[33]

For Hoover, responsibility had always been something to be shared both between individuals and government and between the various levels of government. Insofar as his statements suggested complete reliance on individual and local governmental efforts, they appeared to exempt the federal government from its share of responsibility. In fact, Hoover was talking not of antidepression policy in general, but specifically of "relief," that last-ditch "charity" which represented the failure of all other measures.

Centralizing responsibility for relief, however, would be counterproductive because "opening the doors of the Federal Treasury" would stifle local giving, "destroy far more resources than the proposed charity from the Federal Government," and in subjecting the local community to "a remote bureaucracy with its minimum of understanding and of sympathy" divest that community of "a large part of its voice and its control of its own destiny." The federal government's proper responsibility lay in expanding employment, "affording credit to drought sufferers for rehabilitation," and "cooperation with the community." Complementarity and balance were inseparable from the maintenance of a proper division of responsibilities, whereas an improper division would undermine liberalism, individualism, and progressivism all at once.[34]

Herein both the meaning of Hoover's loss of the progressive and liberal labels and the superficiality of thought underlying that loss become clearer. Panic is seldom conducive to serious reflection; it more frequently propels people down the path of least resistance. All one had to do was correlate the persistence of the depression with Hoover's insistence on individual responsibility and on the individual

33. Myers, ed., *State Papers and Public Writings of Hoover*, 1:496–505.
34. Ibid., pp. 497, 502–503.

as the natural political unit; once this was done, it became all too easy
to believe in the nation as the natural unit and the federal government
as the focus of all responsibility. This at once legitimized demands for
greater federal action and put the primary blame for the depression on
Hoover himself.

The response was not an elegant one, for it not only undercut
complementarity and balance with respect to coercion and freedom,
but wiped out Hoover's careful distinction between "progressivism"
and "liberalism." In short, it was a reaction of panic. Nonetheless, in
view of the earlier interchangeable usage of the two labels by Croly
and others, and because of such precedents as the "New Nationalism"
and Croly's notion of "national responsibility," the reaction was one
that could be indulged without abandoning one's claim to either label.
All that was necessary was to deprive Hoover of both of them. Saddling one man with primary responsibility for so complex a disaster
was of course a remarkably superficial diagnosis, yet it had the irresist-
ible dual appeal of locating a scapegoat and simultaneously allowing
the scapegoater the emotional security of faith in the existing system.

Like many superficial diagnoses, its consequences would be profound. In the short run, it left vacant the leadership of "progressive"
and "liberal" forces, thus creating a vacuum to be filled. In the long
run, it paved the way for ever greater federal regulation in the name of
promotion, ever greater coercion in the name of freedom. It is in this
context that the rise of Hoover's challenger and successor is best
understood.

As governor of New York, Franklin Roosevelt was already an expert
and seasoned campaigner, and he had long made clear his claim to the
progressive and liberal labels. Shortly after the 1924 election, Roosevelt had described the outcome as a victory for "conservatism" and
claimed that the Democrats, though disunited, were still the "party of
progress and liberal thought."

Nonetheless, Roosevelt did not take an aggressively ideological
stance in 1932. His campaign was not remarkable for concrete proposals, consistency, or an ideologized vocabulary. Surrounded by a
variety of advisers, his academic "Brains Trust," personal staff, and a
host of politicians, social workers, and lawyers, Roosevelt tended to
avoid overcommitting himself in any one direction. He kept his own
proposals general, and concentrated his attacks on Hoover's failures.
At various times he did call for "national planning in agriculture" and

for a halt to the "process of concentration" in industry. But on issues such as the tariff, he equivocated to a degree that amazed his closest advisers, and he offered no comprehensive definitions of the major ideological labels to compete with those of Hoover.[35]

In substance, Roosevelt inherited the progressive and liberal labels in 1932 by default. Senator George Norris of Nebraska, a disenchanted Republican, put it simply: "We of the progressive faith have to look to the Democratic Party." In September 1932, Norris became chairman of the National Progressive League, a pro-Roosevelt group formed to bolster the candidate's identification with the progressive label. Roosevelt also received indirect support from Flynn and other columnists who attacked Hoover's liberal credential.

Not all Hoover's critics allowed Roosevelt uncontested accession to the legitimizing labels. As in the early 1920s, there was again an effort to reify old labels in explicitly new ways. "Progressivism today, if we are to revaluate the term," wrote columnist John Chamberlain, "must mean either [Socialist] Norman Thomas or [Communist] William Z. Foster." The League for Independent Political Action, which included a number of prominent self-styled progressives and liberals, endorsed Thomas. Hoover's having been deprived of the labels, however, suggested that they would not be transferred to anyone whose views represented a significant departure from conventional wisdom.[36]

The importance of Roosevelt's inheritance by default should not be underestimated. Although his immediate objective was an electoral prize rather than a verbal one, in the long run both would be significant in the transformation of American society. Inheriting the labels without having to supply detailed information about programs gave him greater freedom of action than he might otherwise have had. Indeed, one cannot understand modern American history without understanding Roosevelt's verbal inheritance.

In the period from McKinley's death to April 1917, there had been two major shifts in American political vocabulary: an existing power structure had survived by twice transforming its idiom. In contrast, from 1919 to 1932 there had been no major shifts; the same power structure had survived without transforming its idiom. This com-

35. Schlesinger, *Crisis of the Old Order*, pp. 103, 424–427.
36. Ibid., pp. 421–422, 435–436.

parison suggests a substantially greater political arousal during the former period and a greater quiescence during the latter.

The two periods had certain similarities: both eventuated in disaster, one in war, the other in economic collapse. From neither disaster had new fundamental categories of thought emerged. The old prewar intellectual categories had resurfaced after the war and been incorporated into a new postwar synthesis. And although the synthesis itself had collapsed with the economy, its intellectual categories had held. Thus neither disaster had led to fundamental questions about the categories themselves or how they influenced political thought and action. In neither case was the process of de-reification sustained, or the harmonization of discordancy consistently exposed. Wilson and Hoover had both had their liberal credentials attacked, but neither attack had led to a sustained analysis of political manipulation through language. In short, both disasters had eventuated in lost opportunities.

There was nonetheless a difference in the two periods and in their respective outcomes. The intellectual ferment of the prewar years had been such that when critics debated the wartime legacy during the 1919-1920 period, they still debated the semantic and political content of the labels themselves. The quiescence of the decade that followed was such that when disaster finally struck, Americans were as unprepared mentally as they were economically, and the panic was as much intellectual as financial. Political debate during the 1931–1932 period tended to turn more on personalities than on the meanings of ideological terms. Conventional categories had become so ingrained, and the need for leadership or personification of those categories so immediate, that the question was more likely to be "who is a liberal?" than "what is a liberal?," and the answer "whoever looks as if he can do something."

Hoover understood the danger of the situation. "We have heard a great deal in this campaign," he declared, "about reactionaries, conservatives, progressives, liberals, and radicals. I have not yet heard an attempt by any one of the orators who mouth these phrases to define the principles upon which they base these classifications." It was in this context that he reiterated his long-held definition of "true liberalism." Opposition statements, he charged, foreshadowed "a profound change in American life—less in concrete proposals, bad as that may be, than by implication and by evasion." Opposition spokesmen were taking advantage of the situation to demand a blank check. For this reason, Hoover warned, the election was "not a mere shift from the ins to the outs," but meant "deciding the direction our Nation will take over a century to come."

Hoover's analysis of Democratic campaign strategy was unflattering but essentially accurate. Immediately after the Democratic debacle of 1924, Roosevelt himself had ruefully remarked that since 1920 the Democrats had "been doing nothing—waiting for the other fellow to put his foot in it." Now that the other fellow had finally done so, Roosevelt was quite willing to let the situation work to his advantage. All that was required was that he not put his own foot in it as well.[37]

It was a situation fraught with contradictions. In the upheaval and arousal occasioned by the depression, Roosevelt's inheritance by default had been made possible only by an underlying intellectual quiescence. While the eclipse of Hoover's individualist label implied a profound readiness for change, survival of the progressive and liberal labels implied an equally profound desire for continuity. The attacks on Hoover's progressive and liberal credentials amounted to an angry exercise in de-reification; yet the simultaneous transfer of those labels to Roosevelt suggested a desperate need to re-embody abstractions in concrete form all over again.

It was also a situation laden with unpredictability. Apart from Hoover himself, probably few people even dreamed what evolution of language and politics was in the offing, or what realignments were in store between nature and artifice, tradition and innovation, promotion and regulation, and especially coercion and freedom. Even fewer likely realized how fully interchangeable the categories would become, or what profound quiescence would develop beneath the extraordinary surface-level arousal of the years ahead.

As for Roosevelt himself, he had no more detailed a vision of how he would use power than did the millions who had elected him. Election Night 1932 was, in his words, "the greatest night of my life."[38] Apart from that, little else was certain.

37. Myers, ed., *State Papers and Public Writings of Hoover*, 2:425, 428; Schlesinger, *Crisis of the Old Order*, p. 103.
38. Ibid., p. 439.

5

The Political Vocabulary
of Franklin Roosevelt

The transformation of the liberal label

Generally speaking, in a representative form of government there are usually two general schools of political belief—liberal and conservative. . . . The liberal party is a party which believes that, as new conditions and problems arise beyond the power of men and women to meet as individuals, it becomes the duty of the Government itself to find new remedies with which to meet them. . . .

The conservative party in government honestly and conscientiously believes the contrary. It believes that there is no necessity for the Government to step in, even when new conditions and new problems arise. It believes that, in the long run, individual initiative and private philanthropy can take care of all situations. . . .

The clear and undisputed fact is that in these later years, at least since 1932, the Democratic party has been the liberal party, and the Republican party has been the conservative party.

Franklin Roosevelt, 1941

In the world of political discourse, the supreme achievement is to make what is partisan and temporary seem universal and timeless. If Roosevelt's definitions of liberalism and conservatism still seem commonplace rather than remarkable, it is not because he defined the terms "correctly" in some abstract sense, but because his usage became and has remained standard in both the political and historiographical arenas. He did not triumph over the linguistic dialectic; he merely participated in it. Yet he did so with such skill and finesse that he temporarily made people forget the dialectic existed. That in itself is a measure of his achievement.[1]

1. *The Public Papers and Addresses of Franklin D. Roosevelt, 1938* (New York: Macmillan, 1941), pp. xxix–xxx.

119

Roosevelt's definitions were neither remarkable nor precise. He qualified their partisan aspects by stating that not all Republicans were conservatives and not all conservatives were Republicans. His definition of liberalism as "the duty of the Government itself to find new remedies" was, as he put it, "general." Both the lack of absolutism and the imprecision were deliberate, however. The purpose of political labeling is not precision but evocation, and what Roosevelt wanted to evoke was a general feeling that New Deal policies represented "true liberalism" and those of his opponents an already-discredited "conservatism."

What difference can it make whether Roosevelt is remembered as "a liberal," or indeed as founder of what is often called "twentieth-century liberalism?" It has long been a cliché of American politics that "nineteenth-century liberalism" is equivalent to "twentieth-century conservatism," whereas "twentieth-century liberalism" differs profoundly from its nineteenth-century namesake. It is also a cliché that "twentieth-century liberalism" began with Roosevelt.

Such clichés do recognize a process of linguistic evolution, but they obscure its political significance. Roosevelt's language did not go unchallenged in the 1930s. His opponents struggled long and hard to prevent his transformation of the liberal label. That their struggle has been nearly forgotten does not attest to its lack of importance but to the completeness of Roosevelt's victory. In transforming the popularly accepted meaning of the word "liberal," Roosevelt transformed people's expectations of government. Americans (and those subject to American power and influence) still live in the shadow of that transformation.

Roosevelt's categories of thought derived in part from Wilson. In introducing the liberal label in 1917, Wilson had implicitly referred to the polarities of freedom and coercion as well as liberty and authority. In international affairs he had leaned heavily on the connotation of defending freedom in order to justify a policy of military coercion. In domestic politics he had demanded great authority in the name of liberty. Embodied in his vocabulary was the assumption that both these discordancies could be harmonized through a judicious use of federal power.

After the war there had been a strong reaction against Wilson's use of the word "liberal." Hoover did not use it in similar fashion. He justified coercive regulation under the progressive label, because for him liberalism "set bounds" to bureaucratic authority. The depression, however, not only cost Hoover his identification with both labels, but brought them and the categories embedded in them closer to interchangeable usage. Where Hoover had tried to maintain the separateness and complementarity of coercion and freedom, the crisis of the depression stimulated renewed belief in their interchangeability. As in earlier crises, people again began to view coercion as the route to freedom, authority as the route to liberty, and regulation as the route to promotion.

Like Wilson, Roosevelt believed he could harmonize these discordancies through a judicious use of power. Confident of his eventual success, he carried the interchangeability of categories to new extremes domestically and internationally. In this sense he built on existing foundations. However, his use of the word "liberal" also set in motion a process that until then had been merely latent, a process centered on the connotation of generosity or "liberality."

The connotation had of course long been attached to the word. During the war, Wilson had invoked it in exhorting Americans to be "liberal" in giving to the Red Cross. In *American Individualism*, Hoover had touched on it in decrying the "perpetual howl of radicalism . . . that it is the sole voice of liberalism—that devotion to social programs is its field alone." In these uses, however, Wilson and Hoover were both defining "liberal" in terms of voluntary action.[2]

Only with the depression did the connotation of generosity become linked to governmental responsibility (exactly what Hoover had feared). Only with the New Deal did two connotations fuse and liberalism emerge redefined as the politics of governmental generosity. This is what the public works programs, the job creation programs, social security, and the various other efforts at redistribution of wealth were all about.

Although belief in governmental generosity sharply reinforced belief in more laws rather than fewer, Roosevelt did not see the new approach as coercive in any sinister sense. In distinguishing between liberals and conservatives, he emphasized that liberals "believed in the wisdom and efficacy of the will of the great majority of the people,

2. Ibid., p. xxxi; Albert Shaw, ed., *The Messages and Papers of Wilson* (New York: Review of Reviews, 1924), 1:490; Herbert Hoover, *American Individualism* (Washington: Herbert Hoover Presidential Library Association, n.d.), pp. 30–31.

as distinguished from the judgment of a small minority of either education or wealth." Liberalism meant majority rule, and the majority
could not be truly sinister. Roosevelt was updating Ely's argument
about "fraternalism versus paternalism" and taking the position that
governmental generosity should not be viewed as coercion ("paternal") but as an expression of democratic freedoms ("fraternal"). Liberalism was not the politics of coercively imposed generosity but of
democratically ordained generosity.[3]

Was Roosevelt's definition of liberalism "legitimate"? To put the
question that way is to enter the realm of reification. The more searching question is: why was it so important to Roosevelt that the New
Deal be labeled liberal?

In labeling his policies liberal, Roosevelt was invoking familiar values. Even in carrying old trends to new extremes, he was operating
within an existing power structure and verbal idiom. By invoking the
value of generosity, however, he was also transforming both the oper-
ation of the power structure and its justification in terms of that same
idiom. In short, he was at once preserving and transforming a power
structure by preserving and transforming its idiom.

To invoke both old and new values by means of a single symbol is to
proclaim continuity and change simultaneously. Depending on the
nature of the change one has in mind, the psychic resistance aroused
may range from minuscule to enormous. Roosevelt needed a symbol
that was sufficiently flexible to minimize resistance. Because it connoted freedom as well as generosity, the liberal label was ideal.

In Roosevelt's transformation of both the liberal label and the
American political system, the complementarity of the two connotations served two important purposes. Hard times notwithstanding,
the idea of governmental generosity was not a politically appealing
one to invoke directly, still less so the prospect of calling it "charity"
(as Hoover had done). Following the language of the preamble to the
Constitution, it eventually became "welfare," and Roosevelt's status
as founder of "twentieth-century liberalism" is usually linked to his
authorship of what is variously labeled "the welfare state," "welfare
capitalism," or "welfare liberalism." Roosevelt himself preferred the
single word "liberal." The connotation of preserving one's freedom, or

3. *Public Papers of Roosevelt, 1938*, p. xxix.

individual dignity, subtly but effectively removed the onus of accepting a certain measure of dependence on government.

By the same token, it was the connotation of generosity that justified placing certain limits on individual freedom. A frequent accusation of Roosevelt's opponents was that New Deal spending programs necessitated a massive and unwarranted confiscation of the people's wealth. Far from being an embarrassment to him, the accusation was a distinct asset because implicit in the idea of the New Deal was the imagery of taking from the rich and giving to the poor by means of the democratic process. Roosevelt's use of the liberal label harmonized not only the discordancy between coercion and freedom, but that between confiscation and generosity. By implying a democratically ordained, downward redistribution of wealth, it made both sets of categories interchangeable: coercion as freedom and confiscation as generosity were the twin hallmarks of a redefined liberalism.

Historian Otis Graham has suggested that prewar self-styled "progressives" who survived into the 1930s tended on balance to disapprove of New Deal programs. The discordancy between confiscation and generosity suggests both a semantic and a political explanation, and perhaps explains why Roosevelt eventually deemphasized the progressive label in favor of the liberal.

Most of the generation whom Graham studied defined "progress" differently from Roosevelt. Although they were imbued with the metaphor of forward motion, they did not think in terms of governmental generosity or liberality, nor did the metaphor itself evoke the latter connotation. As this older generation viewed the New Deal, they were far more struck by its coercive and confiscatory aspects. For his part, Roosevelt seems to have grasped intuitively that there was nothing to be gained from a pitched battle over the definition of progressivism. Like Wilson in 1917, he chose to avoid the debate: he never entirely abandoned the progressive label, but did deemphasize it. The liberal label was far more appropriate for harmonizing the discordancies between confiscation and generosity, and coercion and freedom.[4]

Roosevelt's avoiding a debate with the old self-styled progressives

4. Otis L. Graham, *An Encore for Reform: The Old Progressives in the New Deal* (New York: Oxford University Press, 1967), p. 44.

did not mean that he was averse to verbal battle. In fact he relished it so long as there was some purpose to it. A major attraction of the liberal label was its setting up a ready-made, useful enemy. With Roosevelt identified as the voice of the wise and generous majority, the clear implication was that his opponents, chiefly Republicans and corporate entrepreneurs, constituted a shortsighted, greedy minority.

Of all Roosevelt's verbal strategies, none was more important than conveying an image of antagonism between himself and the large corporations. His own references to "economic royalists" and "the forces of organized money," like Harold Ickes' characterization of Wendell Willkie as a "simple, barefoot Wall Street lawyer," were designed to distance Roosevelt from what he called "the handful of men and corporations that had dominated [the economy] in the false boom days before 1929."[5]

Again one sees the complementarity of "good" and "bad" labels. In describing himself as liberal and his opponents as conservative, Roosevelt was invoking values and summarizing information in a special way. The word "liberal" implied governmental generosity whereas "conservative" implied minimal government and a procorporate perspective. This vocabulary not only reinforced the idea of inevitable corporate combination under minimal government but established Roosevelt as the champion of countervailing power. Even more important, the vocabulary made the New Deal itself synonymous with a more effective and equitable distribution of wealth.

The latter implication was especially crucial in that it assigned both credit and blame: to the extent that the economic situation improved, the New Deal got the credit; to the extent that the depression continued, Roosevelt's use of labels ascribed responsibility to corporate greed and shortsightedness as well as to the intransigence of procorporate politicians (the Republican party). In short, where there was failure, the Rooseveltian vocabulary reassuringly put the blame on the "other fellow."

The liberal label was also useful for undercutting critics who accused Roosevelt of "socialist," "communist," or even "fascist" tendencies. Far from being intimidated by such accusations, he was a master

5. Ickes' reference to Willkie is cited in William Leuchtenburg, *Franklin D. Roosevelt and the New Deal, 1932–1940* (New York: Harper and Row, 1963), p. 319. Roosevelt's reference to the "false boom days before 1929" is in *Public Papers of Roosevelt, 1938*, p. xxi.

at turning them against his accusers. "There is no difference between the major parties," he declared in 1936, "as to what they think about Communism. But there is a very great difference . . . in what they do about Communism." Expanding on this theme, Roosevelt used it to woo opposition faithful. "The true conservative," he noted in the same speech, "seeks to protect the system of private property and free enterprise by correcting such injustices and inequalities as arise from it. . . . Liberalism becomes the protection for the far-sighted conservative. . . . I am that kind of conservative because I am that kind of liberal."[6]

Roosevelt could be at once militantly partisan and ideologically ecumenical. He could also use the liberal-conservative dichotomy to harmonize continuity and change. His rhetorical style was flexible. During the initial "honeymoon" period, when he was still enjoying his inheritance by default, he usually let others do the labeling. His early statements on relief and recovery contained few references to progressivism or liberalism and he responded coolly and calmly to prejoratives. "A few timid people, who fear progress," he remarked in 1934, "will try to give you new and strange names for what we are doing. Sometimes they will call it 'Fascism,' sometimes 'Communism,' sometimes 'Regimentation,' sometimes 'Socialism.' But in so doing, they are trying to make very complex and theoretical something that is really very simple and practical."

Only in late 1935, with the courts striking down major New Deal legislation and the country gearing up for the 1936 campaign, did Roosevelt begin utilizing ideological labels with greater frequency. By the middle of his second term, he was generally on the attack, leaning heavily on the liberal label and hurling such pejoratives as "conservative" and "reactionary" at opponents. By 1941 he had formulated his "classic" definitions of liberal and conservative and was applying Nazi labels to the opposition, accusing opponents of his Supreme Court bill of a propaganda "putsch" and describing opposition to other proposals as having reached "blitzkrieg" proportions.[7]

An inflammatory rhetoric often indicates a defensive attitude, and Roosevelt's later rhetoric suggests that he himself came to perceive

6. *The Public Papers and Addresses of Franklin D. Roosevelt, 1936* (New York: Random House, 1938), pp. 384, 389–390.

7. Mario Einaudi, *The Roosevelt Revolution* (New York: Harcourt, Brace, 1959), pp. 84–85; *Public Papers of Roosevelt, 1938*. pp. 398–399, 515, xxii, xxvii.

growing resistance to his policies and their ideological implications. Much of his early legislative program had resulted in new administrative structures with either broad coercive authority (the NRA and the AAA), or broad spending authority (the CWA and the PWA). In putting such emphasis on discretionary administrative authority, Roosevelt was not merely redefining the duties or responsibilities of government but redefining responsibility itself in terms of prerogative.

Government by administrative prerogative was not new. In carrying it to new extremes, however, and in linking it to the connotation of generosity, Roosevelt was again both preserving and transforming. Hoover's liberalism had implied governmental restraint (the citizen's "freedom from"), whereas Roosevelt's implied license (the government's "freedom to"). Using the same label to subsume both required an extraordinary harmonization of discordancy. Even so, he might have encountered less resistance but for one other factor.

By 1938, it was clear that the New Deal had not succeeded in ending the depression. The massive new structures and spending programs notwithstanding, the country was still faced with severe unemployment. Governmental generosity had aided millions, but had left millions of others substantially untouched. The investment in administrative license was not paying off, and Roosevelt had much to answer for. No matter how he summarized information, he could not fully suppress the inconvenient fact of failure. However, an effective use of words could deflect much of the responsibility and antagonism and undercut a political unrest that was reaching alarming proportions.

The 1930s were years of great public arousal, and Roosevelt is often regarded as a master of rousing rhetoric. If anything, his rhetoric again suggests the interchangeability of arousal and quiescence. Like Wilson, Roosevelt excelled in provoking the public against a variety of foes, thereby undercutting opposition to his own policies. This latter purpose underlay his "classic" definitions of liberal and conservative. Herein the magnitude of Roosevelt's victory emerges most clearly.

When the political categories of political actors become the investigative categories of social science, the very possibility of critical analysis is undercut. Phrases such as "economic royalists" and "the forces of organized money" convey obvious partisanship, and in writing about the New Deal, historians routinely put such phrases in quotation marks. However, they routinely use the words liberal and conservative without quotation marks as supposedly value-free categories. Their usage, moreover, tends to follow Roosevelt's own, with liberalism defined in terms of governmental generosity and conservatism defined in terms of a procorporate, minimal government perspective.[8]

This transference of Rooseveltian usage into social science vocabulary has had an immeasurably powerful impact on American political thought. It reifies labels on Roosevelt's terms, makes supposedly critical scholars into custodians of his definition of the situation, reinforces his intellectual and political victory, and in so doing undercuts the possibility of reassessment. Even to write critically about something called "New Deal liberalism" is not to get to the heart of the matter. So long as one's investigative and analytical categories are Roosevelt's own, one remains imprisoned within a Rooseveltian perspective. Only when one treats political vocabulary as historical data does that perspective lose its imprisoning power. Roosevelt's definitions fall into place as political weapons, as partisan contributions to an ongoing struggle, whereas the objections and rebuttals of his contemporary critics emerge, as in previous cases, replete with lost insights.

The struggles of the 1930s involved a variety of critics. Some, such as Hoover and his protégé Robert Taft, were Republican leaders; others, such as John T. Flynn of the *New Republic* and Oswald Garrison Villard of the *Nation*, were journalists; and still others, including Amos Pinchot (brother of Gifford), were survivors of the 1912 Progressive party crusade. All were labeled conservative by Roosevelt or his supporters; all angrily insisted on referring to themselves as liberals.

As the vocabulary of both sides indicates, the linguistic competition was extraordinarily intense. From Roosevelt's point of view, important as it was that the New Deal be identified as liberal, it was equally important that these critics be identified as conservative. In one sense, the reason was obvious: the label would link them to "economic royalists" and "organized money" and discredit them by association. But this only raises another question. What were these self-styled liberal critics saying that was so threatening to Roosevelt's popularity?

Here the continuity and depth of the struggle become apparent for

---

8. See, for example, Clinton Rossiter, *Conservatism in America* (London: Heinemann, 1955), pp. 173–174, and James T. Patterson, *Congressional Conservatism and the New Deal* (Lexington: University of Kentucky Press, 1967), pp. vii–viii.

what these critics were doing was a continuation of what earlier critics such as Garland, Bourne, and Coblenz had done. They were challenging power in terms of its own vocabulary. As Flynn put it, the point was to show what Roosevelt was really doing "under the label of liberalism."[9]

Like many earlier critics, those of the 1930s tended to fall into the trap of counter-reification, and as in earlier eras, this would be partly responsible for their eventual failure. Like Roosevelt, the critics built in part on previous usage. Thus Hoover told reporters in 1936: "Liberal is an old English term. With the English the accepted definition of a liberal was a man who believed that in the least possible government there was the most freedom. Today it is the man who believes that in the most government there is the greatest liberty that is labeled a liberal." The terms "liberal" and "liberalism," he remarked on another occasion, were being "perverted" and "used as a camouflage for the wholesale violation of the principles of liberty."[10]

At issue was not merely the quantity of government, but its quality as well. In the name of liberalism, Hoover charged, Roosevelt was edging "into a system of government-directed monopolies" and creating "vast political bureaucracies." Hoover was especially irked by the administration's insistence on labeling these things liberal. "If you do not believe these things," he noted, "you will be called bad names, such as 'reactionaries' or 'tories.' These ideas are not American Liberalism."

Pinchot agreed. "No man now can call himself a liberal unchallenged," he wrote in 1939, "unless he is partial, prejudiced, class-conscious, and as intolerant and narrow minded as a backwood Kentucky bishop." Most people who professed to be liberal, he noted, were really "reactionary," in that "they stand for concentration of power in the executive, destruction of power in the legislative branch of the government, coercion, and various things that heretofore have been correctly assigned to reaction."[11]

9. For Flynn's use of the phrase "under the label of liberalism," see his column "Other People's Money," *New Republic*, January 22, 1940, p. 115.

10. Remarks to press, Portland, Oregon, February 12, 1936, PS#2267; "Americanization and American Ideals," statement of November 27, 1935, PS#2235, HHPL.

11. Ibid.; Pinchot is quoted in Ronald Radosh, *Prophets on the Right: Profiles of Conservative Critics of American Globalism* (New York: Simon and Schuster, 1975), p. 324.

There was both strength and weakness in such commentaries. Roosevelt had indeed raised executive and bureaucratic prerogative to unprecedented levels and increased administrative authority both in absolute terms and relative to that of the legislature. Spotlighting the discordancy between authority and liberty was thus an apt criticism. Yet in reifying their own definitions of liberalism and reaction, thereby validating the linguistic competition, Hoover and Pinchot opened the way to a powerful administration rejoinder. New Deal supporters could agree that there really was such a thing as "true liberalism," then argue that it required administrative prerogative to implement its most important element (namely, a liberal or generous redistribution of wealth) and that opposition to such a program was "truly reactionary" or "truly conservative." This in substance was the position Roosevelt himself took from 1938 on.[12]

In so doing Roosevelt was using one connotation to complement another, harmonizing the discordancy between confiscation and generosity as a way of harmonizing that between authority and liberty. Generosity, in short, neutralized whatever sinister implications coercive authority might otherwise have had. And because this complementarity of connotations was central to Roosevelt's strategy, it was central to the critics' strategy that both harmonizations be exposed and discredited, the discordancy between confiscation and generosity laid bare, and Roosevelt's supposed generosity subjected to the closest scrutiny.

The crux of the matter was Roosevelt's relationship to large corporations. Roosevelt himself conveyed an image of antagonism but the reality, critics charged, was exactly the reverse. Roosevelt was using the liberal label to camouflage the construction of an unprecedentedly powerful corporate-government alliance. Far from redistributing wealth and power downwards, he was being extraordinarily generous toward the corporations themselves.

John T. Flynn was among the first to accuse Roosevelt of using liberal rhetoric to camouflage a procorporate policy. Unlike Hoover, Flynn believed in the constructive possibilities of governmental generosity, and in particular advocated job creation through public works

12. *Public Papers of Roosevelt, 1938*, pp. 398–399, 444–445, 515–517, 570–571, 585; *The Public Papers and Addresses of Franklin D. Roosevelt, 1939* (New York: Macmillan, 1941), pp. 62–63, 67, 434–437; *The Public Papers and Addresses of Franklin D. Roosevelt, 1940* (New York: Macmillan, 1941), pp. 88, 166–170, 299.

programs. He also believed that as president Hoover had relied too heavily on corporate power to stimulate recovery, and for this reason Flynn had dismissed him in 1932 as a "bogus liberal." To Flynn, the trouble with the New Deal was not that it promised generosity, but that it failed to deliver.

As early as the fall of 1933, Flynn charged that Roosevelt was cutting back job creation programs while giving more and more power to large corporations through the NRA production codes. Ironically, some of the very trade associations Hoover had helped organize were playing leading roles among code authorities. Now, however, they had the delegated power of law. "It has been sold to our people as a great liberal revolution," Flynn angrily declared. "That is a fraud. It is nothing else than the scheme which the Chamber of Commerce of the United States has been fighting for for twelve years—the modification of the Sherman anti-trust law and turning over the control of industry to the tender mercy of the trade associations." Roosevelt's "liberality" toward labor was spurious. "Employers," wrote Flynn, "are compelled to combine. But laborers are not."[13]

Without accepting Flynn's criticisms of his own presidency, Hoover echoed the latter's attack on the NRA. By setting up code authorities dominated by large corporations, he noted, the NRA was "crushing the life out of small business" while giving little to working people. "NRA's pretended promises to labor," Hoover charged, "were intentionally vague and have never been clarified. They have only promoted conflict without establishing real rights." In a press release issued shortly before the NRA was invalidated by the Supreme Court, Hoover declared: "If all these things are liberal and progressive we need some new definitions of these terms."

Among younger Republican leaders, none was more vociferous than Taft in attacking the supposed generosity of the New Deal. "It is easy," he remarked, "to call oneself a liberal; it is much harder to devise the measures which will really benefit the average man and woman. If the ultimate result of New Deal measures is to deprive the average man of freedom and opportunity, and subject him to crushing taxation and monopoly prices, then it is a false liberalism and the worst kind of reaction." Taft was especially persistent in attacking the financing of social security. "The character of the tax imposed, one

13. Radosh, *Prophet on the Right*, p. 203.

directly on payroll," he noted, "shows who is going to pay the bill." Roosevelt was parading social security as "Something for Nothing," whereas in reality it amounted to forced savings at minimal return. Confiscation it certainly was; generosity it was not.[14]

Whereas Hoover and Taft rejoiced in the Supreme Court decision outlawing the NRA, Flynn had mixed feelings. He strongly believed that the federal government had to have sufficient power to deal with national economic problems. To that extent, he told Senator George Norris, "the decision of the Supreme Court limiting the power of the federal government is deplorable." This, however, "ought not to blind liberals to the appalling danger which has been halted, namely, the delegation of legislative power over our economic life to trade groups."[15]

Challenging Roosevelt in terms of his own vocabulary, exposing the discordancies and contradictions. was a powerful form of attack. Flynn's criticism of the NRA was also powerful. Yet to posit the existence of an identifiable group called "liberals" was still to reify the label and compete for it.

Reification of the "good" label, moreover, was only part of the problem. In any struggle to shape public attitudes, the temptation to hurl "bad" labels is also great. Opposition leaders split on whether to accuse Roosevelt of "socialism," "communism," or "fascism." Taft, a rising star in the Republican party, saw more political payoff in the first two labels, whereas Hoover, reflecting a lifelong belief in the equivalence of all "European patent medicines," used all three labels more or less interchangeably, and even accused Roosevelt at one point of "goosestepping the people under this pinkish banner of Planned Economy." Flynn, for his part, agreed with fellow columnist Dorothy Thompson that New Deal policies were encouraging "the growth of monopolies" under state control. As she wrote in 1936: "The logical end of a growing state control over business without affecting any change in ownership is not socialism. It is fascism. That is what

14. Interview with Hoover in *Baltimore Sun*, May 16, 1935; statement to press on the NRA, Stanford University, May 24, 1935, PS#2197, HHPL; Taft speech to Republican National Convention, Miscellaneous Speeches, 1936, Box 1249, Robert A. Taft Papers, Library of Congress, Washington, D.C. (hereafter Taft MS.); "Something for Nothing," Taft speech to Women's National Republican Club, January 18, 1936, ibid.

15. Flynn to Senator Norris, June 6, 1935, Flynn MS. Also see Flynn to Senator Vandenberg, June 10, 1935, ibid.

fascism is." On reading Thompson's column, Flynn immediately wrote to congratulate her on a "masterpiece."[16]

However scathing the criticism, such statements still ignored the impact of reification itself. In any competition over labels, Roosevelt's initial inheritance by default gave him a tremendous advantage. Reifying the labels demanded an all-or-nothing response. This only reinforced Roosevelt's initial advantage and undercut audience receptivity to specific criticisms of his policies. In Flynn's own terms, the labels themselves blinded audiences.

It was a cruel dilemma, bound to have short-run and long-run consequences. In the short run, reification obscured both the sources and the substance of policy. With respect to sources, it obscured what Flynn called "this continual drawing on Wall Street and its environs for the advisors of the New Deal." Its substantive effects were even more serious. "One of the most amazing illusions I have ever seen," wrote Flynn, "has been the illusion of businessmen that Roosevelt wants to ruin them and the illusion of the liberals that he wants to subdue business." Roosevelt was "against certain individual businessmen who have abused him or insulted him or crossed him." Nonetheless, from the beginning of his first term he had used the Department of Commerce to "do things for business." The problem, reflected in Flynn's own vocabulary, was that so long as one reified a category called "liberals," the polarization of "liberals" versus "businessmen" reinforced the very antagonism Roosevelt himself wished to convey.

Flynn continued to attack Roosevelt's use of language, and by 1939 was accusing him of using liberal rhetoric to camouflage an outright abdication in favor of "big business." Recent antitrust prosecutions and the much-publicized TNEC hearings on corporate power notwithstanding, Flynn charged that Roosevelt was preparing to turn the New Deal over to the "business community" in a desperate effort "to

16. For Taft's accusations of "socialism" and "communism," see speech to Kiwanis Club, reported in Chillicothe (Ohio) *Gazette*, November 20, 1935; "Something for Nothing" speech, cited n. 14, above; and speech to Ohio Republican Convention, September 14, 1938, Box 1250. Taft MS. For Hoover's pejorative use of all three terms, see "Americanization and American Ideals" speech, cited n. 10, above, and address before John Marshall Republican Club, St. Louis, December 16, 1935, PS#2242, HHPL. For his use of the phrase, "goosestepping the people under this pinkish banner of Planned Economy," see address at Lincoln, Nebraska, January 16, 1936, PS#2254, ibid. Thompson's column is in the *New York Herald-Tribune*, May 26, 1936; and see Flynn to Thompson, May 26, 1936, Flynn MS.

do something for business to make it recover." This, he declared, was the strategy behind the appointment of Harry Hopkins as secretary of commerce. Now Roosevelt was in a dilemma: "He cannot surrender to business. He would lose all his liberal following, which is his only real support now. He could not turn the Department of Commerce over outright to a labeled economic royalist. But he could turn it over, and along with it much of his administration, to the conservative business groups through the disguise of Harry Hopkins, who is a liberal left-winger. Hopkins can go much further to the right without a blast from the liberals, than an economic royalist Secretary could go." When Flynn repeated this thesis in the pages of the *Yale Review*, Roosevelt responded by writing personally to its editor Wilbur Cross to suggest that Flynn had become a "destructive rather than a constructive force" and should "be barred hereafter from the columns of any presentable daily paper, monthly magazine or national quarterly such as the *Yale Review*."

Roosevelt's reaction was a handsome if unintended compliment. It also indicated the long-run consequences of the opposition's dilemma. A sustained competition for the liberal label meant that one of two things was bound to happen: either Roosevelt would lose his liberal credential or the challengers would lose theirs. By late 1940, Flynn and like-minded critics would indeed have difficulty finding "presentable" outlets.

Flynn's vocabulary also indicates a further difficulty that faced opposition spokesmen. During the 1930s, an increased American awareness of events in Europe brought the importation of the traditional European "left-to-right" linear spectrum, which in turn subsumed such labels as liberal, conservative, communist, socialist, and fascist. As with the latter labels, reification of the linear spectrum only strengthened Roosevelt's position. The extremes of "left" and "right" evoked frightening European comparisons, yet Roosevelt simply could not be credibly compared to Stalin, Mussolini, or Hitler. The very appeal to such a spectrum, coupled with a lack of credibility of the extreme labels, reinforced Roosevelt's image as a "centrist" or "moderate." As he himself reassuringly put it, the New Deal was "just a little bit left of center."[17]

17. Flynn to Harold Ickes, April 8, 1936, Flynn MS.; Flynn to Wilbur Cross, April 4, 1939, ibid.; and Roosevelt to Cross, July 7, 1939, in Elliott Roosevelt, ed., *F.D.R.: His Personal Letters, 1928–1945* (New York: Duell, Sloan, and Pearce, 1950), 2:904.

In short, the opposition's vocabulary played into Roosevelt's hands in several ways. It was not that opposition spokesmen had failed to understand New Deal policies, nor were they insensitive to Roosevelt's use of language. Challenging him in terms of both liberty and liberality was a thoughtful and courageous thing to do. Yet the trap of counter-reification was a serious one, and none of his major critics entirely escaped it.

Even so, Roosevelt's triumph might not have been so complete, indeed he might not have triumphed at all in the long run, had not circumstances also played into his hands. By 1938 he was on the defensive. His popularity was ebbing. The New Deal had not cured the depression. Just at that point, however, events abroad began shaping up in a way that would ultimately rescue both his political fortunes and his definition of the situation.

The remarkable label nobody wanted

The wholesale eclipse of democracy must concern us. Our national mission is to keep alight the lamp of true liberalism. But it is in the United States that we must keep it alight.

Herbert Hoover, 1938

Some indeed still hold to the now somewhat obvious delusion that we . . . can safely permit the United States to become a lone island . . . in a world dominated by the philosophy of force.

Such an island may be the dream of those who still talk and vote as isolationists. Such an island represents to me and to the overwhelming majority of Americans today a helpless nightmare of a people without freedom.

Franklin Roosevelt, 1940

Liberal or isolationist—how are Roosevelt's foreign policy critics best classified? To put the question in such terms is to fall again into the trap of reification. The more historical question is: why, when

---

Flynn's article was published under the title, "Mr. Hopkins and Mr. Roosevelt," *Yale Review* 28 (June 1939):667–679. For Roosevelt's description of the New Deal as "just a little bit left of center," see *Public Papers of Roosevelt, 1939*, p. 556.

critics such as Hoover tried to debate foreign policy in terms of liberalism, did Roosevelt insist on the language of isolationism?

To put the question this way is not only to recognize the significance of the linguistic struggle, but to focus specific attention on Roosevelt's transformation of the terms of the debate. That transformation was itself part of a historic pattern of challenge and response that went back to McKinley and America's emergence as a world power.[18]

In 1898, in an attempt to lay bare the discordancy between tradition and innovation, opponents of Philippine annexation had accused McKinley of "imperialism." He in turn recognized the ideological unity of domestic and foreign policy and, knowing his domestic strength as a self-styled conservative, held fast to the latter label and incorporated it into foreign policy debate. The harmonization of tradition and innovation succeeded, the critics' attempt to transform the terms of the debate backfired, and the imperialist label was neutralized indefinitely in American politics.

When Wilson had faced a similar challenge in 1917, he rather than his critics took the initiative in transforming the debate. Instead of arguing foreign policy in the language of progressivism, Wilson shifted to the liberal label. Although his shift, too, was a recognition of the ideological unity of domestic and foreign policy, it was simultaneously an implicit admission of the shakiness of his own domestic position. Successful in the immediate situation, Wilson generated a postwar reaction that led to the short-term eclipse of the liberal label.

Now, in the late 1930s, Roosevelt faced the challenge, and his shifting the terms of the debate also suggests that he, like Wilson, grasped the vulnerability of his domestic situation. Ironically, the liberal label that had served Roosevelt so well in the domestic arena and that Wilson had introduced as his new foreign policy label was the very one Roosevelt avoided in foreign policy debate. Beneath the irony lay an important political fact: Americans had come a long way since 1917 in their appreciation of the danger of war. It would be much harder to harmonize coercion and freedom at the level of preparing people for yet another war.

Although Roosevelt's position was partly similar to Wilson's, the

18. Hoover speech to Council on Foreign Relations, March 31, 1938, reprinted in *Congressional Record*, 75th Cong., 3rd sess., *Appendix*, p. 7168; *Public Papers of Roosevelt, 1940*, p. 261.

variance in circumstances spotlights an important difference in their approaches. When Wilson had shifted labels, he had focused on a new "good" label for himself and had stated his case in positive terms. By contrast, Roosevelt focused on saddling his opponents with a "bad" label. He used what Garry Wills calls the "denigrative method," the hallmark of those who lack a positive program of their own. The evolution from McKinley's bold statement of unity to Wilson's careful adoption of a new positive label to Roosevelt's resort to denigrative vocabulary says a great deal both about the declining popularity of war in America and about the significance of Roosevelt's eventual victory.[19]

As in domestic policy, Roosevelt was successful not only in defining the foreign policy situation but in endowing a partisan and temporary definition with apparent universality and timelessness. The foreign policy label he chose for his opponents passed into social science literature as a supposedly value-free term of classification, and it was forgotten that his opponents did not generally apply it to themselves.

The history of the isolationist label is instructive in that there were some public figures during the mid-1930s who occasionally identified with it in a carefully qualified way. For example, Senator Borah noted in a 1934 speech that although Americans had "never been isolationist" in matters of trade, commerce, finance, or humanitarian assistance, "in all matters political, in all commitments of any nature or kind, which encroach in the slightest upon the free and unembarrassed action of our people, or which circumscribe their discretion and judgment, we have been free, we have been independent, we have been isolationist." Even in 1934 Borah's usage was rare, however, and by 1938 it had all but disappeared among leading critics. In line with Roosevelt's usage, the label had become a pejorative that connoted an attitude of unreality, willful ignorance, and an inability to face facts. It is therefore hardly surprising that from the late 1930s onward few if any of Roosevelt's leading opponents ever labeled themselves "isolationists."[20]

That Roosevelt's usage nonetheless became social science usage again indicates the extent of his triumph. Indeed, what makes the isolationist label so remarkable is that in using it, scholars have over-

19. Garry Wills, *Nixon Agonistes* (New York: Signet Books, 1970), pp. 76–82.
20. Borah is quoted in Manfred Jonas, *Isolationism in America* (Ithaca: Cornell University Press, 1966), p. 5.

whelmingly failed to recognize its pejorative implications. In so doing, they have likewise failed to recognize their custodial relationship to Roosevelt. As in the case of his domestic vocabulary, they have shown far less political sensitivity than did his contemporary critics. The effect has been the same in both cases: reification on Roosevelt's terms, reinforcement of his political victory, and loss of the independent perspective necessary for reassessment.[21]

Again, the main element in that loss of perspective is the obscuring of the fact that a struggle over language took place. In foreign as in domestic policy, Roosevelt's use of terms met with fierce resistance. If the pejorative nature of the isolationist label were not reason enough to resist it, opponents also reacted because it failed to capture and indeed distorted their own frame of reference.

A case in point is that of historian Charles Beard, who in a series of books published between 1934 and 1940 developed an analysis that made him one of the leading foreign policy critics of the era. At first, Beard's attitude toward the isolationist label was neutral. In *The Idea of National Interest* (January 1934), he expressed support for what he saw as Roosevelt's "conception of [a] national economy which does not turn primarily on foreign trade." Roosevelt's approach, he wrote, fixed the "center of gravity for American policy" within the United States itself: "Such a course may be called the 'national attitude,' or it may be termed 'isolation' or 'nationalism,' according as those terms are interpreted by various observers; but no matter what name may be applied, the policy itself is clear."

Even when Beard began questioning Roosevelt's commitment and saw him moving back toward a traditional Open Door approach, however, he did not himself adopt the isolationist label. In *The Open Door at Home* (November 1934), Beard continued to argue for an internal economic "center of gravity" as a basis for what he now called "an American commonwealth." He specifically denied that this repre-

21. After the war, historian Harry Elmer Barnes made a brief effort to bring to public attention the custodial implications of the isolationist label. See his *Perpetual War for Perpetual Peace* (Caldwell, Idaho: Caxton Printers, 1953). p. 34. His effort was unsuccessful. See, for example, the recent sympathetic study by Justus D. Doenecke, *Not to the Swift: The Old Isolationists in the Cold War Era* (Lewisburg: Bucknell University Press, 1979), as well as the more critical study by Wayne S. Cole, *Roosevelt and the Isolationists, 1932–1945* (Lincoln: University of Nebraska Press, 1983). Both authors recognize the pejorative implications of the terms "isolationist" and "isolationism," but continue to use them as analytical categories.

sented "traditional isolation," and argued that the "leading sponsors of isolation" in American history had been Theodore Roosevelt, John Hay, Calvin Coolidge, "and men of this type," whose policy amounted to "a free hand for capitalism at home and abroad, with government support for it." Like La Follette, Beard defined isolation in ideological terms, and explicitly feared isolating America ideologically from the subject peoples of the world.[22]

By 1939, Beard was calling for a "continental policy" of self-defense and maximal self-sufficiency, and attacking the "Wilsonian creed of world interventionism and adventurism." To him, this was not isolation, and the point was not "to withdraw from the world" but "to deal with the world as it is and not as romantic propagandists picture it." In *A Foreign Policy for America*, published in 1940, Beard noted that "the founders of the Republic did not coin the word 'isolation' in referring to foreign policy.

Indeed that term would have been, in their view, inappropriate to their theory and practice, had it been in general usage for any purpose at the time. . . . The leaders who created [the American system] were not isolationists. They were noninterventionists in respect of European wars which were not projected into the western hemisphere. They were also noninterventionists in respect of the purely domestic conflicts arising in other countries everywhere. . . . It was, therefore, unfortunate and unhistorical when, long afterward, the policy so established and so pursued was ineptly and inexactly branded by a false name—"isolationism."[23]

As Beard explicitly repudiated the isolationist label and its implied frame of reference, so did such critics as Hoover, Taft, and Flynn. Long afterward, Hoover continued to defend his belief that "the long-view contribution to preserving peace would be for America to stand on moral forces alone in support of law between nations." This, he

22. Charles Beard, *The Idea of National Interest* (New York: Macmillan, 1934), pp. 543–545; Charles Beard, *The Open Door at Home* (New York: Macmillan, 1934), pp. 268, 300–301, 131.

23. Charles Beard, *Giddy Minds and Foreign Quarrels* (New York: Macmillan, 1939), pp. 75, 23, 86; Charles Beard, *A Foreign Policy for America* (New York: Knopf, 1940), pp. 32–33. After the war, Beard made one effort to neutralize the isolationist label by offering supposedly value-free, contrasting definitions of "isolationism" and "internationalism." See his *American Foreign Policy in the Making, 1932–1940* (New Haven: Yale University Press, 1946). pp. 1–2 n. 1, p. 17 n. 2. This attempt also failed.

wrote, "was not isolationism" but "a belief that somewhere, some-how, there must be an abiding place for law and a sanctuary for civilization." Taft's repudiation was equally explicit. "While I cer-tainly do not consider myself an isolationist," he wrote in April 1940, "I feel it would be a great mistake for us to participate in the European war." Taft occasionally made the mistake of allowing others to label him, as in September 1941 when he responded to what his biographer accurately describes as "the epithet 'isolationist' that critics were hurl-ing at him." "If isolationism means isolation from European wars," Taft remarked, "I am an isolationist."24

As their own vocabulary suggests, some critics were not fully sen-sitive to the language issue. In setting up the category of "noninter-ventionists," Beard was falling into the trap of counter-reification. In simply denying the charge of "isolationism," or even in redefining the term, Hoover and Taft were inadvertently validating it as a political category.

In much of the literature, the standard investigative categories are "isolationist" and "internationalist." As the former was a pejorative used against Roosevelt's critics, so was the latter the self-designation of his supporters. To analyze the conflict as one between isolationists and internationalists is thus to become a custodian of the pro-Roose-velt perspective. The implications of that custodianship become clear-er when one considers how history books would read were they gener-ally written in the vocabulary of the critics. In his 1940 volume, Beard warned of a resurgence of American "imperialism." Throughout 1941, both Taft and Flynn repeatedly used that term to describe Roosevelt's foreign policy. All three critics described themselves as "noninterven-tionists." The impact of a generally accepted scholarly vocabulary pitting noninterventionists against imperialists, as supposedly value-free categories, hardly requires elaboration.

The full implications of the labeling process cannot be understood, however, unless one also recognizes the linkages so often made be-tween domestic and foreign policy labels. By late 1940, or so the argument often goes, the "isolationist movement" was dominated by "conservatives," the "internationalist movement" by "liberals."

24. Hoover, *Memoirs: The Cabinet and the Presidency*, pp. 377–378; James T. Patterson, *Mr. Republican: A Biography of Robert A. Taft* (Boston: Houghton Mifflin, 1972), pp. 216, 247.

Scholars such as Manfred Jonas have shown that a number of self-styled liberals, progressives, and socialists remained opposed to military involvement right up to Pearl Harbor. Although Jonas disputes traditional linkages, however, he does not eschew the idea of linkage itself and cites in particular Hoover and Taft as "unquestionably the key figures among the conservative isolationists."[25]

Here the problems of custodianship and reification are compounded. To label as "conservative isolationist" a person who described himself as a "liberal anti-imperialist" or "liberal noninterventionist" is not merely to adopt a custodial relationship to the views of his detractors, but to perform a double reification—to use one reification to build an intellectual fence around the other. To adopt the categories "conservative isolationist," "progressive isolationist," "liberal isolationist," and so on, is to remove oneself that much further from questioning whether there is such a thing as "an isolationist" at all. This in turn reinforces the custodial relationship. Only by moving from reification to critical analysis of language can the cycle be broken.

The moment one embarks on such an analysis, two things become apparent. First, in foreign as in domestic policy, the struggle over language involved a critical challenge to Roosevelt's invocation of values and summarizing of information. Second, the evolution of that struggle took place over a period of years, and involved several stages.

In the early New Deal era, foreign policy debates centered not on the isolationist label at all, but on the term "neutrality." Despite the growing revulsion against the "war profiteering" of 1914–1918 and the widespread belief that such activities had helped spur American entry into war, few people wished to isolate the country economically. Most preferred to maintain foreign trade without becoming militarily committed to either side in case of war. The term "neutrality" reflected this preoccupation, as did the popular phrase "taking the profits out of war." The so-called Neutrality Acts of 1935–1937 were attempts to meet this concern by permitting nonmilitary trade while embargoing arms sales to belligerents. In short, the terms "isolation" and "neutrality" were not used interchangeably.[26]

At first Roosevelt, too, carefully distinguished between them. "We

25. Jonas, *Isolationism in America*, p. 88.
26. See, for example, Bernard Baruch, *Taking the Profits out of War* (New York, 1935).

are not isolationists," he announced at Chautauqua in 1936, "except in so far as we seek to isolate ourselves completely from war." He called for a "more liberal international trade," warned that without it "war is a natural sequence," and praised Congress for giving him "new weapons with which to maintain our neutrality." Even in taking this position, however, Roosevelt took pains to distinguish his version of neutrality from that of Congress. In signing the 1935 act, he warned that its inflexible provisions might "have exactly the opposite effect from that which was intended." In the Chautauqua address he noted that despite the new laws the effective maintenance of American neutrality depended "on the wisdom and determination of whoever at the moment occupy the offices of President and Secretary of State." As in domestic policy, discretionary administrative authority was the key.

By the fall of 1937, with the advance of Nazi power in Europe and Japanese power in Asia, Roosevelt's use of terms was already shifting. In his "quarantine address" on October 5, he called for a "concerted effort" to restrain those "creating a state of international anarchy and instability from which there is no escape through mere isolation or neutrality." The move toward an interchangeable, pejorative usage of both terms was not accidental, but reflected Roosevelt's political sympathies as well as the changing state of the world. This change also indicated that the word "neutrality," taken alone, was harder to reify on his terms. From the outset, people had defined the word differently and had differed on which policies best embodied it.

By January 1939, Roosevelt was arguing that neutrality could not be legislated and that "when we deliberately try to legislate neutrality, our neutrality laws may operate unevenly and unfairly—may actually give aid to an aggressor and deny it to the victim." Although he still occasionally used the word itself in a positive way even after the onset of war, he no longer linked it to legislation. By 1941 he was using quotation marks to refer disparagingly to "the 'neutrality' laws" and "the 'neutrality' legislation." By then he was also using the isolationist label as his chief pejorative.[27]

Roosevelt's changing usage well illustrates his evolving strategy with respect to foreign policy. When he spoke disparagingly of "mere

27. *Public Papers of Roosevelt, 1936*, pp. 288, 290; Robert A. Divine, *The Reluctant Belligerent* (New York: John Wiley, 1965), p. 22; *The Public Papers and Addresses of Franklin D. Roosevelt, 1937* (New York: Macmillan, 1941), p. 408; *Public Papers of Roosevelt, 1939*, pp. 3–4, xxxi, xxxvii–xxxviii, 387, and esp. 522–524.

isolation or neutrality," his language indicated a major conceptual shift, for he was no longer defining American foreign policy in terms of staying out of war, but of preventing war. The new assumption was that the United States might not be able to keep out of war no matter how the legislation was written, and therefore government had the responsibility, hence the prerogative, to try to prevent war. Not only was this a shift in policy conceptualization, but one which again defined a problem in terms of an absence of government. The problem was keeping the peace; the apparent answer was more government power.

Here one confronts not only the issue of more government versus less, but Roosevelt's tendency to define more government as more executive power. Neutrality laws were additional legislation, yet from his point of view they diminished government power because they curtailed *his* freedom of action. His pejorative references to that legislation were his way of asserting this view. Herein lies the emerging significance of the isolationist label. Although the word "neutrality" invoked this value of keeping out of war, it did not invoke that of actively trying to prevent war. The latter required a different vocabulary, one which asserted Roosevelt's prerogative and denigrated those who challenged it.

Because of the advent of World War II and America's subsequent participation, it is easy in retrospect to view Roosevelt's triumph as inevitable. In reality, international events and the congressional definition of the situation both played into his hands, particularly because congressional leaders agreed with Roosevelt in defining the maintenance of neutrality as a governmental rather than an individual responsibility. This common definition rested on two assumptions: first, that individuals could commit an entire nation, and second, that as things stood the government had insufficient power to prevent such a commitment from occurring.

The congressional frame of reference reflected a popular summarizing of historical information. By 1935, there was a widespread awareness that Wilson had faced powerful economic pressures in 1914–1917, had attempted at first to meet those pressures through a "moral embargo" on loans and contraband goods, and eventually had reversed himself and committed his administration to protecting American trade to the point of military action. However, in 1935 the Congress did not conclude that the government should be given less power either to restrict private enterprise or to defend it militarily, but more. The implication was that Wilson had lacked sufficient authority to deal with private interests, and that those interests, operating unchecked, had inevitably forced the nation into war.

There was one way in which the Neutrality Act of 1935 spotlighted both executive discretion and individual responsibility. The act allowed the president, at his discretion, to warn American citizens that they traveled on belligerent ships at their own risk and without government protection. In 1936 Senator Homer Bone proposed an amendment to the effect that American goods shipped to belligerents likewise traveled at the risk of the shipper, but neither event established a trend. Bone's "ship-at-your-own-risk" amendment was supported by only eighteen senators, and the "travel-at-your-own-risk" provision was reversed in 1937 when the law was amended to prohibit travel by American citizens on belligerent ships. As the language of embargo and prohibition suggests, the main thrust of the Neutrality Acts was to mandate increased governmental control.[28]

This mandating of governmental control ultimately played into Roosevelt's hands because by interpreting history to justify increased governmental power, congressional leaders reduced their argument with Roosevelt to one of means rather than ends. That his definition of the situation was as arbitrary as theirs was beside the point. The consensus on the fundamental issue meant that when their option was discredited, his was the only apparent alternative.

In this connection the Spanish Civil War emerges as a turning point. Ironically, it was Roosevelt himself who precipitated the crisis. Not daring for domestic reasons to veto the 1935 act, he took the lead, largely for the same reasons, in extending its coverage to the Spanish situation. In January 1937, at Roosevelt's urging, Congress enacted a joint resolution applying the arms embargo to Spain; it passed with but a single dissenting vote.[29]

At few times in twentieth-century American history has political language operated in a more subtle fashion. The debate over Spain reveals a contradiction in congressional usage of the word "neu-

28. Thomas A. Bailey, *A Diplomatic History of the American People*, 7th ed. (New York: Appleton-Century-Crofts, 1964), pp. 701–702; Jonas, *Isolationism in America*, p. 181.

29. Robert A. Divine, *The Illusion of Neutrality* (Chicago: University of Chicago Press, 1962), pp. 168–172.

trality." As embodied in the act, the word implied balance and noninvolvement, for the purpose of the embargo was to preserve both. Superficially, the two were in harmony, but in fact, governmental action to preserve balance necessarily implied involvement.

This contradiction between balance and noninvolvement explains what followed. Unlike the Italo-Ethiopian War of 1935, in which the Neutrality Act had first been applied, the Spanish Civil War generated intense political passions within the United States. In the former case, the theme of noninvolvement had predominated in public discussion of the issue, but in the latter, the element of balance became predominant. Despite virtually unanimous congressional support for the joint resolution, sympathies within Congress and among the public at large were sharply divided between the Spanish government and rebel forces under Francisco Franco. Attitudes toward the embargo tended to reflect strategy rather than indifference.

Here the subtle impact of language becomes apparent. The putative purpose of the embargo was to preserve a balance, and whatever their actual sympathies or strategic calculations, members of Congress were forced to argue in such terms. This enforced rhetorical emphasis on balance gave Roosevelt his opening.

Having initiated extension of the arms embargo to Spain, he, too, was forced to defend it in terms of balance. That very emphasis, however, shifted the focus of debate away from noninvolvement, and without ever acknowledging the shift directly, Roosevelt exploited it very effectively. When Japan invaded China in July 1937, he simply refused to invoke the Neutrality Act, arguing that an embargo would tip the balance in favor of Japan. When asked how this squared with the legislation, he blandly replied that he was "maintaining, in fact, a neutral position . . . . despite the neutrality law." That, he added, was the trouble with legislation that attempted to "tie the hands of an administration for future events and circumstances that no human being can possibly guess." Roosevelt's choice of words was brilliant. Without ever abandoning either the rhetoric of neutrality or the assumption of governmental control, he neatly undercut both the congressional perspective and the original emphasis on noninvolvement.[30]

Apart from Roosevelt's having initiated the Spanish embargo, there

30. *Public Papers of Roosevelt, 1938*, p. 287.

was a further irony. Throughout the war private citizens who wished to sell arms to the Spanish government argued that they should be allowed to do so on their own responsibility and at their own risk. By January 1939, Roosevelt himself had concluded that the embargo had been a "grave mistake" because it had helped weaken the Spanish government. At no time during or after the war, however, did he question the assumption of governmental control or its attendant denial of individual responsibility and risk. Indeed, as the international situation continued to deteriorate, he became increasingly insistent on expanding his own discretionary authority in foreign affairs.[31]

Here the power of denigrative vocabulary becomes apparent. To rely on denigrative labels is to define one's position negatively (in terms of what one is against), concede the intellectual initiative to one's opponents, and admit one has no positive program. Roosevelt's vocabulary in the "quarantine" speech was not entirely negative; he spoke in general terms about international "solidarity and interdependence," and thereby suggested a positive image of a world system. When pressed by reporters for details of a positive program, however, he immediately backed away. "It is an attitude," he remarked, "and it does not outline a program; but it says we are looking for a program." It was a refreshingly candid admission. Even so, it indicated that Roosevelt knew more clearly what he opposed than what he favored. He was against his being indefinitely restricted by legislative mandate, that was the point of the denigrative vocabulary.[32]

To accomplish a de facto release from such restriction was itself no mean feat. Throughout late 1937 and early 1938 Roosevelt remained under tremendous pressure to invoke the embargo in the Sino-Japanese conflict. That he ultimately succeeded in resisting the pressure indicates both his own tenacity and the degree to which events in Spain had discredited the congressional perspective. Even so, his achievement was a negative one, couched in negative terms. Through an effective use of denigrative language, he had successfully refused to take an action mandated by Congress.

31. Harold L. Ickes, *The Secret Diary of Harold L. Ickes: The Inside Struggle, 1936–1939* (New York: Simon and Schuster, 1954), pp. 569–570; *Public Papers of Roosevelt, 1939*, pp. 428–429 (especially the phrase "they have tied my hands"). At the same time, Roosevelt was careful to argue that repeal of the Neutrality Act would not give the executive branch increased "power of action" (ibid., p. 386).

32. *Public Papers of Roosevelt, 1937*, pp. 409, 423.

His simultaneous move toward rearmament is best understood in this same context of negativity. Because rearmament required a direct initiative on his part, it can be interpreted as a positive action. Yet it, too, was merely a general response that bespoke no specific intent on Roosevelt's part other than to widen his options. This, however, was precisely the point. Rearmament could widen the government's options only if it carried the implicit threat of war, and by having no positive foreign policy program yet demonstrating a willingness to go to war, Roosevelt was making himself vulnerable to powerful critical attack. For this reason, he had to preempt that attack by discrediting opponents in the broadest possible terms; thus at the same time he began referring disparagingly to "isolation" and "the 'neutrality' law," he also began talking more and more of the danger of "fascism."

Roosevelt's usage here illustrates one of the most important phenomena of modern American politics; namely, the successful use of a negative label as a self-designation. McKinley's opponents had attempted such usage in 1898, explicitly styling themselves "anti-imperialists." By contrast, Roosevelt did not explicitly label himself "antifascist," but simply used the term "fascist" as a pejorative, so that his adoption of the "antifascist" label was implicit rather than explicit. The indirection was a deliberate way of defining his position on specific issues in negative terms without defining *himself* negatively in any direct or explicit way.

Roosevelt used the word "fascist" in a broad issue-oriented fashion. During a 1938 press conference, he remarked on the tendency, "every time we have trouble in private industry, to concentrate it all the more" in New York State. "Now that is," he observed, "ultimately, fascism." The next day he told the Daughters of the American Revolution of the need to teach "the boys and girls of this country today . . . the reasons that impelled our Revolutionary ancestors to throw off a fascist yoke."[33]

To label George III a "fascist" was rather superficial, yet it had potentially profound consequences. If Roosevelt could establish his own "antifascist" credentials and claim the label as his own, he would have another extremely effective denigrative weapon at his command. Having a recognizable foreign policy label would also make it easier to

33. *Public Papers of Roosevelt, 1938*, pp. 255, 259.

meet the challenge from critics such as Hoover who wanted to debate foreign policy in the language of liberalism.

The connotations of the antifascist label were especially useful in this regard. Although Roosevelt used it with reference to both domestic and international issues, it was primarily a foreign policy label in that it evoked primarily European images. Also, because the word "fascist" implied extreme coercive authority, his denigrative usage implied opposition to such behavior, and neatly complemented his domestic liberal label.

Roosevelt's being perceived as both "liberal" and "antifascist" enabled him to do indirectly what he could not do directly; namely, meet Hoover's challenge on the ideological unity of domestic and foreign policy. And as the antifascist label evoked primarily foreign dangers, it did not invite critical analysis of Roosevelt's own domestic use of coercive authority. On the contrary, the label externalized the enemy and denigrated those who refused to focus their attention on that enemy. Not only did the antifascist label mesh with Roosevelt's pejorative use of the isolationist label, but his self-designation as a "liberal antifascist" set the stage for further denigrative linkages to be built around the isolationist label.

Again, Roosevelt's language did not go unchallenged. What one sees from 1938 on, apart from the controversy over the isolationist label, is a developing struggle between Roosevelt and his critics over both the liberal and antifascist labels. Like Roosevelt, critics such as Hoover, Flynn, and Taft all described themselves as both "liberals" and opponents of "fascism." From their point of view, the most dangerous aspect of Roosevelt's antifascist rhetoric was its obscuring the underlying direction and long-run consequences of his own domestic policy.

To examine the critics' vocabularies from 1938 on is to confront once more insightful policy analysis undercut by insufficient linguistic analysis. Flynn and Hoover were particularly adept at calling attention to Roosevelt's *choice* of labels, yet they failed to show *how* his vocabulary worked to legitimize his policies while confusing and dividing his opposition.

For Flynn, rearmament joined the issues of depression economics, foreign policy, and executive power. In a letter to Senator Borah, written in January 1938, Flynn pooh-poohed the idea of the United

States "uniting with the great democracies of the world to save democracy and to check fascism." Roosevelt's real purpose, he noted,
was to use rearmament "as a means of creating employment." The
danger in such an approach was twofold. First, Roosevelt would have
to "keep on using war scares in order to keep public sentiment behind
these expenditures." Second, "building any part of a recovery program on armament industries" would become irreversible. "We will
not be able to stop it; it will get all mixed up with our thinking; it will
thrust forward into the solution of our domestic problems foreign
quarrels with which we should have nothing to do."

By November, Flynn was publicly castigating Roosevelt for promoting "recovery through war scares." Rearmament, he noted sourly, had
the support of both the American Communist party and the "extreme
right-wing internationalists of our Eastern border who would press in
the same direction but for a different reason." The rearmament program, however, was not being controlled by either the Communists or
anti-New Deal industrialists, but "by a Democratic administration
supposedly in possession of its liberal wing."[34]

In calling attention to Roosevelt's combined antifascist and liberal
rhetoric, Flynn was spotlighting the breakdown of Roosevelt's most
important linguistic harmonizations. With the failure of New Deal
social programs, the harmonizations between coercion and freedom
and confiscation and generosity were weakening. New formulas were
needed. As rearmament replaced the New Deal, "antifascism" began
to emerge as both the new freedom and the new generosity.

The antifascist rhetoric also camouflaged Roosevelt's surrender to
large corporations. Rearmament was the ultimate abdication to "big
business," which was why "extreme right-wing" elements applauded
it. That all groups "from the tip of the right wing to the tip of the left"
were now "clamoring for war preparations" put the country in danger
of accepting military spending as the only remaining route to generosity. Moreover, if Roosevelt's rhetoric were successful, public hostility would be directed not at those promoting this solution but at those
resisting it.

Not only was Flynn's analysis prescient, but on occasion, even an
administration supporter would corroborate it. "The reason for all this

    34. Flynn to Borah, January 7, 1938, Flynn MS.; Flynn, "Recovery through War
Scares," *New Republic*, November 2, 1938, pp. 360–361.

battleship and war frenzy is coming out," observed Congressman Maury Maverick of Texas. "We Democrats have to admit we are floundering. The Democratic administration is getting down to the condition that Mr. Hoover found himself [in]. We have pulled all the rabbits out of the hat and there are no more rabbits."[35]

Yet, Flynn's own vocabulary still limited his understanding. His conceding the internationalist label to his opponents was an error he later rectified. What continued to handicap him was his reification of the linear spectrum and its cognates, for this more than anything else kept critics like Flynn from seeing or explaining *how* Roosevelt's rhetoric worked. So long as people thought in terms of "communists" on the "left," "fascists" on the "right," and "liberals" in the "center" Roosevelt's use of labels would effectively assure him the "anti-extremist," sensible position and the implications of his use of power remain camouflaged.

Equally important was the critics' continuing to compete on Roosevelt's terms by reifying the liberal label and challenging him for it because as long as they did so they would reinforce his advantage in the situation. What was needed was a frame of reference that would transcend Roosevelt's and at the same time allow the critics to expose the implications of his approach.

Hoover came the closest to transcending conventional vocabulary. By January 1938, he was having serious doubts about the wisdom of the Neutrality Act. "If enforced," he remarked, "it will sometimes place us in practical economic alliance with the aggressor." The solution, however, was manifestly not in the direction of either greater executive power or military buildup, for neither option would enhance individual liberty, ensure a more generous distribution of wealth at home, or contribute to world peace. The most constructive step the government could take in both domestic and foreign policy, he told the Council on Foreign Relations in March, would be to set an example of adherence to "true liberalism."

Despite his continuing reification of the liberal label, it was here that Hoover at least implicitly departed from the traditional linear spectrum. "True liberalism," he declared, "is not a mere middle ground between fascism and socialism. Both fascism and socialism hold to the other concept—that the individual is but the pawn of an

35. Maverick is quoted in Williams, *Tragedy*, p. 162.

all-wise, omnipotent State. Liberalism has no compromise with either of these two forms of the same concept." The linear image of "right" and "left" as ideologically poles apart was a false one and so, too, was Roosevelt's "centrist" image. The linear spectrum, in short, was a conceptual trap.[36]

Hoover's comment contained the seeds of a major conceptual breakthrough, but he did not follow it up, and his continued reification of the cognate labels undercut not only his insight into the linear spectrum, but the impact of his argument on the unity of domestic and foreign policy. All Roosevelt had to do was hold fast to the antifascist label while continuing to define his opponents in terms of "isolationism," and Hoover's point would be neatly obscured. This in fact is what happened. From 1939 on, critics fought a losing battle to define foreign policy in terms of liberalism, while Roosevelt swept them aside with his antifascist, anti-isolationist rhetoric.

This is not to say Roosevelt immediately got everything he wanted from Congress. Indeed not until after the Nazis had invaded Poland in September 1939 was he able to muster sufficient votes to repeal the arms embargo. Once the war began in Europe, however, it became increasingly difficult for critics to focus public attention on the domestic implications of his foreign policy approach. By January 1940, Flynn was publicly accusing Roosevelt of moving steadily toward "militarism," while the "bland complaisance of almost all the progressive groups" had "allowed an old-fashioned Mark Hanna Republican program, including a runaway military and naval spree, to be put over on them under the label of liberalism." Rather than debate on Flynn's terms, Roosevelt simply ignored such challenges and substituted his own categories.

There were those, Roosevelt noted in his annual message that month, "who wishfully insist, in innocence or ignorance, or both, that the United States of America as a self-contained unit can live happily and prosperously, its future secure, inside a high wall of isolation, while outside the rest of civilization and the commerce and culture of mankind are shattered." A few minutes later he added, "I hope that we shall have fewer American ostriches in our midst. It is not good for the ultimate health of ostriches to bury their heads in the sand." The

36. Divine, *Illusion of Neutrality*, p. 221; address to Council on Foreign Relations, in *Congressional Record*, 75th Cong., 3rd sess., *Appendix*, p. 7168.

term "ostrich isolationist" quickly became a part of popular vocabulary.[37]

By the summer of 1940, Roosevelt's anti-isolationist rhetoric was taking its toll within the opposition itself. At the Republican convention in late June, party leaders carefully bypassed Taft and nominated corporation executive Wendell Willkie for president. Willkie, in turn, carefully refrained from opposing the peacetime conscription bill introduced that summer. Meanwhile, Taft joined Bone and twenty-six other senators in an unsuccessful effort to prevent the confirmation of Republican Henry L. Stimson, a conscription supporter, as secretary of war.

The critics were equally unable to undercut Roosevelt's anti-isolationist rhetoric or prevent him from advertising "antifascism" as both the new freedom and the new generosity. During an inspection tour of the Norfolk Navy Yard in late July, Roosevelt carefully pointed out to reporters that much of the battleship construction work was being done by former WPA labor. Forty percent of WPA workers, he noted, had been absorbed as "permanent employees" in defense plants. In fact, the Norfolk installation alone had increased its roster from 7,600 to 12,000 men in one year. The Norfolk tour became the first of over a dozen such tours conducted between late July and election day.[38]

For Flynn, conscription and rearmament constituted a gross betrayal of both freedom and generosity. Conscription, he warned Willkie, would mean "crushing taxation" as well as other "inescapable" evils: "It means creating new kinds of heroes and ideals—love of military glory, of drilling, military pageantry in order to keep people pleased with the burden. It means a foreign policy with frequent alarms about our safety, playing a part to keep people frightened and willing to be taxed. Enemies will become essential to us. It means building a huge military industry and budget as a prop under our economic system." To label this as "antifascism" was simply a fraud. "Hitler," Flynn noted, "is a menace. But there are other menaces far more imminent." Willkie, however, refused to budge, and conscription passed by large majorities.

By mid-September, with Willkie effectively neutralized on foreign

37. See Flynn's column, *New Republic*, January 22, 1940, p. 115; and *Public Papers of Roosevelt, 1940*, pp. 2, 4.

38. On the Stimson nomination, see *Congressional Record*, 76th Cong., 3rd sess., pp. 9310–9311; and *Public Papers of Roosevelt, 1940*, pp. 307, 312–313.

policy issues and Roosevelt on his way to a third term, Flynn summed up his own response to Roosevelt's foreign policy approach. "I see the whole liberal movement," he wrote, "utterly in eclipse. . . . I see the standard of liberalism that I have followed all my life flying over a group of causes which, as a liberal along with all liberals, I have abhorred all my life."[39]

However poignant, Flynn's plea revealed the underlying weakness in his critical approach and that of his colleagues. In foreign as in domestic policy, counter-reification was a trap, and to fall into it was to play into Roosevelt's hands. The full consequences would soon become apparent.

War and the American language

> One of the things I cannot understand is that a liberal writer who is saying now the same things he said five years ago and ten years ago . . . should be accused of holding these views because of a personal feeling against the President. I held these views before Roosevelt was President and I have now lost my liberal credentials because I do not agree with the New York Times, the Herald-Tribune, Mr. Harry Stimson, Mr. Franklin Roosevelt and Wendell Willkie about the war.
>
> John T. Flynn, 1940

The risk had been there all along. So long as critics competed for the labels, rather than analyzing and exposing the labeling process itself, sooner or later someone was bound to lose the competition. For Flynn, losing his "liberal credentials" had specific consequences. As early as July 1939, Roosevelt himself had suggested that Flynn be barred from "presentable" outlets. In November 1940, readers of the *New Republic* learned that Flynn's regular column had indeed been discontinued.

Nor was Flynn the only critic so treated. By the end of the year, Oswald Garrison Villard had been dropped from the *Nation* (terminating an association of over forty-six years), while historian Harry Elmer

---

39. Telegram, Flynn to Willkie, August 14, 1940, Flynn MS.; Flynn to Jerome Frank, September 18, 1940, ibid. Also see "Other People's Money," *New Republic*, July 22, 1940, p. 117.

Barnes had been removed from the Scripps-Howard newspapers. Roosevelt's definition of the situation was becoming the only "presentable" one.[40]

As Flynn himself pointed out, war was the catalyst in these developments. Ever since 1933, he and others had challenged Roosevelt's language and policies, and by 1938, Roosevelt had been on the defensive in domestic policy. The war had not only restored his economic and political leverage, but had validated his intellectual categories. As if in stark reminder of Bourne's earlier warning, war had again emerged, economically, politically, and linguistically, as "the health of the State."

Again, because America was eventually drawn into the "shooting war," it is easy in retrospect to view Roosevelt's triumph as inevitable. Considering the nature of the enemy, it is also easy to view it as fortunate. From this latter perspective, not only was Roosevelt's antifascist rhetoric more legitimate than that of his critics; their protests notwithstanding, it was equally fortunate that he was able to pin the isolationist label on them. Otherwise Hitler might have conquered all of Europe and perhaps America as well. Moreover, subsequent misuses of American power cannot be laid at Roosevelt's door; nor do they invalidate his use of terms.

Such a perspective is open to two criticisms. First, it assumes Hitler could not have been stopped without American military participation. Apart from the fact that Soviet armies had turned the tide of war long before June 6, 1944, the assumed need for American troops has since become subject to serious question.[41] Second, by making the war itself the single focus of attention, the perspective ignores the critics' central argument.

Although Flynn rejected the isolationist label, his main concern was not with having that label thrust on him, but rather losing his "liberal credential." The point of debating foreign policy in the language of liberalism was not merely to stress the relationship to domestic policy but to confront the effects of "militarizing" the country. Those effects would be disastrous whether or not the United States ever went to

40. Ronald Radosh, *Prophets on the Right: Profiles of Conservative Critics of American Globalism* (New York: Simon and Schuster, 1975), pp. 215–216, 80–82; *New Republic*, November 18, 1940, p. 677; and *Nation*, June 29, 1940, pp. 773–774, 782.

41. See Bruce M. Russett, *No Clear and Present Danger: A Skeptical View of U.S. Entry into World War II* (New York: Harper and Row, 1972).

war. War itself, Flynn argued, was temporary, whereas "militariza-
tion" and "war scares" would be permanent, especially if they were
needed to rationalize a prosperity permanently built on the military
industry.

This was why the struggle over the liberal label was so vital. Because the New Deal had failed to end the depression, Roosevelt had
turned to "war preparations" as both the new freedom and the new
generosity. A permanently war-oriented economy, however, would
inevitably require permanent coercion (conscription) to justify it.
Moreover, one could not expect the "forces of organized money" to
foot the bill for the new generosity. The cost would inevitably be
passed on to the American people, who would find themselves subjected to permanent confiscatory taxation. It was essential that both
these discordancies be exposed.

Needless to add, Flynn and like-minded critics also specifically
opposed American entry into the war. Once the country was involved
in military hostilities, they feared, the public would be much easier to
manipulate. Moreover, given Roosevelt's anti-isolationist rhetoric, it
was much less likely that there would be an early postwar demobiliza-
tion such as had followed the last war. At the same time, as Flynn's
vocabulary suggests, the critics were thinking far beyond the immediate emergency. As early as September 1940, Flynn anticipated a later
generation of critics in referring sarcastically to "the terrible scourge
of peace." Given a permanent reliance on military spending, peace
would be an "economic calamity" whether it occurred before or after
American entry into war.[42]

In the immediate situation, however, Flynn's analysis was already
too late. As his lament for his "liberal credentials" indicates, the battle
was over long before Pearl Harbor. Once Roosevelt's self-styled liberal critics had been silenced, there could be no further effective opposition to his definition of the situation. The transformation of the liberal
label was complete. Consequences alone remained.

There was fine irony in the situation. By 1940 it was impossible to
make a positive case for war preparations using the liberal label directly. Thus critics like Flynn were denied the label by people who

42. Flynn, "Other People's Money," *New Republic*, September 16, 1940, pp. 384–
385. Also see his columns for June 10, 1940, p. 792; August 26, 1940, p. 276; September 9, 1940, p. 352; September 23, 1940, p. 416; and October 14, 1940, p. 525.

dared not debate military spending and conscription in the language of liberalism. Because their method had to be denigrative, they, like Roosevelt himself, insisted on debating these issues in terms of "anti-fascism" and "anti-isolationism." Not once in any of their public or private exchanges with Flynn did the editors who fired him ever use the word "liberal." Indeed, his very complaint about losing his "liberal credentials" was at once an extrapolation and a challenge.[43]

That the challenge was ignored suggests more than irony, however. For self-styled liberals, refusing to debate in the language of liberalism was a confession of bankruptcy. This in turn underlines two other aspects of the language of the time: the use of separate foreign policy labels on one hand and the emergence of linkages on the other.

Again it was Roosevelt himself who took the lead. To read his 1940 speeches is to confront a carefully crafted vocabulary. Rather than debate military spending and conscription in terms of liberalism, he defined them as "defense" or foreign policy issues and attacked critics as "isolationists," "appeaser fifth columnists," and "propagandists of fear." He also insisted that those opposing "total defense" were the same "reactionaries" who had opposed social progress at home. Americans should take warning, he noted, from the fate of European nations led to ruin by "reactionary men who . . . could not see the real danger that threatened" because they "were afraid of losing their own selfish privilege and power." There was, in short, a universal linkage between "isolation" and "reaction."[44]

The effectiveness of Roosevelt's language is evident in the fate of the America First Committee. Given that the committee was not formed until September 1940, by which time Flynn was already lamenting the loss of his "liberal credentials," its fight to keep the country out of war was anachronistic. Roosevelt's definition of the situation had already triumphed, and this success made it easier to saddle the committee with the intended pejoratives. In this respect, the fate of the committee both reflected and reinforced Roosevelt's linguistic victory.

America First supporters overwhelmingly rejected the isolationist label. In publicly announcing his support for the committee, Charles

43. Ibid., November 11, 1940, p. 660, and November 18, 1940, p. 677. Also see Radosh, *Prophets on the Right*, pp. 215–217.
44. *Public Papers of Roosevelt, 1940*, pp. 261, 302, 415, 495, 507, 534.

Beard explicitly noted that it contained "no 'ostrich isolationists.'" In addition, several leading committee supporters including Flynn, Villard, Pinchot, and Taft had long contested the liberal label with Roosevelt. Nonetheless, historians have tended to label the committee both "isolationist" and "conservative." Such labeling not only mirrors that of the committee's detractors, but perpetuates the intellectual evasiveness of the detractors themselves.[45]

In labeling America First "isolationist" and "conservative," its detractors evaded the very issue its members were most anxious to debate; namely, the impact of war on domestic American society. The conservative label deflected their challenge with respect to freedom and generosity whereas the isolationist label ascribed a lack of realism with respect to foreign policy. Reification by present-day scholars not only reinforces the success of this labeling but mirrors the failure of the committee's supporters to respond effectively. Even the committee's most sympathetic and insightful historian describes it as consisting mainly of "conservatives" and "liberals." Most committee members did espouse reified labels and in so doing repeated the basic error of prewar years by failing to confront the labeling process itself.[46]

Given this failure, it is not surprising that the process quickly evolved to the point where administration supporters defined the situation in terms of two contrasting linkages: "conservative isolationists" versus "liberal internationalists." As early as 1937, Roosevelt had talked in the "quarantine address" about the "maintenance of international morality." By 1941, the term "internationalist" had acquired the far broader connotations illustrated in publisher Henry Luce's *The American Century*, which appeared early in that year.

America, Luce argued, faced two choices. One was an already bankrupt "isolationism," which unfortunately had "infected an influential section" of Luce's own Republican party. The sounder alternative was "internationalism," which in practical terms meant "exert[ing] upon

---

45. Beard's statement is in the *New York Times*, September 9, 1940, p. 7. For representative labeling of America First by historians, see Wayne Cole, *America First* (Madison: University of Wisconsin Press, 1953), passim.; Selig Adler, *The Isolationist Impulse* (London: Abelard, Schuman, 1957), pp. 299–301; Divine, *Reluctant Belligerent*, p. 99; Dulles, *America's Rise to World Power*, p. 200; and, most recently, George Brown Tindall, *America: A Narrative History* (New York: Norton, 1984), p. 1120.

46. Michele Flynn Stenehjem, *An American First: John T. Flynn and the America First Committee* (New Rochelle: Arlington House, 1976), pp. 15–17.

the world the full impact of our influence, for such purposes as we see fit and by such means as we see fit." Luce called for a postwar "world-environment" shaped by American power and ideals, and particularly by the American commitment to "a system of free economic enterprise." His definition of internationalism, in short, went far beyond participation in the war and amounted to a blueprint for what Luce called an "American Century."

Because of Luce's influential position, his analysis would have been significant in any case, but it gains even greater significance in retrospect as a measure of the degree to which the war had rehabilitated Roosevelt's definition of the situation. That rehabilitation is well illustrated by the reaction of one of Roosevelt's severest prewar critics.

In 1936, Dorothy Thompson had suggested that the "logical end" of New Deal economic policy was "fascism." By February 1941, Thompson had become convinced that "this century will either be a Nazi century or an American century." Luce, she noted, had drawn "objectively the two pictures: isolationism and internationalism."

Accepting Luce's categories, Thompson also accepted Roosevelt's linkages. In America as elsewhere, she remarked, the "tory parties" had been "those most willing to sacrifice the national honor, power, prestige and eventually existence out of the fear of revolutionary developments at home." To "Americanize enough of the world so that we shall have a climate and environment favorable to our growth," she added, "is indeed a call to destiny. It means some reforms . . . but those reforms are in the cards and a clear international policy will make them easier, not harder." Not since Croly had anyone made the connection so boldly.

Both Luce's analysis and Thompson's response predated Pearl Harbor by more than half a year, so the linkages were in place well before America entered the war. Moreover, these linkages were related not merely to the immediate issue of the war itself, but to a remarkably long-term future. The "natural" unit of time had now become the century, just as the "natural" political unit had again become the world. Not surprisingly, Luce summoned up an earlier "American internationalist" vision: Roosevelt, he wrote, "must succeed where Wilson failed." Equally as predictable, neither Luce nor Thompson ever used the word "liberal."[47]

47. Henry Luce, *The American Century* (New York: Farrar and Rinehart, 1941), pp. 24, 23, 32, 35, 48, 49–51, 27.

One of Luce's critics almost did. To journalist John Chamberlain, the real lesson of the war had been misplaced in Luce's analysis. "Our responsibility," wrote Chamberlain, ". . . should be for our own behavior; we should teach by example, not by verbal subscription to ethical abstractions." Chamberlain not only feared seeing Luce's program "fall into the hands of the hypocrites who are skilled in using the great slogans to heil nefarious purposes"; the greater danger was that America would "turn to an imperialism that will fail in *liberality* and become something very close to the Nazi thing." Governmental generosity, the putative hallmark of the New Deal itself, would be as spurious internationally as it had been domestically.[48]

In general, administration critics no more accepted the Rooseveltian linkages than they accepted the isolationist label. To review American political vocabulary during the balance of 1941 is to observe an ongoing competition for both the liberal and antifascist labels. When philosopher John Dewey charged the America First Committee with being a "Nazi transmission belt," Flynn wrote back arguing that entry into war would lead to "fascism" at home. In early December, when historian Arthur Schlesinger, Jr. publicly linked "noninterventionism" with "conservatism," Taft angrily responded that it was the "most conservative members of the [Republican] party—the Wall Street bankers, the society group, nine-tenths of the plutocratic newspapers, and most of the party's financial contributors" who favored entry into the European war.

Meanwhile, historian and former Scripps-Howard columnist Harry Elmer Barnes warned in the December 6 issue of *Progressive* of the imminent possibility of war with Japan. "For this country to enter war over Far Eastern issues," Barnes wrote, "would be the supreme folly of all American experience in foreign affairs." A Far Eastern war, he noted, "viewed against the background of the disasters which would befall our country on the domestic front . . . must be branded as nothing short of sheer national idiocy."[49] The following morning, Japanese planes bombed Pearl Harbor.

Senator Arthur Vandenberg later wrote in an oft-quoted diary entry

---

48. Ibid., pp. 67–69, 71. (italics added)
49. Radosh, *Prophet on the Right*, pp. 219–220; *Nation*, December 6, 1941, pp. 561–564, and Dec. 13, 1941, pp. 611–612; and Warren I. Cohen, *The American Revisionists* (Chicago: University of Chicago Press, 1967), pp. 231–232.

that Pearl Harbor had "ended isolationism for any realist." But the label had always been a reification, and far from ending its use as a political weapon, Pearl Harbor made it remarkably easy to hurl the isolationist label at anyone who had ever opposed entry into war. Most self-styled noninterventionists remained unrepentant, however. A statement released by America First headquarters declared: "Our principles were right. Had they been followed, war could have been avoided."

The struggle to define the situation in terms of "good" and "bad" labels also continued unabated. To critics such as Villard, wartime developments were all too predictable. Condemned by former friends for associating with "extreme reactionaries," Villard kept up his own attack on Roosevelt's "liberal credentials." He noted the president's tendency to surround himself at strategic moments with military and corporate personnel and observed that "Mr. Roosevelt has never been more of a liberal than he felt he could afford to be at any given moment." By late 1943, Villard was angrily pointing to an emerging corporate-government partnership in the field of Middle Eastern oil development. In an article titled "Head On for Imperialism," he warned of the danger of "permanent conscription and a seven-ocean navy."[50]

Taft agreed that entry into war had heightened an "imperialist" drift in American policy. In his Grove City College address in May 1943, he warned against trying to run the world, however benevolently. The only result, he predicted, would be "a permanent army a good deal larger than 11,000,000 men" and suspension "for a long time [of] any renewal of freedom in the United States." Taft openly attacked Luce's *American Century*, terming it a call for an "American raj." There would be "constant protest in this country," he added, "against any act which smacked of imperialism."[51]

To Flynn, wartime policies more than justified his prewar fears. The purpose of his book *As We Go Marching* (1944) was to define "fascism" and "search for its elements in America." Flynn found those

50. Arthur H. Vandenberg, Jr., ed., *The Private Papers of Senator Vandenberg* (Boston: Houghton Mifflin, 1952), p. 1; Cole, *America First*, p. 195; Radosh, *Prophets on the Right*, pp. 82, 88–89; Oswald Garrison Villard, "Head on For Imperialism," *Christian Century*, November 10, 1943, pp. 1300–1302.

51. The Grove City College address is reprinted in *Congressional Record*, 78th Cong., 1st sess., vol. 89, pp. 5092–5094.

elements in what New Dealers called "planned economy," a "form of
society in which the government would insert itself into the structure
of business, not merely as a policeman, but as partner, collaborator,
and banker." He found them in the creation of a debt-ridden war
economy in which planning agencies functioned "with almost totalitarian power under a vast bureaucracy." He found them in the government's plans for continued postwar conscription and military
spending, the latter being "the one great glamour public-works project upon which a variety of elements in the community can be
brought into agreement."

To keep this system going, Flynn warned, the government would
have to encourage fear of other people's aggressive ambitions while
Americans "embark[ed] upon imperialistic enterprises" of their own.
"We must have enemies," Flynn prophesied. "They will become an
economic necessity for us." The "test of fascism," he wrote, "is not
one's rage against the Italian and German war lords:

The test is—how many of the essential principles of fascism do you accept and
to what extent are you prepared to apply those fascist ideas to American social
and economic life? When you can put your finger on the men or the groups
that urge for America the debt-supported state, the autarchical corporative
state, the state bent on the socialization of investment and the bureaucratic
government of industry and society, the establishment of the institution of
militarism . . . and the institution of imperialism; under which it proposes to
regulate and rule the world . . . then you will know you have located the
authentic fascist.[52]

Again, Flynn's insight was perscient in several respects. The problem of communication remained the same, however. If it had been
impossible to win the competition over labels in peacetime, it was
worse in wartime. As Bourne had noted, "In a time of faith skepticism
is the most intolerable of all insults." To a nation that defined itself as
committed to total war against "fascist imperialism" the suggestion
that the nation's own elected leadership was adopting "fascist imperialist" policies was most unwelcome. Thus Flynn's warnings about the
future of American society were rejected, and the labels he used in
expressing them were turned against him.

52. John T. Flynn, *As We Go Marching* (New York: Doubleday, 1944), pp. vi, 193,
207, 213–214, 224–226, 251–252.

In general, the reification trap sprang ever more tightly shut during the war years. Critics like Taft and Flynn stood no chance of defeating Roosevelt in a battle for the liberal and antifascist labels. At the 1944 Republican convention, Taft was again passed over in favor of Governor Thomas E. Dewey of New York. Returning home to campaign for reelection to the Senate, Taft found himself under attack as an "isolationist," the "Number One Tory conservative," and the "Number One opponent of the President." He was narrowly reelected, winning only 50.5 percent of the vote. Flynn, for his part, also remained under attack for having opposed the war. When he spoke at the University of Illinois in 1944, his appearance was protested on the grounds that he was "anti-Semitic" and "profascist" and that it "was not good for the war effort to have him there."[53]

The wartime battle over labels was more than a short-term event, however. From the perspective of a half century, the battle revealed a great deal about the evolution of American politics. In one sense, there was a striking parallel between the vocabularies of the McKinley era and the New Deal era: if McKinley could not be at once conservative and imperialist, neither could Roosevelt be both liberal and imperialist. In both cases the domestic label remained the label of primary potency. As the traditionalist connotation of McKinley's conservative label overwhelmed the pejorative charge of innovation, so the connotation of freedom attached to Roosevelt's liberal label overwhelmed the charge of coercion. In both cases the discordancy remained successfully harmonized.

There was, however, a difference in the two situations. Although both men enjoyed considerable labor support they did so under different banners—McKinley under that of conservatism, Roosevelt under liberalism, which in this case stood for generosity. The change in labels reflected a major evolution in American politics: half a century earlier generosity could be assumed to be part of the tradition; now it had to be asserted and argued.

The language of the argument masked an important development, however. It was military spending, not the New Deal, that ultimately rescued Roosevelt's "liberal credential," for the military spending was the basis of the generosity. Even so, it was the New Deal that remained associated with the liberal label. New Deal social programs

53. Patterson, *Mr. Republican*, pp. 274–278; Radosh, *Prophets on the Right*, p. 238.

were based on distribution, and generous distribution was impossible without the production of sufficient wealth to distribute. Military spending provided that production, and together they operated as a system. Yet Roosevelt never debated military spending in the language of liberalism. When he used liberal rhetoric, it was always with respect to the distribution aspect. His vocabulary thus worked to camouflage the fact that a dependence on military spending was now the foundation of the American economic system.

It was Hoover who finally provided the most poignant and revealing epitaph for the entire New Deal era. By 1945 Hoover had become thoroughly embittered. He had irrevocably lost his fight to preserve "true liberalism" and was being referred to not merely as a "conservative" but as a "reactionary." The designation of reactionary he still indignantly rejected, but now, at the age of seventy-one, he accepted for the first time the designation of conservative. "Being a conservative," he wrote, was "not a sin." It was not fascism or reaction: "It means today the conservation of representative government, of intellectual freedom and of economic freedom within the limits of what does not harm fellow men. It means the conservation of natural resources, of national wealth, education and employment. A conservative is not allergic to new ideas. He wants to try them slowly without destroying what is already good." Hoover suggested that the Republicans openly accept the conservative label, inasmuch as the Democrats were "holding the radical fort." Republicans, he noted, "should have the courage to adopt the word that means what a large part of the American people are—Conservative."

It was clear, however, that Hoover was accepting the label only reluctantly. He would still have preferred to have been called a liberal, but the New Dealers, who were now linked in his mind with "socialists and communists," had stolen his preferred designation. In an angry postscript he vented his feelings on the subject.

P.S. We do not use the word "liberal." That word has been polluted and raped of all its real meanings. The fundamentals of political liberalism were established by Morley, Gladstone, John Stuart Mill, in the nineteenth century in England. Liberalism was founded to further more liberty for men, not less freedom. Therefore, it was militant against the expansion of bureaucracy, against socialism and all of its ilk. The conservatives in America are akin to the nineteenth century liberals of England.

Lenin's instructions on propaganda included the deliberate distortion of accepted words and terms and Lenin has surely had his way with the word "liberalism." The Socialists and Communists daily announce that they are "liberals." They have nested in this word until it stinks. Let them have the word. It no longer makes sense.[54]

Once again, even in defeat, Hoover had tried to give concrete meaning to his position, but his definition of conservatism was yet another exercise in reification. What was poignant and revealing, however, was his belated abandonment of the liberal label. It was understandable that after twelve years of frustration he should have concluded that the Roosevelt administration be allowed to "have" the label. This, however, was what the struggle had been all about: the word no longer made sense to Hoover, but it still evoked a positive response from a majority of Americans.

To concede the liberal label to Roosevelt and his supporters was not only to aid them in justifying all sorts of government action in the name of liberalism, but to validate their long-standing claim that opponents of their policies were, after all, self-confessed opponents of liberalism. During the postwar period, as more and more critics joined Hoover in adopting the conservative designation, administration supporters would eagerly seize on the opportunity thus provided.

Beyond this, Hoover's insistence on linking New Dealers with "socialists and communists" was to be equally self-defeating. Superficially, the charge often appeared to put the administration on the defensive, but in reality, these postwar efforts of self-styled conservatives to equate the New Deal with socialism and communism would provide administration officials with an important political asset they would utilize again and again.

54. "The Republican Party and the Democratic Process," *Los Angeles Times* editorial sent to Norman Chandler, October 14, 1945, PS#2871, HHPL.

6

The Struggle for

the Anticommunist Label

Symbol words and thinking

Such words are symbol words, used to influence mental and emotional
attitudes. How can they be precisely defined? Moreover, can you
imagine the Republican Party being able to agree on what they mean,
e.g., isolationist or liberal? . . . Symbol words not only keep people
from thinking; they keep us from thinking too.

Garet Garrett, 1943

It was a curious dichotomy to propose: "people" versus "us." Yet
veteran journalist Garet Garrett knew what he was trying to say.
"Symbol words" created confusion in the minds of both hearer and
user. Now, more than ever, opposition leaders could ill afford such
confusion. America's future was at stake, and clarity was of the
essence.

Garrett's injunction to "stop using" symbol words and use descrip-
tive phrases instead missed the point politically, however. Administration rhetoric was full of symbol words, both positive and negative.
To ignore the intellectual categories of the powerless was one thing; to
ignore the loaded weapons of those in power was quite another. What
was needed was active de-reification, a public process of spotlighting
the symbol words of the powerful and openly exposing the contradictions therein. What was needed was a direct confrontation with the
politics of language.[1]

Such a confrontation never took place, however. As wartime gave
way to the exigencies of the postwar era, the administration's critics

1. Garrett to James P. Selvage, August 31, 1943, in Post-Presidential Individual
File–Garrett, Garet, HHPL.

became caught up in their own symbol words, especially in their own denigrative vocabulary. They became increasingly desperate in their efforts to pin "bad" labels on those in power. Despite fanfare, they won no major victories. On the contrary, they brought disastrous defeat on themselves. As Garrett had warned, their symbol words kept them from thinking, and they paid dearly for it. They failed in the most important political process of all, the process of self-reflection.

Of all the symbol words that crippled critical thinking in postwar years, the most important were "communist" and "anticommunist." Indeed, much of the history of postwar American politics is a history of struggle over the anticommunist label, the effects of which can be understood only through an historical analysis of language.

A review of the opposition's vocabulary in 1944 and 1945 shows a shift as abrupt as Wilson's shift from the progressive to the liberal label. Throughout the late 1930s and early 1940s, such critics as Hoover, Taft, and Flynn had challenged Roosevelt for the antifascist label. For Flynn, the culmination had come in his book *As We Go Marching,* in which he had attempted to expose "fascist" elements in the administration's policy. By December of that year, Flynn was demanding a "rescue [of] labor from the leadership and hands of Communist revolutionaries," and urging opposition leaders to tell returning servicemen "what the Communists and their New Deal allies have been doing in this country while they have been away fighting to preserve its freedom." Flynn's hope was that "we can fasten upon the Communists and New Deal organization the guilt for the conditions which the soldier will meet."[2]

At first glance, Flynn's language would suggest his political perspective had changed dramatically in a very short time. In fact, it had not changed at all. Like Hoover and Taft, Flynn had long considered himself both antifascist and anticommunist. He saw important similarities in the behavior, if not the rhetoric, of those he labeled fascists and communists, and recognized that the two groups were quite capable of working together to achieve their respective ends.

What had changed was not Flynn's perspective, but the political situation at home and abroad. The impending Axis defeat and the

2. Confidential memo by Flynn, undated (December 1944), Flynn MS. Also see notes on "Lunch at University Club," New York City, December 6, 1944, and "Memorandum from John T. Flynn," circulated to those present at that meeting, ibid.

westward advance of Soviet armies had already caused many people to begin thinking about a postwar world in which "communism" would be the chief international threat to American security. Meanwhile, the rapid growth of the American Communist party's influence in certain trade unions, and the conspicuous backing given Roosevelt in the 1944 campaign by the C.I.O. Political Action Committee, which many regarded as "communist dominated," raised the spectre of a New Deal–Communist party alliance. For critics such as Flynn, this meant a growing preoccupation with "communist" influence in postwar America.

It would be hard to find a more salient example of symbol words leading to self-defeating political behavior. Increasingly convinced of their charges of "communism" in government, the administration's critics became ever more strident in their efforts to make political capital of the issue. Except for a brief period of success brought on by American military reverses abroad, such efforts failed miserably.

However sincerely critics believed that Roosevelt and his successor, Harry Truman, were "soft on communism," it was extremely difficult to make the accusation credible. First, it was no easier in the late 1940s than in the mid-1930s to persuade Americans that anti-depression spending was "socialist" or "communist." Second, many of Truman's domestic and international policies were advertised under the anticommunist label. The opposition's rhetoric tended to validate Truman's perspective and thereby assisted him in co-opting Republican leaders into supporting some of his most important policies.

Like Roosevelt, Truman defined himself positively as a "liberal," yet anticommunist rhetoric was one of his chief political weapons. As Flynn had presciently observed, enemies would "become an economic necessity" for any administration that failed to find a substitute for military spending or wished to maintain a permanent, conscript military establishment. Because anticommunist rhetoric posited a permanent enemy, it was indispensable to Truman on both counts.

When Roosevelt had first moved toward massive military spending in the late 1930s, he had done so under the antifascist label. In part, it was the Axis defeat and the rise of Soviet power that expedited the shift from antifascist to anticommunist rhetoric. Yet there was another, more fundamental reason why the anticommunist label was more politically appropriate in the long run. It involved the historic connotations embedded in the label.

Like the word "fascist," the word "communist" suggested to most Americans extreme coercive authority, primarily because of the American image of the Soviet Union. There was a second, equally important connotation, however, that the word "fascist" did not evoke nearly so readily as did the word "communist": the connotation of government ownership of the means of production.

Without knowing a great deal about Karl Marx, most Americans nonetheless tended to define communism as the antithesis of the free market, private enterprise system. They also understood the putative purpose of government ownership to be a more generous distribution of the "communal" wealth. But conditions in the Soviet Union seemed to belie the promise, and when Americans put together the connotations of extreme coercion and government ownership of production, their image of communism was of a system of extreme privation and false generosity.

Communism, in short, was the exact opposite of the genuine generosity that Roosevelt had instituted under the liberal label. Moreover, where Roosevelt's "true liberalism" occurred within a free market, private enterprise framework, the "false liberalism" of communism relieved people of both the right and responsibility of private ownership and initiative. This image of communism made anticommunist rhetoric important to Truman not only because it distinguished the American system from that of the Soviets, but because it helped summarize and justify his policies in a particularly useful way.

The relationship between the anticommunist and liberal labels was likewise vital to Truman. During his presidency, governmental generosity continued to depend on military spending, and like Roosevelt, Truman carefully avoided debating military spending in the language of liberalism. Whereas Roosevelt had justified military spending under the label of antifascism, Truman did so under that of anticommunism. As antifascist rhetoric had eventually become indispensable in maintaining Roosevelt's "liberal credential," so anticommunist rhetoric fulfilled the same function for Truman. In short, as the liberal and antifascist labels had been complementary during the war, so were the liberal and anticommunist labels after it.

The anticommunist label was equally useful for what it conveyed and suppressed. If communism connoted a thoroughgoing interference with the free market mechanism, anticommunism connoted opposition to such interference. If communism connoted extreme confiscation and false generosity, anticommunism connoted true generosity without confiscation. If communism connoted the complete centralization of economic and political power, anticommunism connoted a commitment to a dispersion of power. However, an economy perpetually based on military production could not be sustained without massive interference with the market mechanism, permanent confiscatory taxation, and centralization of production in the hands of large corporations. The anticommunist label was the perfect label for camouflaging all three contradictions.

Insofar as it helped·harmonize the discordancies between coercion and freedom as well as confiscation and generosity, the anticommunist label, like the antifascist label, nicely complemented the liberal label. Moreover, in the postwar context there was one additional purpose that neither of the other labels could serve. Although opposition to centralized power was to some extent implicit in both the liberal and antifascist labels, it was far more explicit and timely in the anticommunist label. As a postwar pejorative, the latter label directly singled out the Soviet Union as a negative role model with respect to centralization of power.

Again the value of denigrative vocabulary is apparent. Despite his liberal label, Truman came to the presidency without a positive program of his own. What he had was what Roosevelt had bequeathed to him. In domestic policy, he had a system dependent on military production of wealth and government distribution of it. In international affairs, he had a network of shaky alliances backed by American military power. The fledgling United Nations Organization was not a program. As Senator Vandenberg candidly noted, its only practical utility was "to have a mechanism that [could] mobilize the world against" the Soviet Union if necessary. Nor did Truman ever develop a program for a truly nonmilitary prosperity.[3]

3. Vandenberg Diary, May 19, 1945, Arthur H. Vandenberg Papers, University of Michigan Library, Ann Arbor, Michigan (hereafter Vandenberg MS.).
Early in September 1945, Truman presented Congress with a series of legislative proposals which, in the words of historian William Leuchtenburg, "consisted largely of Roosevelt's unfinished agenda." See Leuchtenburg's *In the Shadow of FDR: From Harry Truman to Ronald Reagan* (Ithaca: Cornell University Press, 1983), p. 8, and *Public Papers of the Presidents of the United States: Harry S. Truman, 1945* (Washington: Government Printing Office, 1961), pp. 263–309. These proposals were designed to extend the government's role in the distribution of wealth as in Truman's later "Fair Deal" proposals.

This lack of a program necessitated language that would justify high levels of military expenditure. Like the antifascist label before it, the anitcommunist label directed attention toward an external threat and denigrated those who refused to focus on that threat. And because of the relative prominence of the American Communist party, the anticommunist label also identified a domestic enemy that could be treated as an extension of the foreign enemy. This identity not only reinforced concentration on the external threat but provided the complete alibi for domestic difficulties. All postwar domestic problems could ultimately be attributed to an external enemy and its internal agents. Anticommunist rhetoric thus allowed Truman to externalize responsibility for whatever went wrong under his administration even as it camouflaged his own reliance on the centralization of economic and political power.

In short, the anticommunist label was central to Truman's vocabulary, and only when this is understood can one appreciate how self-defeating it was for critics to build their own positions around anticommunist rhetoric. In so doing, they played into Truman's hands. As prewar critics had undercut themselves by competing with Roosevelt for the antifascist label, so postwar critics undercut themselves by competing with Truman for the anticommunist label. There was an important difference, however. During prewar years, critics had recognized the complementarity of the liberal and antifascist labels and had competed with Roosevelt for both of them. By the postwar era, as Hoover's 1945 statement indicates, critics were beginning to abandon the liberal label to Truman. This was a crucial development.

Of the three options open to critics—de-reification, competition over labels, and abandonment of the field—the third was even more self-defeating than the second. To abandon all claim to a positive self-designation and retreat entirely to denigrative vocabulary was not

---

However, Truman was no more successful than Roosevelt in realizing an adequate program for the production of wealth on a nonmilitary basis. "Reconversion" was never more than partial, and the "sixty million jobs" remained a dream. The "Full Employment Bill" of late 1945 was finally enacted simply as the Employment Act of 1946, omitting "the government commitment to full employment." See Alonzo Hamby, *Beyond the New Deal: Harry S. Truman and American Liberalism* (New York: Columbia University Press, 1973), p. 69. For John T. Flynn's comments on an "economic equivalent for armaments," see Flynn to Norman Thomas, April 2, 1947, Flynn MS.

merely to adopt a negative position on specific issues but to define
oneself negatively, to declare ideological bankruptcy. As Roosevelt
had once put it with regard to his own party, it was to sit around
"waiting for the other fellow to put his foot in it." That the denigrative
vocabulary focused on an external enemy only made the declaration of
bankruptcy that much more obvious because it left critics with nothing constructive to say about the domestic situation.

This retreat to negative self-definition did not occur all at once.
Taft, for example, continued to compete for the liberal label as late as
1948. Hoover, having abandoned the liberal label, immediately
adopted the conservative label as his self-designation. Other critics
later joined him. Despite Hoover's efforts to give the conservative
label positive content, however, the Rooseveltian definitions had already triumphed. For most Americans, the conservative label was no
longer a positive self-designation at all because it connoted no more
than opposition to the New Deal. And although Taft's definition of
liberalism embodied insightful criticisms of Truman's policies, it likewise dated from the prewar era. Thus while it indicated Taft's continuing awareness of the need for positive self-definition, it offered no new
alternative to Rooseveltian vocabulary.[4]

The history of early postwar American politics, then, is that of an
opposition in deep intellectual disarray. Failing either to confront the
politics of language or offer a competitive definition of the situation,
opposition leaders retreated to an entirely negative approach. That
their chief pejorative was the same one chosen by the administration
itself only indicates how little they understood Truman's strategy. In
such circumstances, the ease with which they were co-opted into
supporting so many of the administration's measures is understandable. So, too, is their increasing stridency, bitterness, and ultimate
self-destructiveness.

This is not to deny the acuity of many of their criticisms of Truman's
policies, nor to suggest that opposition leaders immediately accepted
whatever Truman proposed in the name of anticommunism. Taft,
Flynn, Vandenberg, and Villard were among many who opposed
Truman's early call for permanent universal military training, or UMT.
Throughout the late 1940s, Taft remained highly skeptical of "cold

4. See Taft's "What Is a Liberal" speech, February 13, 1948, Box 1271, Taft MS.
The speech is analyzed in detail later in this chapter.

war" thinking and even voted against ratification of NATO. Flynn continued to castigate Truman for failing to find an "economic equivalent for armaments" and by 1950 was attacking Truman's support of French "imperialism" in Indochina and demanding the United States "make an end of the cold war."[5]

Despite such views, however, the administration's critics were never entirely able to overcome their own susceptibility to anticommunist arguments. Although they feared the growth of the domestic military establishment, they also feared the growth of Soviet power. Moreover, once they had given away all other domestic political weapons, anticommunist rhetoric was all they had left, and as time went by they tended to cling ever more tenaciously to it.

This situation created a dilemma for individual critics, for it was difficult to reconcile an increasingly militant anticommunist rhetoric on domestic issues with a belief in limiting America's "anticommunist" commitments abroad. For Republican leaders such as Taft, the dilemma was particularly painful. Although he never missed an opportunity to criticize Truman on domestic issues for supposed "softness on communism," he was nonetheless extremely wary of provoking the Russians. Thus he agonized at length about the Truman Doctrine and the Marshall Plan and eventually supported the requisite appropriations only with great reluctance.[6]

Taft's dilemma was a microcosm of the opposition's larger problem. There was a certain logic in arguing that the chief threat of "communism" was domestic rather than international. As Hoover had argued during the prewar era, America's task was to set a proper example rather than attempt to run the world, and anything that threatened the integrity of that example was a primary danger. Yet because of the link both the administration and the opposition drew between the American Communist party and the Soviet Union, it was difficult not to treat both with equal militance. So long as one took the symbol words seriously, the dilemma was insoluble. It was more than an

5. James T. Patterson, *Mr. Republican: A Biography of Robert A. Taft* (Boston: Houghton Mifflin, 1972), pp. 392–393, 435–439; Flynn to Vandenberg, October 30, 1945, and Vandenberg to Flynn, October 31, 1945, both in Flynn MS.; Ronald Radosh, *Prophets on the Right: Profiles of Conservative Critics of American Globalism* (New York: Simon and Schuster, 1975), pp. 98, 167–171, 251–255. For Flynn's comment on an "economic equivalent for armaments," see Flynn to Norman Thomas, April 2, 1947, Flynn MS.

6. Radosh, *Prophets on the Right*, pp. 94–104, 154–167, 244–245.

individual dilemma, however. Ultimately, it split the Republican party wide open, not only paving the way for many of Truman's most spectacular foreign policy successes but fatally weakening opposition to his domestic policies.

The split that developed within the Republican party in the late 1940s centered on Taft and Vandenberg. Although not as spectacular as the three-way battle that had occurred in 1912, it was equally important in the long run because it allowed Truman to set the tone for American policy for over a generation.

Ironically, the Taft-Vandenberg split was rooted in their common acceptance of, and dependence on, anticommunist rhetoric. Had both men not retreated to this particular negative self-definition, the split might not have occurred or might not have had the same consequences. Their clash is often described as one between an unrepentant "isolationist" and a former "isolationist" turned "internationalist" (neither of which descriptions either man applied to himself), but is better understood in terms of their differing definitions of the "communist threat."

To Taft, the clash between "communism" and "liberalism" was that between coercion and freedom—a contradiction that could not be camouflaged and could be resolved only by the victory of one perspective over the other. The clash had always been chiefly ideological in nature, however. Like Hoover, Taft viewed history as primarily a contest of moral forces rather than of naked power. Hence for him the essential danger of "communism" was domestic and moral. Taft did not ignore concrete points of conflict between the United States and the Soviet Union, but neither did he wish to see those points artificially magnified in order to justify "illiberal" or coercive government at home. Thus although he could attack Truman for "appeasing" Russia, he preferred not to counter aggressive power with aggressive power but rather to take a moral stand and oppose any agreements that might make things worse.

Vandenberg agreed that "communism" was a moral danger. The Republican party, he wrote privately in early 1945, would have to "reeducate the American people" if it was to "recapture the soul of the nation." The "brutal, naked truth," he noted, "is that we confront the necessity for saving America from *Communism*." Vandenberg was nonetheless more prone than Taft to see Soviet power as the immediate, overriding threat to American security and was therefore more ready to grant Truman enlarged powers to fight "communism" abroad.[7]

Because of their shared anticommunist rhetoric, the split between the two men was more a matter of emphasis than anything else: Taft defined the threat as primarily internal, Vandenberg as external. Yet this difference had profound consequences, for it not only made Vandenberg more willing to countenance enlarged international commitments abroad but rendered him far more susceptible to arguments favoring "bipartisan cooperation" in foreign policy. "I think it would be sheer political suicide," he wrote in September 1946, ". . . for the Republicans, after two years' forbearance, to be the ones who should wreck the non-partisan character of our official attitudes toward America's foreign policy."

Taft disagreed. He feared that a blanket commitment to "bipartisanship" would cause the Republicans to lose their independence and yet have to share the blame for policy failures. Still, he feared allowing the administration to take sole credit for "saving America from communism." Without recognizing it, both men had allowed their receptivity to symbol words to place them in extremely uncomfortable positions.[8]

Truman was delighted to utilize the Taft-Vandenberg split. Following Roosevelt's lead, he quickly adopted the practice of using Vandenberg as Republican senatorial "adviser" on foreign policy, thus allowing him as much prominence as possible without giving him any real influence on policy formulation. Vandenberg was easily flattered and quickly convinced himself that his "bipartisan cooperation" was essential to the future of both the country and his own party. That Vandenberg should have been so easily co-opted is understandable. What is more striking is the degree to which important elements in the pro-Republican press were similarly co-opted.

In an article published in October 1946 in *Life* magazine, Joseph and Stewart Alsop analyzed the growing differences between Vandenberg and Taft. Labeling Taft "a singularly complete symbol of American conservatism," they began by reviewing his record as Republican

7. Ibid., pp. 154–168; Patterson, *Mr. Republican*, pp. 295–296; Vandenberg to James H. Sheppard, January 2, 1945, Vandenberg MS.

8. Vandenberg, ed., *Private Papers*, pp. 311–312; Patterson, *Mr. Republican*, pp. 339–340.

leader on domestic issues. "By studying this record and the climate of business opinion," they noted, "one could make a fairly confident forecast of coming Republican programs—if it were not for one other factor. More and more, the political weather at home is made abroad. More and more, domestic policy must reflect the success or failure of foreign policy, which is the field of operations of Taft's coleader, Vandenberg."

The Alsops praised Vandenberg's conversion from "blind provincialism" in foreign affairs and contrasted his new "constructive" attitude with Taft's stubborn "isolationism." They attacked Taft's recent address to the Ohio senatorial nominating convention. On the one hand, they wrote, "he took a more sternly anti-Soviet line than any responsible American politician has yet taken." On the other, he had suggested that "the most necessary instruments of foreign policy should be lightly cast aside, ridiculing the draft and generally echoing the mood of the early '20s." Should Taft "insist on asserting his views on foreign policy," they warned, there would be "trouble ahead—trouble for Vandenberg and Taft themselves, bad trouble for the Republicans, and worse trouble for the country."[9]

Although the Alsops' analysis supported Vandenberg's views, their vocabulary nonetheless reflected Truman's definition of the situation. To posit the primacy of international affairs and label the draft a "necessary instrument of foreign policy" was to summarize the current scene virtually in Truman's terms. To warn of a return to the "early '20s" was also to echo Truman's version of recent history.

Most important, however, was the way in which the Alsops presented Taft's position. By labeling him "conservative" and "isolationist," they were not only perpetuating the Rooseveltian linkages in the postwar era but ignoring Taft's own analytical categories. To Taft, the whole point of both "liberalism" and "anticommunism" at home and abroad was to minimize the realm of coercion and maximize that of freedom. One did not promote liberty by either emulating the Russians or giving in to them. Nor did one simply retreat from international problems: the point was to take a moral stand rather than rely merely on force.

As the Alsops' article suggests, by late 1946 Taft was having increas-

9. Joseph and Stewart Alsop, "Taft and Vandenberg," *Life*, October 7, 1946, pp. 102–104.

ing difficulty communicating his definitions of both anticommunism and liberalism. Whereas his position was more morally searching, Vandenberg's was more reassuring. By externalizing responsibility for current international problems, Vandenberg implicitly absolved the United States of any immorality. The more courageous Taft's challenge of this perspective, the more it was to cost him politically.

In a speech delivered at Kenyon College two days before the Alsops' article appeared, Taft noted that America's "whole attitude" since V-E Day constituted "a departure from the principles of fair and equal treatment" that had made America respected before the war. "Today," he charged, "we are cordially hated in many countries." Even the current Nuremberg war crimes trials violated America's constitutional ban on *ex post facto* laws. A trial of "the vanquished by the victors" could not be impartial "no matter how it is hedged about with the forms of justice."

Later defended by many legal experts, Taft's position on the Nuremberg trials provoked great hostility at the time. Most Republicans, including Dewey, quickly dissociated themselves from it, while leading Democrats accused Taft of "pro-Nazi" sympathies. In response to such attacks, Taft noted that he had no objection to having the Allied powers "shut these men up for the rest of their lives as a matter of policy and on the ground that if free they might stir up another war." His "big objection," he wrote, "was to "the use of the forms of justice to carry out a predetermined policy." That, he charged, was "the Russian idea of a trial."[10]

Both the speech at Kenyon College and Taft's subsequent defense of it show the fundamental consistency of his position. His attacks on the Truman administration and the Russians sprang from a common premise that he still defined as liberal; namely, that no government had the right to use coercion in defiance of freedom even if the coercion were "hedged about with the forms of justice." His argument that emulation of Russian tactics could not be "liberal" was largely overshadowed by the furor over the Nuremberg reference, however, and the only tangible result of the speech was to increase the distance between Taft and most other Republican leaders regarding foreign policy.

10. "Equal Justice Under Law: The Heritage of the English-Speaking Peoples and Their Responsibility," October 5, 1946, Box 210, Taft MS.; and Patterson, *Mr. Republican*, pp. 327–328.

By early 1947, that distance was becoming increasingly useful to the administration. In February, Truman and his advisers decided that Britain's cutting back aid to beleaguered "anticommunist" governments in Greece and Turkey necessitated America's moving in to fill the gap. On February 27, Truman called in congressional leaders from both parties for "consultations." Vandenberg was invited; Taft was not. Hearing no strong objection from those present, Truman decided to go ahead with his plans. On March 12, he appeared before a joint session of Congress and not only requested $400,000,000 in emergency aid to Greece and Turkey, but enunciated the general "anticommunist" foreign policy that became known as the Truman Doctrine.[11]

Vandenberg was not entirely pleased with the result. He wrote in his diary: "The trouble is that these 'crises' never reach Congress until they have developed to a point where Congressional discretion is pathetically restricted." Were Congress to turn Truman down after the March 12 speech, "we might as well either resign ourselves to a complete Communist encirclement and infiltration or else get ready for World War No. Three." Although his comment on congressional discretion was very much to the point, Vandenberg had missed a key aspect of the situation. His hand had been forced not by the speech itself but by the February 27 meeting from which Truman had excluded Taft.

At Vandenberg's suggestion Taft was included in a second meeting on March 10, two days before the speech was delivered. Immediately after the meeting, Taft publicly expressed serious reservations about the administration's "policy of dividing the world into zones of political influence, communist and anti-communist." Were America to assume a "special position" in Greece and Turkey, he argued, "we can hardly longer reasonably object to the Russians' continuing their domination in Poland, Yugoslavia, Rumania, and Bulgaria." Emphasizing that he did not "want war with Russia," Taft wondered aloud whether "our intervention in Greece tends to make such a war more probable or less probable."

11. Walter LaFeber, *America, Russia, and the Cold War, 1945–1980* (New York: John Wiley, 1980), pp. 52–59; Herbert Feis, *From Trust to Terror: The Onset of the Cold War, 1945–1950* (New York: Norton, 1970), p. 190; Dean Acheson, *Present at the Creation: My Years in the State Department* (New York: Norton, 1969), p. 219; Vandenberg, ed., *Private Papers*, pp. 339, 343; *Public Papers of the President of the United States: Harry S. Truman, 1947* (Washington: Government Printing Office, 1963), pp. 176–180.

There is no way of knowing what might have happened had Taft been present on February 27 to express these reservations. By March 10, however, assured at least of Vandenberg's tacit support, the administration had generated sufficient momentum so that the speech could not be called off. In contrast to the first meeting, the second was largely pro forma, and once the speech had been delivered, as Vandenberg himself acknowledged, it was virtually impossible to disown the president. Even Taft eventually voted for the aid appropriation on the grounds that Truman had "committed the United States to this policy in the eyes of the world, and to repudiate it now would destroy his prestige in the negotiations with the Russian government on the success of which ultimate peace depends."[12]

The events surrounding the formulation and initial implementation of the Truman Doctrine were to have profound implications. The administration had adroitly utilized both the split between the two Republican leaders and their shared susceptibility to anticommunist arguments, and established the Truman Doctrine not only as firm national policy but as a policy to be personally identified with the president rather than with his critics. Henceforth it would be even harder to impugn Truman's "anticommunist credential" or offer effective opposition to his "anticommunist" programs. Moreover, Truman's solicitous treatment of Vandenberg would pay off handsomely in future confrontations with the Taft wing of the Republican party. Indeed, by the time the aid appropriation came to a vote, Taft had already been defeated in open confrontation with Vandenberg regarding the integrity of the administration's "anticommunist commitment."

The April 6, 1947 issue of the New York *Herald-Tribune* carried the bold headline: "Vandenberg Now Senate's 'Strong Man': He Carried Off All Honors in Head-On Clash with Taft over Lilienthal." The issue over which the two leaders had clashed was Senate confirmation of former TVA director David Lilienthal as chairman of the newly formed Atomic Energy Commission. Vandenberg supported the nomination; Taft opposed it.

Lilienthal, Taft charged, was a "devotee of public ownership" and "soft on the subject of communism." Vandenberg angrily retorted that his own position "in the top bracket of all Communist blacklists" showed he was "not calculated to be 'soft' on such a subject." Lilienthal's experience with public ownership, he added, was a prime qualification for the job. The Senate, Vandenberg observed, had unanimously endorsed a law making atomic energy "the tightest government monopoly" in American history.

Although Taft carried thirty Republicans with him against seventeen for Vandenberg, solid Democratic support ensured Lilienthal's confirmation. "The vote," reported the *Herald-Tribune* approvingly, "suggested, at least, that on any future issue involving international co-operation and fundamental liberalism, Senator Vandenberg will be able to carry a majority of the Senate with him."[13]

The reference to "fundamental liberalism" spotlighted Taft's increasingly uncomfortable position. Both he and Vandenberg had argued in the language of anticommunism. Not only had Vandenberg carried the day, he had won acclaim as a "liberal" whereas Taft was again denied that designation. Indeed, the Lilienthal controversy, together with the Truman Doctrine debate, sharply underlined Taft's weakness in his ongoing competition with Truman for both the liberal and anticommunist labels.

Taft's attempt to make an issue of Lilienthal's New Deal background was yet another effort to equate the New Deal with "communism." As the *Herald-Tribune*'s reaction indicated, far from injuring either Lilienthal or Truman, such efforts only weakened Taft's credibility among those who continued to define liberalism in terms of governmental generosity. At the same time, the assumption of nuclear secrecy seemed to suggest the appropriateness of powerful, centralized governmental control in fighting "communism." Growing public acceptance of this idea and a growing belief that massive government spending abroad would undercut the appeal of "communism" suggested that as "Cold War" thinking took hold, it was Truman rather than Taft who was gaining recognition as more effectively "liberal" *and* "anticommunist."

Vandenberg's position was hardly more comfortable. He worried not only about splitting his own party but about the long-term issue of public ownership. Lilienthal's "liability under other circumstances,"

13. *New York Herald-Tribune*, April 6, 1947.

he told the Senate, "thus becomes an asset for the time being."
Though Vandenberg still hoped that Republican cooperation on foreign policy would be rewarded at the polls, neither he nor Taft
seemed to realize how their own anticommunist rhetoric continued to
play into Truman's hands. [14]

During the spring of 1947, Taft and Vandenberg took time off from
their foreign policy differences to enjoy one seemingly major Republican victory in domestic affairs. Solid Republican majorities in
Congress pushed through the Taft-Hartley labor bill, then joined with
dissident Democrats to repass it over Truman's veto. From Taft's
point of view, his sponsorship of the bill belied the conservative label
frequently thrust on him. He saw the bill as liberal in that it protected
the liberties of nonunion labor and rank-and-file unionists against the
arbitrary power of union executives. Not surprisingly, most union
leaders and many other self-styled liberals hotly disputed Taft's definition of liberalism. He would shortly pay heavily for it. [15]

Meanwhile, as early as July, Taft was receiving warnings that the
anticommunism issue was going to backfire badly against the Republicans, especially in foreign policy. Ohio congressman George
Bender, who had vigorously opposed the Truman Doctrine, wrote to
Taft urging him to come out squarely against "the whole Truman
policy . . . of military aggression." He warned Taft that he did "not
see any way to keep foreign policy out of the 1948 campaign," and told
him frankly: "It seems to me that it is wrong to let Vandenberg
continue to push us into the arms of the Democrats under the guise of
this phony bi-partisan foreign policy."

To counter the recently proposed Marshall Plan, under which
Truman planned to "squander" some "five or ten billions a year,"
Bender urged the announcement of a "Taft Plan," which would put
economic policy on a "solid business basis" and handle international
disputes through the United Nations. Decrying a global anticommunist crusade, he insisted that the United States could and should
do business with those "large hunks of the world which have adopted
some type of economy other than ours." Such an approach required
neither coercion nor governmental generosity. Bender predicted that

14. Patterson, *Mr. Republican*, p. 345; Vandenberg, ed., *Private Papers*, pp. 354,
356, 340.
15. Patterson, *Mr. Republican*, pp. 352–366.

foreign policy would be "overriding everything else by November 1948" and called on Taft to take the offensive and "give affirmative direction through a Taft Plan." He emphasized that both the nation's future and Taft's own hung in the balance, and warned that there was "no good reason to let Vandenberg make suckers out of the Party and swing votes for Dewey."

For his part, Taft continued to speak throughout 1947 against conscription, American "imperialism," and those who "talked of war with Russia." He agreed with Bender that foreign policy "should be one of the main issues in the next election, and the sooner we get free from the idea that we are bound to cooperate in everything, the better off we will be." Yet, Taft made it clear that his attack on Truman's foreign policy would be partly based on Secretary Marshall's failure to combat "communism" effectively. Marshall, he charged in November, had "made a complete failure of himself in China," and were his policy continued there it would "hand China over to the Russians."[16]

As the 1948 campaign approached, one thing was clear. Symbol words would be playing a particularly important role. What was not clear was whom they would aid, and whom they would keep from thinking.

A linguistic last stand

[T]he Republicans have tried to identify the Administration with the domestic Communists. . . . If [Henry Wallace's] third party effort fizzles, it is quite possible the Communists will try to deliver the unions they dominate to the Republicans. The shoe may conceivably be on the Republican foot by election time—and it will be the Democrats' turn to emphasize the red lining on the opposition banner. . . .

President Truman must carry the West to win. To carry the West, he must be "liberal". . . . [The Republicans] are chasing votes in earnest. And it emphasizes the only tenable Democratic strategy, which is to continue to stay to the "left" of them . . .

In the Land of Electoral Votes, the West is the "Number One Priority" for the Democrats. Its people are more liberal because they

16. Ibid., p. 384; Radosh, *Prophets on the Right*, pp. 157–159; speech to the Missouri Republican Club, Kansas City, December 29, 1947, Box 1270, Taft MS.

need the economic help of government and in the years of the New Deal have come to understand how it functions. . . .

There should also be a *Taft* expert. The President is running against the Taft record no matter who his opponent is.

Clark Clifford, 1947

What is a Liberal?

Robert Taft, 1948

Clark Clifford and Robert Taft would have been formidable antagonists in any era. To read through Clifford's now famous memorandum on "the politics of 1948" is to discover a blueprint that the Democrats followed with remarkable fidelity and devastating results. With this memorandum the young White House staff lawyer established himself as one of the most brilliant strategists in his party.

Taft was no intellectual slouch either. When he stood before Republican party faithful in mid-February and asked the single most important question in American politics, he was doing so not merely for rhetorical effect, but attempting most searchingly to lay bare the underlying trends and contradictions of the day.[17]

The distance between the two men represented more than just another partisan disagreement. One of the most important lessons historical analysis of language teaches is how to recognize the end of an era. Some eras end with the breakdown of an old label and its replacement by a new one. Some end with a transformation in the popularly accepted meaning of a label. Others end when one side or the other abandons the competition to be publicly identified with a label. The vocabularies of Clifford and Taft indicate the final stage of a vital era in modern American politics; namely, that of competition over the liberal label.

In this case, the end of the competition over one label was intimately linked with continued competition over another. Taft's last defense of his liberal designation was closely tied to his struggle for the anticommunist designation. Both struggles were part of his continuing fight to reverse the direction of domestic and foreign policy.

17. "Memorandum for the President," November 19, 1947, pp. 15, 24, 32, 38, 42 (italics in original), in Clark M. Clifford Papers, Harry S. Truman Library, Independence, Mo. (hereafter Clifford MS.); "What Is a Liberal?" February 13, 1948, Box 1271, Taft MS.

Conversely, Clifford's rhetoric was designed to ensure policy continuity.

One way of gauging the significance of a political confrontation is to see how many major linguistic variables are present and how they are used. Clifford opened his memo by warning against "original or unusual thinking." Electoral strategy memoranda, he noted, must "be devoted to a review of the *usual*." The memo not only contained all the major labels then in use, but reflected what had become by then their "usual" meanings. Thus when Clifford talked about "liberals," "conservatives," "progressives," "isolationists," and so on, his definitions were Roosevelt's. For example, "liberals" were people who needed and appreciated governmental generosity; "conservatives" those who did not. Although the progressive label did not feature as prominently as the liberal, the two were used interchangeably. Henry Wallace's third-party candidacy would receive support from "die-hard isolationists." President Truman could not "afford to be shackled with the Wall Street label."[18]

Clifford also incorporated the "usual" usages of the linear spectrum. Wealth and "conservatism" were on the "right," whereas those more amenable to governmental generosity were on the "left." The Republicans would "push some sort of a housing bill" in 1948 as part of their "general strategy . . . to move somewhat more to the 'left'," and to undercut them Truman would have to "continue to stay on the 'left' of them." He could also undercut Wallace by moving "to the left," though not so far "left" as Wallace.

Also important was the way in which Clifford integrated deliberately conventional vocabulary with shrewd policy proposals. The "high cost of living," which included the high cost of housing, would be "the *only* domestic issue" in 1948. For Truman to "stay to the 'left'" of the Republicans, to protect his "liberal credential," would require more than a "negative" attack on the "Real Estate Lobby." The Administration, wrote Clifford, "*must* take an affirmative position on housing." A "liberal credential" required tangible generosity.[19]

Most important of all, however, was Clifford's integration of liberal and anticommunist rhetoric, the linear spectrum, and foreign policy. "There is considerable political advantage to the Administration in its battle with the Kremlin," he wrote. "In times of crisis the American

18. Clifford memo, pp. 1 (italics in original), 6, 24.
19. Ibid., pp. 17, 23, 35 (italics in original).

citizen tends to back up his President." Moscow was "sufficiently aware of American politics to perceive that a Republican administration would be rigid and reactionary, and would fail to take those governmental steps necessary to bolster the capitalist economy in time of crisis." That is, the Russians realized that if the Republicans won, they would bring about another depression, and the best way to make this happen would be to support Wallace and "split the Independent and labor union vote," that is, the "liberal and progressive" vote.

Although this possibility represented a danger, it also created an opportunity. At the proper moment, "the Administration must persuade prominent liberals and progressives—*and no one else*—to move publicly into the fray. . . . [to] point out that the core of the Wallace backing is made up of Communists and the fellow-travelers." If Wallace then "fizzled," and "the Communists" wound up supporting the Republicans directly, that would be even better. One way or another, the strategy would be to paint an unholy alliance of "far left" and "far right" against "true anticommunist liberals" in the "center." This proved to be the strategy Truman followed.[20]

That Clifford described Truman as "running against the Taft record no matter who his opponent is" indicates Clifford's assessment of Taft's prominence and vulnerability. To read Taft's 1948 "liberal" credo is to appreciate both aspects of that assessment. Taft's "What Is a Liberal?" speech, delivered at Omaha on February 13, was his last and most comprehensive attempt to lay bare the contradictions in Roosevelt's definition. Although he succeeded in doing so to some extent, he also revealed the limitations of his own predominantly negative approach and, most important, again revealed the inadequacy of counter-reification itself.

Because of the misuses of recent years, Taft began, a word "which used to be a sound Anglo-Saxon word with a clear meaning, has lost all significance today. It has even acquired Russian overtones." Contrary to the administration's use, he declared, "the word 'liberal' in the political sense certainly does not connote 'generous' or 'lavish.' It does not mean a man in favor of giving away his own or other people's money." Despite the passage of time, the "basic meaning" of the word remained what it had always been: "someone in favor of freedom."

Many self-styled liberals, however, were now advocating "measures

20. Ibid., pp. 15, 36, 4, 23 (italics in original).

seriously reducing freedom of the people or freedom of thought." Taft hit out at Roosevelt and Truman for holding that "it was liberal to subject employers to a loss of their liberty, liberal to deprive the individual worker of his private and separate liberty, liberal to enhance the liberty of labor union leaders to 'do as they please with other men, and the product of other men's labor.'" At the same time, Taft criticized "special interest organizations" for being "likely to concede a good deal to totalitarian regulation if it moves in the direction of their interest."

Taft listed several "infractions of freedom" that were being "gradually accepted in America as a matter of course," including governmental interference with the right to own gold coins as "proof against inflation or devaluation," and interference with the right to travel freely abroad. He also attacked proposals such as those for renewed price controls, compulsory federal health insurance, and peacetime conscription as "illiberal" limitations on individual freedom.

Of conscription in particular, Taft remarked: "It seems to me that in a liberal country there ought to be such an intense resentment against this totalitarian measure that the necessity for it would be everywhere doubted until clearly proven." Instead, he declared "those who accept the government dogma consider themselves to be liberals." Taft candidly noted the coercive nature of American intervention in Greece. American policy there, he declared, "may be necessary from a foreign policy standpoint; I believe that it was. But certainly there is nothing liberal about it. Those who opposed it have far more claim to be called liberals than do those of us who supported it."

As a credo, the Omaha speech was in many respects both courageous and effective. Taft was at his best in exposing the contradiction between coercion and freedom inherent in policies such as peacetime conscription and the Truman Doctrine, and forthright in challenging the Rooseveltian connotation of generosity. Yet he failed to follow up his own remark about "giving away other people's money" and failed to expose the contradiction Flynn and others had hammered away at in the 1930s; namely, that under the banner of generosity Roosevelt was confiscating from the many for the benefit of the few. Even in criticizing "special interests" for accepting self-serving "regulation," Taft never made the connection between this and the "false generosity" that earlier critics had tried so hard to unmask.

His was a failure of omission. Even so, in the context of his insistence on "liberalism" simply as "freedom of the people or freedom of thought," the omission came across as an anachronistic evasion of the major economic issues of the day. Indeed, by combining this approach with criticism of the Roosevelt-Truman record on labor legislation, Taft inadvertently set himself up as an apparent advocate of generosity for the few. This was precisely the image of the Republicans that Clifford hoped to convey.

Taft's most untimely failure, however, lay in his continuing attempt to compete with the administration in the combined use of liberal and anticommunist rhetoric. His suggestion that the word "liberal" had "acquired Russian overtones" was merely a reprise of his stock effort to equate the New Deal with "communism." By describing American involvement in Greece as "illiberal" and then defending it as "necessary," he also indicated his readiness to compromise "liberalism" for the sake of "anticommunism."

This was a particularly grievous error because in admitting the necessity of intervention in Greece, Taft again validated Truman's anticommunist rhetoric. Even worse, in making "liberalism" and "anticommunism" contradictory rather than complementary Taft undercut his own strategy. Finally, he showed himself completely unprepared for Clifford's projected strategy of depicting "the Communists" as the chief beneficiaries of a Republican victory.[21]

Altogether, the Omaha speech suggested that Clifford had already stolen a march on Taft in the combined use of liberal and anticommunist rhetoric. As in the Roosevelt years, the game of reification and counter-reification would remain much more useful to the administration than to its critics. Far from challenging or exposing the verbal competition itself, Taft showed once more how symbol words had confused his thinking, and how susceptibility to anticommunist rhetoric in particular had clouded his political judgment.

Taft continued to receive warnings on the latter subject. One of the most prescient came from editor Felix Morley. In a letter to Taft, written in mid-March, Morley pointed out that Dewey was making the fatal mistake of competing with Truman's anticommunist rhetoric. That was "Truman's only card now," Morley warned, "and the aspirant can't play it as well as the man in power." He advised Taft to "move in actively on the field of foreign policy" with a "series of major

21. "What Is a Liberal?" pp. 1–6, passim.

speeches. . . . on the necessity of saving ideals which are as much menaced by domestic stupidity as by any threat of external aggression."

Morley's appeal was a moment of truth for Taft. Though critical of Truman's foreign policy, Taft believed that he himself did not have as many facts at his disposal as did the president and he feared making "some mistake which [could] easily be shown up." He agreed to "do everything possible to discourage war excitement and hold us back from any action which will bring war about," but he could not "be against full preparedness."[22]

While events were demonstrating Taft's ambivalence on political strategy, they were also demonstrating how conventional or "usual" vocabulary was continuing to play into the administration's hands. By early 1948 a diverse coalition was shaping up, as in prewar years, to oppose peacetime conscription. Some of its leaders, like Taft, had also led the opposition in the earlier era, whereas others, like Wallace, had supported conscription in 1940, but had since switched sides.

To compare the vocabulary of the prewar conscription debate with that of the postwar is to note several parallels and one obvious contrast. The contrast is that whereas Roosevelt's prewar rhetoric centered on the antifascist label, Truman's centered on the anticommunist. The very starkness of the contrast helps spotlight the parallels.

In both debates, each side claimed the liberal label and competed for the same positive linkages—"liberal antifascist" in the prewar case, "liberal anticommunist" in the postwar. Both times the administration denounced the opposition as "isolationist," and the opposition retorted by rejecting that label and denouncing the administration as "militarist" and "imperialist." On both occasions the administration attempted to draw denigrative linkages between the opposition's supposed "isolationism" and its supposed attitude on domestic issues.

These denigrative linkages bring the contrasts and parallels into clearest perspective. When Roosevelt argued a link between "isolation" and "reaction," he was suggesting, not too subtly, that opponents of peacetime conscription were little better than "fascists." Similarly, in the 1948 debate Truman turned his anticommunist rhetoric

22. Morley to Taft, March 18, 1948, and Taft to Morley, March 23, 1948, Box 797, Taft MS.

on the opponents of conscription. In the same March 17 speech in which he asked Congress to approve UMT, he announced that he did not want and would not accept "the political support of Henry Wallace and his Communists." These were "days of high prices for everything," Truman declared, "but any price for Wallace and his Communists is too much for me to pay."[23]

Although the denigrative linkages were different in the two fights, the purpose of using them was the same. As the isolationist label assumed the opposition's lack of realism in foreign policy, the denigrative domestic labels evaded the opposition's challenges regarding the impact of conscription and war on American society. In neither case did the administration wish to call attention to the contradictions within its own definition of liberalism.

There was one other important parallel between the two situations. In his memo to Truman, Clifford noted that in 1940 Roosevelt had tried to bring to public attention the fact that certain well-known "communist" labor leaders were supporting Willkie. That is, Roosevelt had attempted to paint himself as victim of a combined assault from the "far left" and the "far right." The charge, wrote Clifford, "was so new and unexpected, and the Communists so adroit in executing their directives, that the Democratic assertion, although true, just wasn't believed by a naive public." Should a similar situation arise in 1948, "it might prove invaluable, particularly as the American public is more sophisticated and more sensitive to the red issue than it then was."[24]

By early 1948, however, the administration's supporters were not waiting for the situation to develop but already using the conscription issue and the Marshall Plan to set up this "both-ends-against-the-middle" argument. Shortly after Truman's March 17 address, *Washington Post* columnist Marquis Childs wrote that in addition to "dissenter" Wallace, people at the "opposite pole" of the spectrum, such as Taft, were helping lead the fight to prevent conscription and cripple the Marshall Plan.

According to Childs, while Truman was working on both economic and military levels to prevent "the conquest of western Europe by

23. *Public Papers of the Presidents of the United States: Harry S. Truman, 1948* (Washington: Government Printing Office, 1963), p. 189.
24. Clifford memo, p. 15.

communist tyranny," Taft was expressing "the same kind of isolationism that [he had] expressed in the years before Pearl Harbor . . . to the effect that Japan had no aggressive intentions." Taken together, the references to Wallace, Taft, the linear spectrum, "communist tyranny," Japanese "aggression," and "isolationism" combined to produce an image of a beleaguered Truman trying desperately to defend the "liberal anticommunist" wisdom of the "center."[25]

In reality, Truman was far from being on the defensive, but making him appear the victim of a squeeze play was nonetheless a useful device. Indeed, Childs's vocabulary reflected what was actually a brilliant offensive strategy on Clifford's part; namely, that of actively playing the "middle" against "both ends." Childs need not have been privy to Clifford's memo. The whole point of the strategy was that once the themes of governmental generosity and the "communist threat" were hammered home, the "usual" vocabulary would do the job quite naturally. Nor did all of the administration's supporters have to be privy to the strategy to help it along. Truman's being privy to it meant only that he used it more consciously and with greater effectiveness. It was the strategy he followed all year, and it worked superbly.

The strategy worked for a number of reasons: because Roosevelt's self-identifying and denigrative vocabulary remained the "usual" vocabulary of American politics; because, as in prewar years, the critics failed to lay bare the full range of contradictions within that vocabulary; and because reification of the linear spectrum kept opposition spokesmen divided not only in "people's" minds but in their own minds. In failing to de-reify the terms "left" and "right," the opposition's leaders failed to break down the barriers between them and thus presented Truman with that most useful of all political gifts, a fragmented opposition.

Finally, Clifford's strategy worked because so many of the opposition's leaders, Taft included, remained caught up in their own symbol words. Part of Taft's motivation stemmed from fear. "I have had more criticism for my very mild appeals to look the whole situation over before acting," he told Morley, "than I have had for anything else I have done." Taft was also genuinely unable to transcend his own anticommunist rhetoric. Having failed to reduce and limit the dura-

25. Radosh, *Prophets on the Right*, pp. 165–166.

tion of the Marshall Plan's commitments, Taft finally voted for the full appropriation with the remark that some aid was necessary to fight "communism." That June, after much soul searching, he voted with the majority to renew peacetime conscription for two years, and thereby forfeited any hope of offering a clear alternative to Truman's foreign policies.[26]

That Taft was co-opted on conscription in 1948 but not in 1940 was a direct result of his differing susceptibilities to different symbol words. In June 1941, just after the German invasion of Russia, he had declared that a "victory of communism in the world outside of America would be far more dangerous to the United States from an ideological standpoint than the victory of fascism." His premise that "fascism" held no popular appeal whereas "communism" was a "false philosophy which appeals to many" was an implied compliment to "communism." Understandably, his contemporary detractors preferred to interpret him as harboring latent sympathies for "fascism."

To accept the latter interpretation is merely to get caught up once more in the reification process. Taft had no sympathy for Hitler or Stalin. At the same time, he did have a stronger emotional reaction to the word "communism" than to the word "fascism." In this, he typified millions of Americans for whom the connotation of government ownership of production was uniquely frightening. Again, this fear was what made anticommunist rhetoric at once so attractive to opposition leaders and so useful to Truman.[27]

Taft's support for conscription sounded the death knell for his presidential ambitions. The combination of his "antilabor" image and his increasingly uncertain foreign policy stance proved much too risky for Republican party leaders, and they again rejected him in favor of Dewey. With the defection of the southern "Dixiecrats" from the Democratic party, Truman now faced three badly divided opponents.

To read Truman's 1948 campaign speeches is to observe him following Clifford's strategy to the letter. The campaign, he told a Los Angeles audience early in September, was a "crucial struggle between the forward forces of liberalism and the backward forces of reaction." There were "some people with true liberal convictions," he noted, "whose worry over the state of the world has caused them to lean

26. Ibid., pp. 165–167; Taft to Morley, cited n. 22.
27. Radosh, *Prophets on the Right*, p. 129.

toward a third party." Asking these people to "think again," Truman warned: "The fact that the Communists are guiding and using the Third Party shows that this is not a party which represents American ideals." A vote for the "third party" would only weaken Democratic efforts to build a "peaceful world" and thus play into the hands of "the Republican forces of reaction, whose aims are directly opposed to the aims of American liberalism."

Following the strategy of identifying Wallace with "the Communists," "the Communists" with a Republican victory, and a Republican victory with "Wall Street domination," Truman neatly updated the strategy by including the Dixiecrats. The Republicans, he declared in Des Moines, were receiving help from "some strange quarters" in the campaign: "The Southern party called Dixiecrats have made common cause with Wall Street, because they would deny the Civil Rights guaranteed by the Constitution for all Americans. *The Communists have lined up solidly behind the new Third Party, whose aim is to defeat the Democratic Party.*" The "Communists," Truman charged, were "counting on a Republican administration to produce another economic crash, which would play into the hands of world communism."

Stressing his domestic and international "anticommunist" programs, Truman was careful not to use language that would lend credence to charges of "warmongering." His administration's foreign policy program, he told a New York audience late in October, was a peace program, and he contrasted the constructive approach of the Democrats to the irresponsible "isolationism" of the Republicans. Truman also reminded his listeners that it had been Roosevelt and Hull, not the Republicans, who had initiated bipartisanship in foreign affairs during the war.[28]

Right up to the end of the campaign, Truman continued to make excellent use of international crises, particularly the Berlin Blockade and the ensuing Berlin airlift. By election day, his position was unchallengeable, and Truman not only was reelected but swept his party into control of the Congress as well. The victory was regarded as a stunning upset, but was really the logical result of the ongoing competition over the liberal and anticommunist labels.

28. All quotations from original drafts in Presidential Secretary's File (PSF), Harry S. Truman Papers, Harry S. Truman Library, Independence, Mo. (hereafter Truman MS.) Original drafts contain italics as indicated. Also see *Public Papers of Truman, 1948*, passim.

Taft was mystified by the outcome. "It defies all common sense," he remarked, "for the country to send that roughneck ward politician back to the White House." From the comparative quiet of retirement, Herbert Hoover sketched out an explanation focused on domestic issues. Truman, he wrote, "had pounded the country with the statement that the Republican Party was the party of big business and private interest." The Republicans, Hoover noted, should have met the charge head-on and taken credit for generous tax revision, farm price supports, and labor legislation that had benefited all workers. Although he no longer used the liberal label, Hoover insisted that the Taft-Hartley Act had contributed to the "liberation of the American workman." Republican orators, he argued, should have discussed the act paragraph by paragraph and demanded of each successive point, "did it benefit the American workman and make a free man of him?"

To former Kansas governor Alfred Landon, the election result underlined the importance of the question "Who's liberal now?" The "meaning of that grand old label," he observed, "has been almost completely destroyed." Landon blamed the "collapse in the liberal leadership in the Republican Party" largely on the "phony issue of isolationism v. nationalism." The "social and economic views of candidates in recent years," he wrote, "has all been obliterated in the one issue of isolationism."

To independent journalist Lawrence Dennis, the message of the election was clear. The Republicans, he noted, had opposed increased federal spending, higher taxes, new controls, and welfare legislation, "but they fall, like the suckers they are, for the war and anti-red-sin features." There was "nothing you can't put over on American conservatives," Dennis observed, "if you spice it with war and anti-red" rhetoric. In short, the "dumb Republicans thought they would win on a pendulum swing to the right and as an anti-communist party. What saps!"[29]

A tale of two labels

There is one thing that the American people know about Senator [Joseph R.] McCarthy; he, like them, is unequivocally anti-Commu-

---

29. Eric Goldman, *The Crucial Decade* (New York: Vintage Books, 1960), p. 90; Hoover, "Memorandum on Election (confidential)," November 17, 1948, PS#3108, HHPL; Landon to Felix Morley, November 5, 1948, Felix Morley Papers, HHPL (hereafter Morley MS.); Radosh, *Prophets on the Right*, p. 310.

nist. About the spokesmen for American liberalism, they feel they
know no such thing.

                                                     Irving Kristol, 1952

Liberalism and McCarthyism. In the history of American politics, it
is unlikely that two labels have been more generally viewed as polar
opposites. Simply stated, few Americans would ever think of calling
Joe McCarthy a liberal. Yet, the enduring polarity between liberalism
and McCarthyism has not been matched by a similarly enduring polarity between liberalism and anticommunism.

What Irving Kristol described in 1952 was a temporary loss of public faith in the "anticommunist credentials" of the Truman administration and its supporters. Like the rise of McCarthy himself, that loss of
faith was brought on by Truman's post-1948 foreign policy reverses—
chiefly the "loss" of China, the Soviet achievement of a nuclear capacity, and the Korean War stalemate—and like McCarthy's popularity,
that loss of faith was brief. Within a few years it would again be
possible, indeed mandatory, for self-styled liberals to win recognition
as "anticommunists." In contrast, it would be very difficult for anyone
who had conspicuously supported McCarthy ever again to be recognized as "a liberal."[30]

Unlike many labels, the word "McCarthyism" is of known origin. It
was coined early in 1950 by *Washington Post* cartoonist Herbert Block
("Herblock"). Although the coining of the word increased McCarthy's
prominence, its acceptance into the language suggests an immediate
negative response to his behavior. Some scholars have argued that
many people supported McCarthy's tactics as much as his professed
goals because his style gave the average American a chance to identify
vicariously with a "tough guy." Although plausible as a sociological
hypothesis, this explanation does not account for the immediate and
enduring presence of the word "McCarthyism" as a pejorative, even
at the height of the senator's popularity. Several public figures encouraged or imitated McCarthy's tactics. Few, apart from the senator
himself, ever identified with the label.

One who did was a young Yale graduate named William F. Buckley,
Jr. "McCarthyism," wrote Buckley, "is a movement around which

30. Kristol is quoted in Lawrence S. Wittner, *Cold War America: From Hiroshima
to Watergate* (New York: Praeger, 1974), p. 102.

men of good will and stern morality can close ranks." Buckley was later to emerge as a leading self-styled conservative. Most who used the word "McCarthyism," however, used it in a context of sharp criticism.[31]

If Buckley typified anything, it was a tendency among McCarthy's supporters to identify themselves as conservatives. Prominent among this group were several former self-styled liberals such as Hoover, Flynn, and Taft, who finally gave up his fight for the liberal label after 1948. Because of Truman's identification with the latter label and McCarthy's antipathy to the administration's policy, it was hardly likely that McCarthy's supporters would call themselves liberals. Nonetheless, short of a permanent reversal of prevailing American attitudes toward the word "liberal," the presumed incompatibility of McCarthyism and liberalism was bound to be a long-run liability for McCarthy's supporters. Similarly, the link between McCarthyism and conservatism would be a liability to self-styled conservatives.

Although this link between McCarthyism and conservatism does not explain why people like Hoover, Flynn, and Taft chose to support McCarthy, it does shed light on the results of their support. By reinforcing the polarity between McCarthyism and liberalism, they helped absolve Truman of responsibility for creating the atmosphere in which McCarthy thrived. Indeed, long after Truman had left the White House, continuing support of McCarthy by self-styled conservatives helped ensure that "liberals" received credit for anticommunist "successes" while "conservatives" got blamed for the "excesses."[32]

To focus on the behavior of McCarthy's supporters is not to neglect the equally important contribution of his self-styled liberal anticommunist detractors. In setting up the polarity between McCarthy and the "spokesmen for American liberalism," Kristol was not merely describing the situation, but advising self-styled liberals to validate their "anticommunist credentials" by joining more enthusiastically in

31. Goldman, *Crucial Decade*, p. 145; Daniel Bell, ed., *The New American Right* (New York: Criterion Books, 1955), pp. 21, 64, 71, 90, 102–103, 211; Buckley is quoted in Wittner, *Cold War America*, p. 100.

32. For Buckley's continuing support of McCarthy, even after McCarthy's death, see his *Up from Liberalism* (New York: Hillman Books, 1959), and various articles in Buckley's self-styled "conservative" journal, *National Review*, e.g. Frank S. Meyer, "The Meaning of McCarthyism," June 14, 1958, p. 565.

the anticommunist crusade. The clear implication was that if they failed to do so, they ran the risk of falling victim to McCarthy.

However ineffective such advice may have been in the short run, it had a remarkably subtle long-run effect, for it enabled self-styled liberal anticommunists to argue that their anticommunist militance had been forced on them—that they had been, in effect, hostages of "McCarthyite conservatives." This hostage theory not only absolved its authors of any responsibility for encouraging McCarthy but was easily generalized to define postwar "liberal anticommunism" as a defensive reaction born of fear of the domestic "conservative" opposition.

Set in the context of the linear spectrum, the hostage theory neatly reinforced Truman's definition of the postwar situation. Just as Truman was able to use "communists" on the "left" as an excuse for his policy failures, so the hostage theory complemented this by setting up "conservatives" on the "right" as the reason for his adoption of anticommunist policies. As in Clifford's scenario, this explanation left Truman squarely in the "center" to defend against the combined assaults of "left" and "right."

As in the Roosevelt era, the opposition's failure in the Truman era was not exposing the contradictions in the administration's vocabulary. Reimposition of conscription to fight a war was as much coercion in the name of freedom as in Roosevelt's time. Taft's cooptation in the case of conscription was probably the central event in muting the opposition's challenge in this regard. Equally important was the opposition's failure to deal with Roosevelt's notion of generosity.

When McCarthy talked of "twenty years of treason," he was reviving Taft's old charge that the New Deal was equivalent to "communism." That charge had not only failed to overthrow the New Deal, but failed even to call attention to the contradiction between confiscation and generosity. Reviving the charge in the 1950s only further obscured the critiques Flynn and others had so painfully developed in the 1930s and 1940s concerning the actual relationship between the New Deal and large corporations. In this respect, it was ironic in the extreme that Flynn himself ultimately became one of McCarthy's staunchest supporters, though one can readily understand the frustration and bitterness that led him, Hoover, and Taft to adopt such a position. The consequences of their actions emerge as no less tragic.

The central event in this context was Taft's linguistic shift. Through

1948, he, like Truman, had argued his case in both liberal and anti-communist terms, but having been rejected by his own party again, Taft decided to change his rhetorical strategy. Both before and after the election, he had been warned that it was the anticommunist rhetoric that was backfiring. Taft, however, apparently believed that he had said all he could by way of competing for the liberal label, and by now he agreed with Hoover and Landon that the label had been robbed of all meaning. "Anticommunism" was admittedly a dangerous issue, subject to misuse by administration supporters and critics alike. Even so, whereas liberal rhetoric had been exhausted, anticommunist rhetoric still seemed to have political possibilities. Thus it was the liberal label rather than the anticommunist label that Taft abandoned after 1948.

With this change Truman's leading critics now united around the argument Hoover had advanced as early as 1945 that so-called "liberals" *were* actually "socialists" and "communists" in fact if not in name. At the same time, Taft finally joined Hoover and other critics in reluctantly accepting the conservative designation that had long been thrust on him. Henceforth, the consensus among the critics would be that "conservatism," not "liberalism," was the "true anti-communist" philosophy.[33]

Throughout these events the underlying purpose of Taft and his fellow critics (the overthrow of the New Deal) remained constant. The change in their treatment of the liberal label nonetheless signified both a momentous shift in rhetorical strategy and a major gamble. They were hoping to reverse popular understanding of the most important, heavily freighted label in American politics. Failure to do so would not only cement the validity of the Roosevelt-Truman usage but reinforce the administration's long-standing claim that the "conservative" opposition consisted of people who were against constructive "liberal" programs but had nothing positive to substitute.

Along with their abandonment of the liberal label came a renewed attempt by opposition leaders to establish their preeminent claim to the anticommunist label. Despite the warnings they had received, the logic of their post-1948 strategy dictated a redoubling of their efforts to use the "anticommunism" issue against the administration. The sup-

33. By the mid-1950s, this definition of the situation would result in an open competition for the conservative and anticommunist labels. See Chapter 7, below.

port given by Taft, Hoover, and Flynn to McCarthy was not merely the result of frustration and bitterness but represented a last, desperate effort to use anticommunist rhetoric to reverse the New Deal and its consequences.

Journalist Richard Rovere later wrote that Taft confronted McCarthy's approach the way an alcoholic confronts the bottle: reluctant at first, he eventually found it impossible to resist. Taft's support for McCarthy was based on two factors. First, McCarthy's tactics, however repugnant, got results. In the 1950 midterm elections, the Wisconsin senator's intervention helped defeat administration supporters in several major Senate races. Second, McCarthy's basic argument that American defeats abroad resulted from "communist" subversion at home differed only in degree from what Taft and like-minded critics had been saying for years.

By 1950, when McCarthy first achieved national prominence, Taft had been hurling the socialist and communist labels at the administration and its supporters for over a decade. Caught up in his own symbol words, Taft already believed that such foreign policy disasters as the "loss" of China and the outbreak of war in Korea were strongly linked to what Flynn called in 1949 "this whole great Socialist thrust" at home. Thus although Taft's initial, private reaction had been that his Wisconsin colleague was putting on a "perfectly reckless performance," eventually there was no blinking the fact that on balance McCarthy seemed an asset in fighting the right enemy. One could not spend fifteen years developing a certain viewpoint without sooner or later coming to support someone who used the same vocabulary in the same way both literally and figuratively, and seemed to speak it so effectively.[34]

In the long run, however, McCarthy's approach was a disaster for both Taft and his supporters. Although it was useful to the Republicans for short-term partisan purposes, it utterly failed to reverse the basic trends of the Roosevelt-Truman years. Indeed, the long-run effect of McCarthy's approach was to make Truman's own "anticommunist" policies look moderate and sensible by comparison.

Moreover, Taft and his fellow critics never escaped the pre-1948

34. Richard Rovere, "What Course for the Powerful Mr. Taft?" *New York Times Magazine*, March 22, 1953, p. 9; Flynn to Senator Styles Bridges, March 1, 1949, Flynn MS.; Richard M. Fried, *Men against McCarthy* (New York: Columbia University Press, 1976), p. 68; Patterson, *Mr. Republican*, pp. 444–446.

dilemma of arguing an anticommunist rhetoric at home while trying to limit America's economic and military commitments abroad. Indeed, in supporting McCarthy they worsened their dilemma by widening the gap between their rhetoric and their specific policy positions. For example, Taft opposed both American entry into NATO in 1949 and the commitment of ground troops to Europe in 1951 as financially costly and unnecessarily provocative to the Russians—the same grounds on which he had initially objected to the Truman Doctrine in 1947. He also criticized Truman's unilateral commitment of American combat troops to Korea as yet another executive usurpation of congressional authority.

Flynn, for his part, continued to attack Truman's military spending as economically and politically disastrous. The "military industry," he announced in January 1951, was already the "biggest industry in the United States." Liquidating it would be equivalent to closing down the entire auto industry, the petroleum industry, and the food and clothing industries. America, Flynn warned, was at the "edge of the precipice."

Flynn also echoed Taft's argument that the struggle between the United States and the Soviet Union was primarily ideological rather than military, and he agreed with Taft on the unconstitutionality of Truman's Korean commitment. After June 1950 Flynn warned repeatedly against American support of French "imperialism" in Indochina. In December 1950, Hoover added his voice to this dissenting chorus when he attacked Truman's Asian policy as militarily counterproductive and urged a retreat to a "Western Hemisphere Gibraltar of Western Civilization."[35]

As in the pre-1945 period, however, these critics were handicapped by their own susceptibility to anticommunist arguments and the ability of the administration's supporters to turn their anticommunist rhetoric against them. Taft's susceptibility was never more pronounced than at the start of the Korean War when he announced that although he could not accept Truman's unilateral procedure, he nonetheless agreed with the policy of resisting "communist aggression" militarily. Under wartime circumstances, Taft's support for the mili-

35. LaFeber, *America, Russia, and the Cold War*, pp. 112–113; Flynn to Burton K. Wheeler, January 25, 1951, Flynn MS.; Radosh, *Prophets on the Right*, pp. 174, 252–255; Hoover speech, "Our National Policies in This Crisis," December 20, 1950, PS#3262, HHPL.

tary policy amounted to inviting Truman to ignore his procedural objection—an invitation Truman promptly accepted.

Hoover similarly undercut his own call for a "Western Hemisphere Gibraltar" by suggesting in a follow-up speech in February 1951 that "since Red China [was] making war on our American armies, we should free Chiang Kai-shek to do what he wishes in China and furnish him munitions." Even Flynn, while counseling an "end to the cold war," continued to argue in anticommunist terms, blaming the entire Far Eastern situation on Secretary of State Dean Acheson "and his Communist-ridden State Department."[36]

As before, such arguments only invited retaliation in kind. After the outbreak of the Korean War, self-styled liberals had a field day attacking Truman's critics on "anticommunist" grounds. "McCarthyism," announced the *Nation*, "will have a hollow sound when applied to the government that stood up to the Russians." Having thus defended Truman, the magazine's editors now counterattacked with Clifford's old strategy of linking "left" and "right" in unholy alliance. "Many top Republicans," they noted, "are now following a line almost indistinguishable from that of the Communists. The *Daily Worker* agrees fully with the *Chicago Tribune*'s contention that the President's statement 'is an illegal declaration of war.'"

Late in December, when Hoover announced his proposal for a "Western Hemisphere Gibraltar," the *Nation* replied that "world communism" had "captured for its purposes Herbert Hoover and a good section of the Republican Party." The approach that Hoover, Taft, and their supporters were proposing "should set the bells ringing in the Kremlin as nothing has since the triumph of Stalingrad." Combining anti-isolationist and anticommunist rhetoric, the *Nation*'s editors went on: "Actually the line taken by Pravda is that the former President did not carry isolationism far enough."

The *New Republic* echoed this strategy. Old-line "isolationists," it charged, were "getting ready to shape the Hoover doctrine into an instrument of sabotage" against NATO. Presidential power to "send the armed forces overseas," the journal declared, "has been solidly established by history." In a revealing if inadvertent statement of the shakiness of their position, the editors added a new pejorative to the

36. Radosh, *Prophets on the Right*, pp. 173–174, 251, 260; Hoover radio broadcast, "We Should Revise Our Foreign Policies," February 9, 1951, PS#3268, HHPL.

emerging debate. "There has historically been a working affinity," they noted, "between the isolationists and the *legalists*. . . . There are signs that this coalition is again tightening." (italics added) Taft's opposition to sending troops to Europe, the journal went on, was "based on Hoover, the value of the dollar, and a benign image of the Politburo."

Meanwhile, Taft's pro-NATO colleague, Wayne Morse of Oregon, attacked Taft's position for being "what the Russians themselves have been saying." In the event, not only were Taft's objections beaten down, but he again undercut his own argument by agreeing to send four divisions to Europe rather than the six originally requested by the administration.[37]

Ultimately, it was the Korean stalemate that gave McCarthy his temporary advantage in the situation. However much the outcome could be interpreted as a victory of policy, it was clearly a defeat psychologically, especially considering the expectations raised by General Douglas MacArthur's "home-for-Christmas" offensive launched amid much fanfare in November 1950. Indeed, it was Truman's firing of MacArthur in April 1951, in the midst of the stalemate, that brought to a head the entire post-1948 struggle for the anticommunist label.

As Felix Morley noted at the time, the dismissal unleashed a flood of popular emotion that embraced a spectrum of issues far broader than "anticommunism" itself. Morley's analysis, published in the early stages of the controversy, did not in fact mention "communism" or Korea at all. To him, the essence of the public reaction was a moral revolt against the New Deal tradition of executive domination of government. "It may be," wrote Morley, "that millions of jobholders will never really bite the hand that feeds them and that MacArthur's return, in retrospect, will seem what the French call a *divertissement*. Such a conclusion comes naturally to those who for over eighteen years have increasingly assumed that the American people will meekly accept whatever the White House orders. When one considers how Americans have been cozened during these years—'again, and again and again'—it would not be surprising if they should now once more slip back into that apathetic acceptance of guileful promises on which

37. *Nation*, July 8, 1950, p. 25, December 30, 1950, p. 688; *New Republic*, January 15, 1951, p. 7; Radosh, *Prophets on the Right*, p. 183.

executive tyranny has ever based its Machiavellian build-up." Even so, there was "something about the reception of MacArthur" that truly worried "all those who cluster round the fringes of the Welfare State." Could it be, Morley asked, "that Americans are not really as interested in personal 'security' as Mr. Truman thinks? Could it be that they are really ready to make sacrifices for the ideals that President Roosevelt put in mothballs eighteen years ago?"[38]

In short, MacArthur was a catalyst. What his reappearance had precipitated was a long overdue reaction against growing coercion and false generosity. The public response to his dismissal was a roar of disapproval not so much of Truman's definition of anticommunism as of Roosevelt's definition of liberalism. As with earlier critics, however, the acuity of Morley's policy insight was blunted by his failure to address linguistic issues, particularly the relationship between liberal and anticommunist rhetoric. He failed to make the vital connection between the policies he described and the way they had been sold to the American public.

Morley was not alone in this regard. None of the administration's critics addressed the linguistic issues any more effectively. MacArthur himself was of no help because of his preoccupation with his political ambitions and militant stance toward "Red" China. Moreover, Republican spokesmen such as McCarthy and Taft were unable to resist the temptation of making political capital from the apparent collapse of Truman's Far Eastern policy. Rather than focus on the fundamental domestic issues Morley had attempted to raise, they chose instead to echo MacArthur's anticommunist rhetoric.

The result was that opposition leaders again played into the administration's hands. Defining the situation in anticommunist terms was exactly what Truman needed to keep it from developing into a full-blown debate over the Rooseveltian definition of liberalism. Indeed, the ensuing Senate hearings on the military situation in the Far East turned out to fit Truman's purpose expressly, for they allowed the administration to confine the debate to Far Eastern issues and MacArthur's military strategy.

After MacArthur's lead-off appearance in the hearings, Truman sent Acheson, Secretary of Defense Marshall, and General Omar Bradley,

38. Felix Morley, "Squall or Tidal Wave?" in *Spotlight*, no. 34, undated (1951), Morley MS.

chairman of the Joint Chiefs of Staff, to explain the fallacies in Mac-Arthur's call for a more militant Asian policy. Over and over, Truman's spokesmen hammered away at three themes: the "containment" strategy of limited warfare was working in Korea; America was in step with its European allies; and the adoption of MacArthur's plan would wreck both the strategy and the alliance. In Bradley's famous phrase, MacArthur's proposals would "involve us in the wrong war, at the wrong place, at the wrong time, and with the wrong enemy."[39]

The Senate hearings did not end Truman's political problems. The popular frustration remained to plague him for the balance of his term. Even so, the hearings accomplished one vital purpose: they altered the public mood sufficiently to cause Republican leaders to conclude that they should not risk the 1952 campaign on any candidate too closely identified with MacArthur's excessively militant "anticommunism." That decision eliminated Taft, because he had made a major point of taking MacArthur's side in the controversy, and Taft's elimination in turn meant the end of any broadly gauged ideological challenge to the administration's foreign or domestic policies.

It is in this context that the 1952 campaign takes on its historic significance. The real battle that year was not between the Democratic and Republican candidates, Stevenson and Eisenhower. Because of the Korean situation Stevenson was beaten before he had been nominated. The real battle took place within the Republican party and centered on the choice between Eisenhower and Taft.

There was an element of pathos in Taft's rather desperate efforts to use anticommunist rhetoric to win the prize that had so long eluded him. This is not to impugn the sincerity of his statements in his fourth and final try for the nomination. The same heartfelt antipathy to the administration's policies led him to support McCarthy's domestic attacks and MacArthur's foreign policy criticisms. In short, he was completely sincere in his use of symbol words, though by 1952 the words themselves had clearly warped his political judgment.

Taft had hoped to make considerable political capital of MacArthur's dismissal in spite of his doubts about some of the general's specific proposals, particularly the naval blockade of China and the intimations

39. U.S. Senate, Joint Committee on Armed Services and Foreign Relations. *Hearings on the Military Situation in the Far East* (Washington: Government Printing Office, 1951), pp. 43, 325, 352, 370–371, 742–743.

that the United States should use atomic weapons. Even so, Taft supported MacArthur in demanding that the United States "try to win that war by every means at our command," including bombing the rail lines in Manchuria and "going the limit" in assisting Chiang Kai-shek against the Chinese Communists. America should not make peace, Taft declared, "until we are safely guaranteed a complete Korean republic covering all of Korea."

When questioned about the relationship between his cautious approach to Europe and his more militant approach to Asia, Taft responded that America had "repeatedly assumed the risk of war in Europe, and there is no reason why the same policy should not be followed in Asia." Such statements did not enhance his standing as a foreign policy critic. As one Republican wrote to Dewey: "Taft is very badly discredited by the MacArthur show and has forfeited his reputation for intellectual honesty."[40]

Later that year, Taft published his first and only book. Titled *A Foreign Policy for Americans*, its obvious purpose was to refurbish his badly tarnished image as a foreign policy analyst. Although much of it was devoted to a continuation of his attacks on executive usurpation of power in foreign affairs, the bulk of his recommendations pointed toward a greater rather than lesser "anticommunist" militance. Indeed, after blaming Roosevelt and Truman for creating the "Russian menace," Taft now proposed to fight that menace through American-sponsored underground movements in Eastern Europe. He also apparently accepted conscription as permanent. In a particularly infelicitous rephrasing of his earlier comments on Europe and Asia, Taft wrote: "Certainly our program in Europe seems to me far more likely to produce war with Russia than anything we have done in the Far East. I am only asking for the same policy in the Far East as in Europe."

Even while escalating his anticommunist rhetoric, Taft continued to espouse arguments he had advanced earlier in the name of liberalism. Echoes of his lost identity as a "liberal" resounded throughout his calls to end "reckless government spending and taxation," "reverse the trend toward Big Government and Socialism," and restore "liberty to the conduct of the nation." He was still caught in the old dilemma, however. To support both limited government at home and a policy of

40. Patterson, *Mr. Republican*, pp. 393, 488–491.

potentially unlimited conflict in Asia was simply not convincing. Taft could talk of "liberty and peace," but what came across was a combination of McCarthy at home and MacArthur abroad.[41]

By early 1952, Taft had lost whatever credibility he had had with the powerful eastern wing of his party. Belatedly attempting to dissociate himself from Hoover's "Gibraltar" concept, he continued to back MacArthur and even sought McCarthy's support for his candidacy. Attacked as a "concentrated Tory" and a go-it-alone "isolationist," he was also the target of an extended "Taft Can't Win" campaign led by such influential newspapers as the New York Times. In a clear rejection of both Taft's definition of anticommunism and Hoover's call to make the party a bastion of anti–New Deal "conservatism," the Republicans nominated a popular military hero of unknown economic and social persuasion. Narrow partisan advantage rather than broad ideological confrontation would be the order of the day.

Taft's supporters were under no illusion about the meaning of Eisenhower's nomination. "The two parties we now have," wrote John T. Flynn to General Robert Wood, "have no relation whatever to the issues touching our material and political welfare." Flynn called for "a political organ that takes a clear and unmistakable position." Wood, for his part, was "convinced that sooner or later a new party will be formed combining the Conservative Northern Republicans and Southern Democrats."[42]

Taft himself bravely attempted to put the best face on the situation. "We were fighting for a cause," he told Wood, "to keep the Republican Party certainly free of New Deal influences. . . . We can still carry on that fight both before and after the election." After a two-hour discussion with Eisenhower in early September, Taft issued an optimistic statement to the effect that he was "completely satisfied that General Eisenhower will give this country an administration inspired by the Republican principle of continued and expanding liberty for all as against the continued growth of New Deal Socialism which we would suffer under Governor Stevenson."

Eisenhower himself, however, carefully refrained in his own public

41. Robert A. Taft, A Foreign Policy for Americans (Garden City: Doubleday, 1951), pp. 33–34, 17, 113; Taft to General Robert Wood, April 25, 1952, Robert E. Wood Papers, HHPL (hereafter Wood MS.).

42. Patterson, Mr. Republican, pp. 529–538, 547–562; Flynn to Wood, September 9, 1952, Wood to Flynn, September 15, 1952, Flynn MS.

statements from saying anything that could be interpreted as an assault on the New Deal. His own "anticommunist credentials" beyond question, he concentrated instead on the peace issue and shrewdly promised to "go to Korea" to end the war.[43]

On the Democratic side, the campaign rhetoric was equally calculated. "The strange alchemy of time," Stevenson told an Ohio audience, "has somehow converted the Democrats into the truly conservative party of this country—the party dedicated to conserving all that is best, and building solidly and safely on these foundations. The Republicans, by contrast, are behaving like the radical party—the party of the reckless and the embittered, bent on dismantling institutions which have been built solidly into our social fabric." Stevenson's conspicuous omission of the liberal label was a tacit acknowledgment of the unpopularity of the Truman administration. In attempting to identify himself as a "conservative," he was endeavoring to create a psychological distance between himself and Truman. Unlike Hoover in 1945, however, Stevenson was not repudiating the liberal designation. On the contrary, in applying the conservative label to the New Deal itself, he was attempting to update Clifford's strategy, implicitly claiming two "centrist" labels while associating the Republicans with the "extremist" radical label. The ploy was unsuccessful, as Eisenhower was careful not to say anything that might assist it.[44]

Ideological critics of the Truman administration reacted guardedly to Eisenhower's victory. "Maybe among the blessings of the year 1953," wrote columnist David Lawrence, "will come a new understanding of 'liberalism' and a rescue of the word from those who in the recent past have monopolized it while at the same time imposing further and further restriction on the liberty of thought of the individual." However, with Eisenhower having carefully refrained from assaulting the Roosevelt-Truman use of the word, and with so many former self-styled liberal critics now supporting McCarthy, prospects were not bright for a revival of the definition Taft had espoused in the Omaha address.[45]

Indeed, as the Truman era drew to a close, it appeared that a seven-

43. Taft to Wood, August 8, 1952, Wood MS.; Taft, "Statement in Support of the Candidacy of Gen. Dwight D. Eisenhower," September 12, 1952, ibid.; Goldman, *Crucial Decade*, pp. 233–234.

44. Clinton Rossiter, *Conservatism in America* (London: Heineman, 1955), p. 94.

45. David Lawrence, "What 'Liberalism' Really Means," *Washington Evening Star*, January 2, 1953.

year struggle for the anticommunist label had only reinforced the ascendancy of Roosevelt's definition of liberalism. If anything, the result of all the anticommunist rhetoric on both sides had been to draw attention away from the domestic issues the critics themselves had attempted to address, such as the "military industry," executive power, and constitutional safeguards.

Despite the acuity of their specific policy insights, the critics had come up short again. Neglecting to address the basic issue of analytical categories, they developed no greater conceptual clarity than they had during the Roosevelt era. In particular, their failing to de-reify the word "liberal" prevented them once again from exposing the contradictions built into the administration's use of the word. Indeed, their anticommunist rhetoric served only to camouflage existing contradictions even further by reinforcing Truman's use of coercion in the name of freedom and confiscatory taxation in the name of generous "anticommunist" spending. Under the circumstances, the Republican victory of 1952 would prove a Pyrrhic victory for critics of the New Deal.

Perhaps the most poignant irony of the era was expressed, albeit inadvertently, by journalist Garet Garrett. In a penetrating post-mortem on the Truman administration's policies, Garrett, the man who had first proposed the abandonment of symbol words, set forth two analytical categories that in his view provided the best framework for understanding events of recent years. "We have crossed the boundary that lies between Republic and Empire," he wrote. Boldly sketching out the historic "requisites of Empire," Garrett drew a sharp series of parallels between ancient Rome and contemporary America.

The dominance of the executive branch, the arbitrary use of administrative agencies, the technique of the *fait accompli*, the subordination of domestic policy to foreign policy, the ascendancy of the "military mind," the protection of satellites through a "hired guard," and a "complex of vaunting and fear" were among the characteristics Garrett listed in his concept of "Empire." Most dangerous of all these characteristics was one that defined itself only gradually. "When it is clearly defined," he wrote, "it may be already too late to do anything about it. That is to say, a time comes when Empire finds itself—*A prisoner of history.*"[46]

Again, the policy insights were formidable, and Garrett's parallels

46. Garet Garrett, "The Rise of Empire," in *The People's Pottage* (Caldwell, Idaho: Caxton Printers, 1953), reprinted in *Left and Right*, Winter 1966, pp. 36–53.

between ancient and modern institutions were vivid. Yet in attempting to reify another set of critical categories without coming to grips with the politics of language itself, that is, without de-reifying the categories of those in power, Garrett showed himself to be as much the prisoner of history as those whose policies he described. Meanwhile, only one more step remained in the process of cementing the Rooseveltian definitions into American life. That step would soon be taken.

7

Life in the

Middle of the Road

A man for all labels

> It may or may not be too late to separate . . . subject phrase from
> association with the President, but it is worth a try. At least let the
> Boss and associates quit using it.
>
> "Middle of the Road" plays into the hands of the opposition: it is
> easily synonymized with their "government by postponement, by
> hesitancy and delay, by do-nothing". It also semantically undercuts
> our "dynamic, progressive" program. . . .
>
> We still want to do what is best for all Americans. . . . The way to
> do this may well be the mid-way between extremes. In fact, we think
> it is, but let's not call it "Middle-of-the-Road"!
>
> James M. Lambie, Jr., 1953

The subjectivity of metaphor! What strikes one person as a brilliantly
evocative image may seem to someone else a hopelessly banal cliché. In
politics, however, the choice and use of metaphor are not merely
matters of literary taste. They are matters of high policy strategy.
Moreover, in politics one does not ordinarily reach the inner circle by
contradicting "the Boss" on basic strategic issues. If the name of James
Lambie does not spring to mind as one of President Eisenhower's most
influential advisers, it may be for that reason. To Eisenhower, "middle
of the road" was more than an attractive phrase—it was his chief
political self-designation.[1]

Far from connoting postponement, hesitancy, or delay, "middle of

---

1. James M. Lambie, Jr., "Memorandum for C. D. Jackson," December 14, 1953,
Chronological File: November-December 1953 (1), Box 3, James M. Lambie Papers,
Dwight D. Eisenhower Library, Abilene, Kansas (hereafter Lambie MS.).

the road" suggested to Eisenhower dynamic progress along a carefully delineated route. On the "road of life" (coincidentally the name of a popular radio serial of the day), the middle of the road was not a place to sit but rather a path to travel, "mid-way between extremes," in Lambie's own phrase. "Middle of the road" also had reference to velocity, for it was easier to keep to the middle when one was not careening wildly ahead at immoderate speeds. Maintaining the middle position required judgment, caution, and a certain restraint. Although Eisenhower was often pictured by his opponents as a rather muddle-headed type who preferred an afternoon on the golf links to the serious business of the presidency, he was in fact a thoughtful and remarkably clear-headed strategist in political and military matters. "I recall almost daily," he wrote privately six months after taking office, "an observation attributed to Napoleon that went something like this: 'The genius in war is a man that can do the *average* thing when everybody else is growing hysterical or panicky in the excitement of the moment." Life in the White House, he noted, was a daily struggle "to apply common sense—to reach an average solution." The middle of the road was the common sense or average path to travel.[2]

Most important from a political standpoint, the "middle of the road," as Eisenhower was fond of saying, was "the widest part"; it was where "most Americans live." If one were to preside over the affairs of a great nation, it was essential, as a matter of both strategy and principle, to be in touch with the wishes of the majority. To "go to the middle of the road," he remarked during a June 1953 press conference, did not mean "to turn the clock back." Mixed metaphors notwithstanding, Eisenhower was making an important political point. Most Americans did not want a repeal of social security, collective bargaining laws, or any other major New Deal measure. The point was to move forward in such a way that "the whole power does not get into the Federal Government."

According to an October 1953 White House memo, distributed on Eisenhower's orders to all cabinet officers and heads of executive agencies, the phrase "middle of the road" was already "acquiring and should continue to acquire a positive and aggressive significance." He

2. Eisenhower to Capt. E. E. Hazlett, July 21, 1953, Box 2, Dwight D. Eisenhower Diary Series, Dwight D. Eisenhower Library (hereafter DDE Diary MS.).

was hardly going to abandon the phrase because some opposition spokesmen were attempting to turn it against the administration.[3]

To understand Eisenhower's use of "middle of the road" is to understand a good deal about his use of other, more standard political terms, such as conservative, liberal, progressive, and moderate. Where others tended to use terms like conservative and liberal as opposites, Eisenhower carefully and deliberately used them as complements. His administration, he repeated frequently during his first years in office, would be liberal in "dealing with the relationships between the human in this country and his Government," and conservative "when we deal with the economic affairs of this country." At the same time, he insisted that the "great mass of the people of the United States" wanted "progressive moderates handling their business," and hoped "'progressive moderation' in government" would become "synonymous with the [Republican] party label."[4]

Not all observers were impressed with Eisenhower's ecumenical approach. Adlai Stevenson had a field day ridiculing the president's semantic experimentation when he told a Chicago press conference:

I have never been sure what progressive moderation means, or was it conservative progressivism? [Laughter] I have forgotten, and I am not sure what dynamic moderation or moderate dynamism means. I am not even sure what it means when one says that he is a conservative in fiscal affairs and a liberal in human affairs. I assume that what it means is that you will strongly recommend the building of a great many schools to accommodate the needs of our children, but not provide the money. [Laughter]

Stevenson could poke fun all he wanted, but as he well knew, there was method in Eisenhower's apparent semantic madness. As Eisenhower himself understood, labels tended to evoke general attitudes, some of which might indeed conflict with each other, but many of which were reconcilable if placed in the proper context. For example,

3. Press Conference, June 17, 1953, pp. 20–21, Box 69, James C. Hagerty Papers, Dwight D. Eisenhower Library (hereafter Hagerty MS.); White House memo, untitled, October 1953, enclosed in Eisenhower to Gen. Carroll, November 5, 1953, Box 2, DDE Diary MS. Also see Robert H. Ferrell, ed., *The Eisenhower Diaries* (New York: Norton, 1981), pp. 234, 245.

4. Press Conference, January 27, 1954, p. 29, Box 69; December 8, 1954, pp. 8, 26, Box 70, Hagerty MS.

one could have an attitude of generosity or "liberality" when it came to human suffering, yet maintain a cautious (meaning "conservative") attitude when one actually spent one's money to alleviate distress. Similarly, one could accept the metaphor of "progress," or forward motion, yet wish to move forward at "moderate" speeds.

Eisenhower's purpose was not to sharpen political antagonisms by making specifically contradictory promises but rather to blunt antagonisms by using words to reassure a variety of constituents that the "middle of the road" was wide enough to include them all. More than a decade before Lyndon Johnson explicitly and unsuccessfully called for a "politics of consensus," Eisenhower's rhetoric constituted an implicit and far more successful effort in the same direction. On this basis Eisenhower consciously became a man for all labels.[5]

Of course he had preferences regarding the standard political terms. His private correspondence, office memos, and diary notations indicate that he identified most positively with the progressive and conservative labels. As he wrote privately in November 1954, the Republican party "must be known as a progressive organization or it is sunk." This meant ignoring, and when necessary repudiating, the "died-in-the-wool [sic] reactionary fringe" for whom "labor is merely an item in their cost sheets," and according to whom "labor is guilty of effrontery when it questions the wisdom or authenticity or any statement of management or of financiers." He told a friend that December, "if we could get every Republican committed as a Moderate Progressive, the Party would grow so rapidly that within a few years it would dominate American politics."

And yet, Eisenhower consistently objected to the efforts of columnists to place him "in the so-called liberal wing" of the party. He and Senator Knowland, he observed privately, "agree that we are conservatives." What the party most needed was a unity based on "essentially conservative principles applied to 20th century conditions."[6]

A corollary to Eisenhower's "middle of the road" metaphor was his

5. Eric Goldman, *The Crucial Decade* (New York: Vintage Books, 1960), p. 282. Also see Press Conference, January 27, 1954, p. 30, Box 69, Hagerty MS, in which Eisenhower said he hoped "to make certain that the individuals realize that Government is a friend and is not their enemy in any way."

6. Ferrell, ed., *Eisenhower Diaries*, pp. 288–289; Eisenhower to Clifford Roberts, December 7, 1954, Box 5, DDE Diary MS.; Eisenhower to Meade Alcorn, August 30, 1957, Box 15, DDE Diary MS.

use of the linear spectrum. The "true radical," he wrote at one point, "is the fellow who is standing in the middle and battling both extremes." Among the Republicans, he noted, "you find no extreme leftists." On the other hand, he warned against allowing the "Right Wing" to recapture control of the party. For Eisenhower as for Clifford, the linear spectrum was an indispensable conceptual and political tool. Not surprisingly, the center of the linear spectrum was also the "middle of the road."[7]

Eisenhower also recognized labels not merely as designations but as weapons. Years after leaving office, he recalled a conversation with Taft early in 1953 during which the Ohio senator had expressed himself as favoring certain types of federal educational subsidies and pensions.

When I heard these things, I had to chuckle. "Why, Bob, with those views you're twice as liberal as I am. How did you ever come to be called a conservative?"

"Oh, you know how it is," he replied. "A label like that gets applied to you, and afterwards you just have to live with it."

Throughout his presidency, Eisenhower made it his business to be master of political language rather than its victim. Unlike Taft, he never allowed symbol words to cripple his thinking or undermine his political strength.[8]

The purpose of language was more than the mere preservation of power, however; its purpose was to facilitate the use of that power in shaping American society. Although Eisenhower was far from being a systematic political theorist, he had definite convictions about the fundamentals of contemporary American political economy. The evolution of American government, he wrote privately in July 1953, belied Lenin's "contradictions of capitalism." Lenin's claim that "there were no restraints upon the power of the . . . great corporations and the syndicates" simply was not true. Despite the "short-sightedness bordering upon tragic stupidity of many who fancy themselves to be

7. Eisenhower to Gen. B. G. Chynoweth, July 20, 1954, Box 3, DDE Diary MS.; Eisenhower to Hazlett, December 8, 1954, Box 5, DDE Diary MS.; Eisenhower to Gabriel Hauge, September 30, 1954, Box 4, DDE Diary MS.

8. Dwight D. Eisenhower, *The White House Years: Mandate for Change, 1953–1956* (Garden City, N.Y.: Doubleday, 1963), p. 219.

the greatest believers in and supporters of capitalism," most Americans had learned from long experience to accept legislation that embodied "the requirements, desires, and aspirations of the vast majority." In short, America had learned the "great middle way," which not only included the legitimate "regulation" of corporate power and legislative protection for trade unions, but government action to "encourage pension plans and other forms of social security in our industry." In phrases reminiscent of McKinley's earlier solicitude toward labor, Eisenhower stressed the "practical necessity of establishing some kind of security for individuals in a specialized and highly industrialized age."[9]

To compare Eisenhower and McKinley is to do what Eisenhower's critics were fond of doing for denigrative purposes. Such denigration misses the point. Both men sought an ecumenical appeal through ecumenical language and were remarkably successful in so doing. Moreover, the parallel ignores the unique and timely quality of Eisenhower's vocabulary, for if he was as genially ecumenical as McKinley, he was also as incisively partisan as Clifford. Indeed, like Clifford, Eisenhower took equally careful aim at targets within and without his own party.

Here the "middle of the road" metaphor is vital and again the crucial element is the interplay between discordant meanings. To describe the middle of the road as the "widest part" was to imply *in*clusivity while simultaneously *ex*cluding the extremes. This formula was deliberate. Eschewing any contact with "extreme leftists," Eisenhower also understood the danger from "extreme Right Wing" or "Old Guard" Republican elements that still wished to repeal the New Deal.

To be sure, Eisenhower had his own antipathies to certain New Deal creations (notably TVA). Asked at a press conference if his program was "an extension of the New Deal," he replied that "all the way along we have showed the difference between . . . the philosophy of this Government, and that of the New Deal." The only example he offered, however, was his overall budget reduction, and indeed it was in response to this very inquiry that he first talked about being liberal in "human" affairs and conservative in "economic" affairs. In short,

9. Eisenhower Diary memo, July 2, 1953, Box 5, DDE Diary MS.

Eisenhower's answer was a political one, dictated by the logic of the question and designedly vague.

Again Eisenhower had his reasons. Whatever his personal antipathies, he knew that for most Americans Roosevelt's legislation was fact. He believed that if the Republican "Old Guard" recaptured control of the party and attempted to repeal that legislation, they would destroy the party's influence nationally "within a matter of a few brief years." Eisenhower was determined to use all means to prevent such a result, and the stealing of "Old Guard" thunder by adopting vague anti–New Deal rhetoric was one such means.

More important was the "middle of the road" metaphor itself. Its very imprecision and simultaneous connotations of inclusivity and exclusivity made it the ideal verbal weapon because Eisenhower could use it to set the boundaries of political discussion, legitimizing all dissent within those boundaries and illegitimizing whatever took place outside them. Whatever Eisenhower's personal predilections, his boundaries turned out to be in practice those established by Roosevelt's legislation. Far from attempting to demolish the New Deal, Eisenhower consciously and deliberately undercut those who did.[10]

One measure of his effectiveness is the extraordinary quiescence that characterized American politics throughout his presidency. Often attributed to the lingering impact of McCarthy, that quiescence was far more the result of Eisenhower's political shrewdness, as his handling of McCarthy illustrates. Whereas Democratic politicians loudly criticized McCarthy even as they desperately competed for his "anticommunist credential," Eisenhower calmly and deliberately chose silence and inaction.

This was not cowardice, but a frank recognition that time and the prestige of office were on his side. His own "anticommunist credential" was beyond dispute, and he had no need to compete with McCarthy. Instead he simply outlasted him. Eisenhower chose this option despite repeated and at times almost frantic appeals from his advisers to take up the cudgels against McCarthy. In this as in other situations, Eisenhower adhered to a "common sense" solution while many

10. Press Conference, January 27, 1954, pp. 28–31, Box 69, Hagerty MS.; Eisenhower to Hauge, September 30, 1954, Box 4, DDE Diary MS. Also see Eisenhower to Edgar Eisenhower, November 8, 1954, Box 5, DDE Diary MS.

around him were "growing hysterical or panicky in the excitement of the moment." The result was that when McCarthy finally undermined his own credibility, as Eisenhower knew he would, the president calmly stepped out of the shadows to resume business as usual.[11]

Another reason for Eisenhower's silence during McCarthy's "moment" was that he understood McCarthy's utility to "Old Guard" Republican elements that were trying to recapture control of the party. Eisenhower wanted do nothing to assist them and as early as March 1954 confidently predicted to a friend that the "Old Guard [would] disintegrate with the decline of McCarthy." Indeed, he willingly took a tough behind-the-scenes approach to ensure the accuracy of his own prediction. In a strongly worded letter to Republican governor Craig of Indiana, Eisenhower warned that the party must decide "once and for all to make up its mind whether to follow the ludicrous partnership of the Old Guarders and the Mc-Carthyites . . . [or] to stand behind the program of the Administration and the middle-of-the-road philosophy in which we firmly believe." Eisenhower's blunt language helped bring waverers into line, so that when he finally emerged from the shadows it was as undisputed party leader.[12]

The "middle of the road" metaphor was equally vital to Eisenhower's foreign policy approach. His Indochina policy, he remarked in April 1954, lay in "steering a course between two extremes," one "unattainable," the other "unacceptable." To "see the whole anti-communistic defense of that area crumble and disappear" would be unacceptable. "On the other hand," he added, "you certainly cannot hope at the present state of our relations in the world for a completely satisfactory answer with the Communists. The most you can work out is a practical way of getting along." This, he noted, was the essence of his administration's policy in Europe as in Asia.[13]

As always, domestic and foreign policy rhetoric were complemen-

---

11. Hagerty Diary, May 20, 1954, Box 1, Hagerty MS.; Press Conference, November 18, 1953, pp. 27–28, Box 69; June 2, 1954, p. 21, December 8, 1954, p. 8, Box 70, Hagerty MS. Also see Elmo Richardson, *The Presidency of Dwight D. Eisenhower* (Lawrence: Regents Press of Kansas, 1979), pp. 55–58.

12. Eisenhower to William E. Robinson, March 12, 1954, March 23, 1954, Box 2, William E. Robinson Papers, Dwight D. Eisenhower Library (hereafter Robinson MS.); Robinson to Eisenhower, March 17, 1954, Box 3, DDE Diary MS.; Eisenhower to Governor Craig, March 26, 1954, ibid.

13. Press Conference, April 29, 1954, p. 3, Box 70, Hagerty MS.

tary. Americans needed reassurance that they would not be faced again with the threat of either depression or war. Eisenhower knew that he had been nominated and elected in 1952 largely because of his international prestige, and having gained credit during his first months in office for ending the Korean War, he was determined not to undermine his "peacemaker" image. Yet he was not averse to allowing others in his administration to espouse a more militant, anticommunist rhetoric.

This is the context in which Eisenhower's choice of John Foster Dulles as secretary of state is best understood. Often viewed as Dulles' captive in foreign affairs, Eisenhower was nothing of the sort—rather the reverse was true. Eisenhower knew that Dulles was a self-proclaimed champion of the "liberation" of Eastern Europe. He also knew that Dulles had long nursed the ambition of becoming secretary of state and had worked for years to make himself acceptable to both the Dewey and Taft wings of the party. In short, Eisenhower knew that Dulles' rhetoric would be "tough" enough to let Eisenhower look "moderate" and restrained by comparison, while Dulles' instinct for political survival would render him manageable on sensitive issues.

Most important, Eisenhower had sufficient confidence in himself to know he was capable of controlling Dulles. As early as the 1952 campaign, when Dulles made a speech advocating the "liberation" of Eastern Europe by "all means," Eisenhower immediately telephoned to "inform him," in Walter LaFeber's words, "that the phrase should have read 'all peaceful means.'" Dulles never repeated the error. Later on, at several points during the 1954 Indochina crisis, Eisenhower quietly but firmly overruled Dulles. However frightening to some critics, Dulles' rhetoric ultimately operated to reinforce Eisenhower's image of restraint.[14]

The contrasting verbal styles of the two men were never more apparent than with respect to nuclear weapons. While Dulles talked threateningly of "massive retaliation," Eisenhower calmly reassured reporters that the arms race itself was under control. Asked at his April 7, 1954, press conference if he were not "afraid that Russia will make bigger hydrogen bombs before we do," the president replied

14. Walter LaFeber, America, Russia, and the Cold War (New York: John Wiley, 1980), pp. 139–140; on Eisenhower overruling Dulles, see Garry Wills, Nixon Agonistes (New York: Signet Books, 1970), pp. 129–130.

serenely, "No, I am not afraid of it. I don't know of any reason for building a bigger bomb than you find to represent as great an efficiency as is needed or desirable, so I don't know why bigger ones would do." Projecting an image of restraint, however, did not mean abandoning anticommunist rhetoric altogether, and it was only moments later in the same press conference that Eisenhower enunciated the "falling domino" principle in regard to Indochina and the rest of Asia.[15]

Here in particular one sees the long-run impact of Eisenhower's language, for acceptance of the "domino theory" by successive generations of American policymakers would profoundly affect the lives of millions of Americans and Vietnamese alike. However predictable such consequences might have been (and critics such as John T. Flynn had been warning of American involvement in Indochina since 1950), Eisenhower's image of restraint effectively prevented most Americans from associating the "domino theory" with a potentially dangerous or "extreme" outcome.

This is not to say that Eisenhower himself foresaw such an outcome. He was probably as convinced by his own rhetoric as were his listeners. Nonetheless, the striking lack of public opposition to the "domino theory" in the 1950s exemplifies the larger effectiveness of Eisenhower's "middle of the road" metaphor. In using "anti-extremist" imagery to condition public perceptions of himself, he so defined the situation that anyone who accepted that imagery could not possibly view the administration's policy as having potentially "extreme" consequences. Moreover, as the metaphor excluded from respectability those whom Eisenhower defined as extreme, it also excluded the possibility of viewing Eisenhower himself as "extremist," and thus provided remarkably broad license in the very name of "anti-extremism." In short, the metaphor harmonized the discordancies between inclusion and exclusion, and restraint and license.

This use of restrained language to achieve broad license is nowhere more apparent than in regard to Eisenhower's foreign policy. Like Roosevelt and Truman, Eisenhower insisted on maximal autonomy in foreign affairs, and as Roosevelt's successful fight against the Neutrality Act resulted in a sharp increase in discretionary executive authority, so was Eisenhower's defeat of the Bricker Amendment simi-

15. Press Conference, April 7, 1954, pp. 3, 5, Box 69, Hagerty MS.

larly rewarded. The amendment, sponsored by Taft's colleague from Ohio, John W. Bricker, would have placed severe limits on the treaty-making powers of the president. Eisenhower's conduct during the Bricker Amendment fight not only shows him to have been an extremely shrewd political infighter but indicates he was far more sensitive than Dulles to the requirements of verbal strategy.

Indeed, when Dulles prepared a lengthy draft statement on the amendment in March 1953, Eisenhower responded with a terse two-page memo detailing the flaws in the secretary's approach. It would be neither useful nor appropriate, he wrote, to argue that the amendment "would make the President the 'servant' of the Congress." A far stronger argument was that the amendment would "impede and stifle necessary action in the international field." Even if it were true that the amendment would alter the "traditional relationship" between president and Congress, it would still be better not to use that argument before a congressional audience. It "might best be used," he added dryly, "before public audiences."

Most important was Eisenhower's handling of the narrowly partisan approach indicated in Dulles' draft. He remarked on the "plain implication that, with a different kind of administration, it might be a good thing to adopt such a Resolution." Were this true, the president added, *"then I am for the Resolution."* There was great danger, he noted, in opposing the amendment on the grounds that "the current one is a *good* administration." The "whole argument of your paper," Eisenhower bluntly informed Dulles, *"should* be based upon principle and on Constitutional wisdom, rather than personal ability and wisdom of individuals."[16]

Eisenhower's response was a masterpiece of both sophistication and disingenuousness. It was important indeed to be selective about vocabulary and audience. Also, argument from principle was generally more effective than argument ad hominem. And yet Eisenhower well knew that all these elements were not enough: his personal reputation and image were his most important political assets in the fight, for without them even argument from principle would have had little impact.

The defeat of the Bricker Amendment was followed shortly by the

16. Eisenhower, "Memorandum for the Secretary of State," April 1, 1953, Box 4, DDE Diary MS.

Formosa Resolution and eventually by the Middle East Resolution or the so-called Eisenhower Doctrine. These resolutions gave the president what amounted to standby authority to use American combat troops in the Formosa Straits and the Middle East and thereby extended executive discretion far beyond what Roosevelt and Truman had had.[17]

As the fight over the Bricker Amendment demonstrated Eisenhower's acuity regarding immediate verbal strategy, his subsequent recollections of it similarly attested to his continued awareness of the long-term implications of ideological labels. "I have heard it said," he wrote in his memoirs,

> that the struggle over the Bricker Amendment was in reality a contest between "liberals" and "conservatives" or between "isolationists" and "internationalists." Yet [Treasury Secretary] George Humphrey, to name just one, who had always classed himself as a conservative, was flatly opposed to the amendment. And certain senators, usually known as liberals, on both sides of the aisle, voted for the [substitute] George amendment. . . . My brother Edgar, a lawyer who always liked to refer to himself as a "constitutional conservative," argued hotly . . . that the amendment was absolutely necessary to save the United States from coming disaster. My own opinion was that the contrary was true.

The passage is instructive for what it says as for what it omits. Eisenhower refused to be labeled either "liberal" or "internationalist" because of his opposition to the Bricker Amendment and was determined even in retirement not to be boxed in by other people's categories. What the passage omits and in fact camouflages is his mastery in setting forth his own categories as weapons against his opponents: he himself freely utilized the isolationist label as a damaging pejorative, and even more important, he subtly reshaped the conservative label in both domestic and foreign policy.[18]

In fact, one cannot understand Eisenhower's "middle of the road" rhetoric except in conjunction with his use of the conservative label.

17. LaFeber, *America, Russia, and the Cold War*, p. 203; Richardson, *Presidency of Dwight D. Eisenhower*, p. 53.

18. Eisenhower, *Mandate for Change*, pp. 284–285. For Eisenhower's use of the isolationist label, see, for example, Eisenhower to Robinson, March 23, 1954, Robinson MS.

When he told a 1954 Lincoln Day audience of Republican faithful not to be "afraid" to use the word "conservative," he was responding to a pronounced public reaction against the cumulative costs of twenty years of growing federal power. Republicans, he remarked, were not afraid to talk of "balanced budgets," of "cutting expenditures," of "all the kind of thing that means this economy must be conservative, it must be solvent."

To talk of solvency, however, was not to talk of dismantling the New Deal, and Eisenhower was careful never to use the word "conservative" to suggest an attack on basic New Deal legislation or more recent social programs. In the same Lincoln Day speech, he repeated his familiar formula about being conservative in "economic" affairs and liberal in "human" affairs. He assured his listeners that his administration was concerned with "every American's" health, housing, and education and added that the objective of the Republican party was to ensure that "every individual American" would have both "the opportunity of a free citizen" and "a sympathetic partner . . . in the Federal government."[19]

What Eisenhower was doing amounted to stealing Stevenson's strategy, for in claiming both major labels he was leaving his opponents in an ideological wilderness. Unlike Stevenson, Eisenhower was not burdened with responsibility for the Truman record, so the strategy that had not worked for Stevenson worked very well for Eisenhower. Yet, that strategy had more far-reaching implications because in redefining conservatism to make it complementary to liberalism, Eisenhower was bringing the conservative label within the bounds of his "middle of the road" consensus. And in so doing, he was undercutting those "Old Guarders" who still hoped to use the conservative label as an anti–New Deal rallying cry. As Roosevelt had snatched their liberal label twenty years earlier, Eisenhower now took away their conservative label and did so at the very height of its revived popularity.

This was a crucial development. Slowly, carefully, implicitly at first, then more explicitly as time went on the president attempted to reverse the anti–New Deal connotations long attached to the conservative label by New Deal supporters and critics alike. In a diary entry in June 1959,

19. Remarks at Uline Arena, Lincoln Day Supper, February 5, 1954, Box 6, Speech Series, Dwight D. Eisenhower Library.

Eisenhower recalled that exactly six years earlier he had had a long discussion in the White House with former president Hoover about the latter's belief that "for twenty years the conservatives and middle-of-the-roaders, had discerned a drift toward greater governmental controls—or at least interference—in the nation's economy." Hoover had pointed out that "the curve representing the interference of government into private life, private business, and into the responsibilities of states and cities, had risen rapidly and steadily over the past twenty years." The former president had observed that although it was "impossible to take this curve and bend it sharply downward," Eisenhower could certainly strive for "a flattening of the curve in this particular trend." Should he be successful, Hoover added, this would be "an achievement that would be long remembered."[20]

Considering the length of the discussion and the time between its occurrence and Eisenhower's written recollection of it, one may reasonably doubt that his account was accurate in every detail. The very phrase "middle-of-the-roaders," for example, was almost certainly his own rather than Hoover's. The memo is also ambiguous about whether either man expressed a hope that some future administration might be able to start bending the curve downward again. Still, the memo is instructive because although Eisenhower clearly agreed with Hoover's prescription for "flattening out the curve," and also identified with the conservative label, there was a strategic job to be done within the Republican party and Eisenhower was determined to do it. He could agree with Hoover's immediate policy prescription and even identify with the same label, yet the connotations he was already attaching to the label were opposite to those Hoover had attached to it since 1945. In Eisenhower's hands, the conservative label would be refashioned to connote acceptance rather than rejection of the New Deal.

By October 1955 that refashioning was explicit, as evidenced when Gabriel Hauge (Eisenhower's administrative assistant) addressed the Commonwealth Club of San Francisco, the very audience before whom Roosevelt had given one of his most important campaign speeches in 1932. Hauge's address, titled "The Economics of Eisenhower Conservatism," described the president's "philosophy" as "dynamic conservatism." Eisenhower, Hauge announced, had "used a

20. Ferrell, ed., *Eisenhower Diaries*, pp. 364–365.

new term because we live in a day when old labels are no longer understood in the traditional sense, when 'liberalism' and 'conservatism' have taken on new meanings, when millions of Americans are seeking a new way to describe their political faith." The president's "dynamic conservatism," Hauge declared, centered on "conserving" four basic aspects of the American economy: the "system of free markets and private initiative"; the "tradition of incentive and reward"; the "integrity of the people's money"; and the "market mechanism when the government must act to avert a depression or inflation." When either of the latter consequences threatened, the solution was "indirect" stabilization measures such as money and credit policy, tax adjustments and public debt management, rather than direct measures "such as price and wage controls, export-import controls, and materials allocations." Government, in short, "should attempt to influence the economic weather and not try to ration raindrops."

At the same time, Hauge announced, the Eisenhower conservative was "no standpatter" because "history does not stand still," and change was "the law of life and adjustment to it . . . the condition of life." This attitude meant recognizing and accepting the "profound changes [that] have occurred in our habits and institutions in the last quarter century," such as the new governmental programs which "met real needs" and had "been integrated into the American way." Rather than repeal these programs, the Eisenhower conservative proposed "to improve upon them and to adapt them to the needs of a vital, self-reliant, and fundamentally united people."

Beyond this, the Eisenhower conservative believed that although an annually balanced budget was still a primary fiscal objective, an occasional "departure in the direction of overbalance" could offset an "overexpanded economy," and a "departure in the direction of a deficit" could offset an economic contraction. To "keep the economy dynamic" government must provide "appropriate" support for research and development, vigorous leadership in reclamation and conservation, and a "partnership policy" with respect to energy and power. Only an expanding economy could make "economic bulb-snatching . . . as obsolete as it has always been wrong" and create a society "where your 'more' need not be my 'less.'" In short, Eisenhower conservatism envisaged a government "with both a head and a heart."

"Dynamic conservatism" had foreign policy implications as well.

The Eisenhower conservative, Hauge announced, sought "to conserve and strengthen economic ties among free nations" through international trade and competition. An economic system based on international specialization could "contribute more to the health of both the domestic and the world economy than can economic nationalism and autarchy." Hauge's comments specifically reflected Eisenhower's determination to overcome lingering Republican opposition to the reciprocal trade agreements program as well as his larger concern to redefine conservatism as coextensive with his own approach.[21]

In his memoirs Eisenhower described the Hauge address as a "resounding summary of the economic philosophy of my administration," but it was far more than that. The very phrase "Eisenhower conservatism" contained a discordancy in its implying an innovative definition of a term that connoted traditional or unchanging values. The point of the rhetoric was to harmonize the same discordancy between tradition and innovation that McKinley had harmonized. In McKinley's case, the accusations of "imperialism" had constituted an implicit and indirect challenge to his "conservative credential," whereas in Eisenhower's the challenge was explicit and direct, and for this reason the timing of Hauge's address is instructive.[22]

By the fall of 1955, McCarthy was in disgrace and as Eisenhower had predicted, "Old Guard" Republicans were already in a much-weakened political condition. The partnership had cost them heavily, and the success of the president's strategy was now forcing them to seek alternative ways of maintaining an effective opposition to the administration's policies. The ensuing struggle for the conservative label is best understood in this context, for what emerged from 1955 onward was not merely a challenge to one of Eisenhower's many labels, but a challenge to his "middle of the road" rhetoric, his ecumenical appeal, and indeed his efforts to force the Republican party to accept the New Deal. Because of the stakes involved, the struggle invites attention as the most important verbal contest of the decade.

21. Hauge Address, "The Economics of Eisenhower Conservatism," October 14, 1955, Eisenhower Conservatism 1955 Folder, Box 20, Staff Files: Special Assistant Re Government Public Service Advertising, Dwight D. Eisenhower Library.
22. Eisenhower, *Mandate for Change*, p. 488.

The struggle for the conservative label

The commands of common sense call upon conservatives to associate with moderate liberals in "the vital center." The rules of American politics, which they cannot be expected to ignore, force them to associate with immoderate conservatives on the Right, as no one knows better than President Eisenhower. There is no cheap solution to this problem, which in one form or another faces conservatives everywhere in the world, but those who are aware of it will be better prepared to live with it. They must, in any case, temper the "radicalism" of the extreme Right with the long view and steady habits of genuine conservatism. They must find the demagogue of the Right every bit as distasteful and dangerous as the demagogue of the Left.

Clinton Rossiter, 1955

Conservatives in this country—at least those who have not made their peace with the New Deal, and there is serious question whether there are others—are nonlicensed nonconformists; and this is dangerous business in a Liberal world.

William F. Buckley, Jr., 1955

Nothing spotlights the political importance of language better than a pitched battle over definitions, for defining the words defines the situation and shapes people's perceptions of the available options. At first glance, the positions taken by political scientist Clinton Rossiter and publisher William F. Buckley, Jr., appear as polar opposites. For Rossiter, "genuine conservatism" meant associating with "moderate liberals" in "the vital center" and accepting the New Deal. By contrast, Buckley defined conservatives as those "who have not made their peace with the New Deal" and who related to "liberals" only on adversarial terms. Beginning with its inaugural issue in November 1955, Buckley's journal, *National Review*, carried a regular column, "The Liberal Line," written by Willmoore Kendall. In his opening contribution, Kendall castigated Eisenhower as "a dependable anti-Republican Republican."[23]

Although Rossiter and Buckley differed sharply in their attitudes toward the New Deal and Eisenhower, analysis of their respective

23. Clinton Rossiter, *Conservatism in America* (London: Heineman, 1955), pp. 300–301; *National Review*, November 19, 1955, pp. 5, 3.

vocabularies reveals the limits of their debate and the reasons for its outcome. Both writers accepted without question the linear spectrum and its corollary, the reification of "communism." Rossiter referred to the "demagogue of the Left," Buckley to the "practicing Communist, with his inside track to History." To both men, "genuine conservatism" was "genuinely anticommunist."

Viewed from this perspective, Rossiter and Buckley were reenacting the Truman-Taft debate of 1948 with one difference. Truman and Taft had competed over the liberal and anticommunist labels, and agreed that liberalism and anticommunism were complementary. Rossiter and Buckley were competing for the conservative and anticommunist labels on the premise that they were the true complements. There had been a major shift from liberal to conservative rhetoric.

The rhetorical shift was itself political. After 1948, Taft had joined Hoover in giving up the fight for the liberal label and adopting instead the conservative as a rallying cry. In so doing Taft had adopted Hoover's position that conservatism, defined as opposition to the New Deal, was the only true anticommunism. Eisenhower had in turn undercut their strategy by using conservative rhetoric to legitimize the New Deal. Thus in reasserting the opposition between "conservatism" and the New Deal, Buckley was not only attempting to revitalize resistance to the New Deal itself, but challenging Eisenhower's "conservative" and "anticommunist" credentials.

This challenge helps explain the failure of the anti–New Deal opposition during the Eisenhower era. Their struggle for the conservative label was in reality a mere continuation of Taft's struggle for the anticommunist label. They offered nothing more original and nothing more positive. Taft had competed with Truman for the anticommunist label and lost. Competing with Eisenhower for that label was even more of an exercise in futility. After McCarthy's failure, there was no reason why Buckley and his associates should have hoped to succeed. Their very attempt only undermined their credibility while reinforcing Eisenhower's own "middle of the road" image.

Taft himself had stated the problem during the 1952 campaign. Eisenhower, he wrote privately, was "inclined to be conservative," but "four-fifths of his supporters" were not, and it "would be more difficult to combat a Republican New Deal than a Democratic one." In his public statement of support for Eisenhower that September, Taft had attacked the "New Deal Socialism" represented by Stevenson and had stated his conviction that Eisenhower supported the Republican policy statement of February 1950 which presented clearly "the issue of liberty against Socialism."[24]

In noting the difficulty of combating a "Republican New Deal," Taft had effectively pinpointed one aspect of the opposition's dilemma while his vocabulary inadvertently revealed a second. So long as opposition leaders themselves remained susceptible to the lure of anticommunist rhetoric and defined the New Deal as "socialist" or "communist," they would offer only a negative self-definition and alternative. It was a problem neither Taft nor his successors in the anti–New Deal opposition ever resolved. On the contrary, the combination of Taft's death in the summer of 1953, McCarthy's subsequent disgrace, and Eisenhower's shrewdness led a surviving but much weakened opposition to cling ever more desperately to the hope of eventually turning anticommunist rhetoric to political advantage.

Of those in this group who remained active throughout the 1950s, no case was more poignant than that of John T. Flynn. During the 1930s and 1940s Flynn had consistently offered penetrating critiques of Roosevelt's relationship to large corporations as well as the relationship between military spending and an illusory "prosperity." Unimpressed by Truman's efforts to "police" the Far East, Flynn had delivered prescient warnings regarding American support for the French war in Indochina. After attempting to expose the contradictions in Roosevelt's liberal and antifascist rhetoric, Flynn had also attacked Truman's anticommunist rhetoric.

For all his insight, however, Flynn never moved beyond competing for these same labels, never reached de-reification or the confrontation with the politics of language itself. As he grew ever more frustrated and bitter, he became increasingly caught up in his own vocabulary, especially his postwar reification of domestic "communism." By 1951 he was not only supporting McCarthy but writing privately about the need to "purge the Pinkoes out of the Republican Party." By December 1952 he was personally congratulating McCarthy on the latter's plan to "have a look at the Reds in our schools."[25]

For Flynn, now in his seventies, the Eisenhower years were the

24. Patterson, *Mr. Republican*, p. 574; Taft, "Statement in Support of Eisenhower," September 12, 1952, Wood MS.

25. Flynn to Senator Karl Mundt, May 21, 1951, Flynn to McCarthy, December 30, 1952, Flynn MS.; and Ronald Radosh, *Prophets on the Right: Profiles of Conservative Critics of American Globalism* (New York: Simon and Schuster, 1975), pp. 259–260.

most frustrating of all. Although he had supported Taft for the Republican nomination, he initially hoped that anti–New Deal critics within the party would still be able to "reach Eisenhower's mind." But the hope quickly gave way to renewed anger. By March 1954, Flynn was writing to Senator Karl Mundt: "The prosperity built on war by Roosevelt, Truman, and which Eisenhower hopes to continue, is about to crack up." Then in December 1954 came the censure of McCarthy by his Senate colleagues.

Flynn was furious. He voiced particular contempt for Eisenhower's failure to defend McCarthy. Flynn wrote to Mundt ridiculing the president's attitude toward "communism and socialism" and denouncing Republican National Chairman Leonard Hall for making "the ridiculous remark that Eisenhower was fighting communism long before Joe McCarthy was." In further explication of Eisenhower's views, Flynn added: "I think he is very definitely a collectivist, but I am sure he couldn't, if his life was at stake, define it or state with accuracy the limits to his collectivism. . . . I am confident that Eisenhower is now preparing to make a deal of some kind with Russia. The only thing that deters him is a fear of the effect."[26] Flynn's joining in the challenge to Eisenhower's "anticommunist credential" left him, for the moment, firmly in the Buckley-McCarthy camp. In the long run, however, it was an unstable alliance.

Unlike Buckley and McCarthy, Flynn had always recognized the danger of a foreign policy based on ideological crusading. So while Flynn continued to espouse a militant anticommunist rhetoric on domestic issues, he continued his efforts to limit America's international commitments. In contrast, Buckley and McCarthy defined anticommunism as a unitary policy that demanded maximal militance at home and abroad.

By the end of 1956 Flynn was at odds with both men. The split with Buckley came in October when the latter refused to publish an article by Flynn critical of military spending. In Buckley's view, Flynn failed to appreciate the "objective threat of the Soviet Union." Barely a week later, when McCarthy released a statement suggesting that Britain, France, and Israel deserved "moral support" in the Suez crisis for "seeking to curb the power of the communist-supported Nasser re-

26. Flynn to Gen. Robert Wood, December 18, 1952, Flynn to Mundt, March 15, 1954, December 9, 1954, Flynn MS.

gime," Flynn immediately wrote to McCarthy expressing amazement at his position. The invasion, Flynn wrote, was "an appalling example of that age-long policy under which one country after another has felt the heels of these two international marauders." Flynn concluded sadly, "I feel we have lost a great captain."[27]

If the events of 1956 had left Flynn isolated even within the opposition, Buckley and his associates at *National Review* actually fared little better. As the electoral rematch between Eisenhower and Stevenson drew near, the journal's editors found themselves deeply divided over a Hobson's choice between two candidates whom *National Review* had enthusiastically damned as "Liberal." Buckley's approach to the problem was at once courageous and revealing. Rather than attempt to hide the emerging split within his staff, he chose to use it as a vehicle for focusing attention on the issues of the day. Readers of the October 20, 1956, issue of *National Review* found themselves treated to a full-fledged debate between editors James Burnham and William Schlamm on the question "Should Conservatives Vote for Eisenhower-Nixon?"

Burnham argued that they should. "I sympathize," he wrote, "with those conservatives who have become so disappointed with Dwight Eisenhower and his Administration that they refuse to support him, and will either abstain or vote for some . . . third-party try." Such a position, though understandable, was "incorrect" because of "the drive of our opponents who at present prevail . . . in both parties" and whose aim was "to label American conservatives as a 'lunatic fringe,' to push us into a side alley, and to rule out all genuine conservative ideas as 'hopeless extremism'." To combat this drive, "conservative" critics had no alternative but to remain within the two-party system, the "Main Street of American politics."

Burnham tried to sweeten the pill by noting that there was still a difference between the parties and he felt "a little better at having Foster Dulles and Herbert Hoover, Jr., in the State Department, rather than Chester Bowles and Arthur Schlesinger, Jr." On economic issues, the Republican party was "at any rate *less* socialist, *less* statist than the Democratic Party." Finally, Burnham argued, there was the all-important question of whom "the Communists" would support.

27. Radosh, *Prophets on the Right*, pp. 272–273; teletype press release by McCarthy, November 2, 1956, and Flynn to McCarthy, November 2, 1956, both in Flynn MS.

"We should not underestimate the political intelligence of the Communists," he noted. "The analysis that has led the Communists, without ceasing to be Communists, to support Stevenson-Kefauver, calls with equal cogency for conservatives, without ceasing to be conservatives, to support Eisenhower-Nixon." The "negative lineup" was in fact a "conclusive consideration."

Schlamm presented the counterargument. "Mr. Dwight Eisenhower, an inconsistent Liberal," he wrote, "is in firm control of the Republican Party. For conservatives, the strategic job in this year's election is to break that control. It can be broken only by defeating Mr. Eisenhower." Stevenson, Schlamm contended, was "*not* the greater evil." Indeed, "conservatives" ought to "prefer a Liberal Administration *opposed* by the Republican Party to a Liberal Administration *supported* by it." He warned against supporting "a Liberal President who can deliver *both* parties to the Liberal Establishment." Stevenson, Schlamm argued, would "do plenty of damage, but his Administration will be neither much less nor, indeed, much more revolutionary than Mr. Eisenhower's." In fact, there was a "good chance that Mr. Stevenson would be chased out of town for a policy that Mr. Eisenhower gets away with."

After acknowledging that he could not bring himself to vote for Stevenson, Schlamm announced that he would vote only for congressional candidates and abstain from the presidential contest, thereby indicating that he did not harbor a secret wish for an Eisenhower victory. Eisenhower's reelection bid, Schlamm concluded, was "indeed the bid for final Liberal control of the Republican Party." Therefore whoever wished to "rally American conservatism around and within the Republican Party" would necessarily "wish for the defeat of Mr. Eisenhower."[28]

The Burnham-Schlamm debate well illustrates the difficult situation in which Eisenhower's competitors for the conservative label found themselves in 1956. Burnham's fear of becoming isolated from the "Main Street" of American politics was an inadvertent acknowledgment of the effectiveness of Eisenhower's strategy. By forcing the bulk of the Republican party to come to terms with the New Deal, he had placed any remaining anti–New Deal critics squarely on the defensive. As Burnham put it, the danger was that in staking out their own

28. *National Review*, October 20, 1956, pp. 12–14.

competing claim to the conservative label, critics were rendering themselves vulnerable to the charge of "extremism."

What Burnham failed to realize was that it was not their opposition to New Deal legislation per se, but rather their militantly pro-McCarthy, anticommunist rhetoric that made critics so vulnerable. Their very competition for the anticommunist label, and in particular their attempts to label the New Deal "socialist" and "communist," made the charge of "extremism" credible even while reinforcing Eisenhower's own "moderate" image. Of equal importance in this context was the negativity of the critics' approach. Conservatism defined as anticommunism was still conservatism defined negatively, whereas Hauge had defined "Eisenhower Conservatism" positively and listed a broad range of achievements Eisenhower wished to "conserve."

Schlamm had a clearer grasp of the situation. Where Burnham defined the problem in anticommunist terms, Schlamm saw it as one of breaking Eisenhower's control of the party, which could not be broken if Eisenhower were allowed a second term. Accepting Eisenhower meant falling into the "middle of the road" trap, which anti–New Deal critics could not afford. The strategic enemy was not "Communism" but "Liberalism," and only by defeating Eisenhower could critics hope to save the Republican party from the permanent control of "the Liberals."

However insightful of intraparty politics, Schlamm's analysis still left self-styled conservative critics facing two difficulties. One was the dilemma of opposing Eisenhower himself. If he lost, they could be blamed for his defeat and drummed out of the party, whereas if they opposed him and he won, they could find themselves discredited and isolated entirely. The second difficulty was no less severe. Although not based on anticommunist rhetoric, Schlamm's position was nonetheless a negative one in that conservatism defined as opposition to "the Liberals" was still conservatism negatively defined.

In the event, Eisenhower was overwhelmingly reelected, winning even more decisively than in 1952. However one assessed the difficulties facing his self-styled conservative critics, it was clear that negative self-definition had not strengthened them, for only in time of imminent or actual castastrophe could such an approach be politically effective, and Eisenhower had neither lost a war not presided over a depression. Like Truman in 1948, Eisenhower undoubtedly benefited in 1956 from tensions abroad, particularly the Hungarian and Suez crises. As in Truman's case, the benefits accrued to Eisenhower because he combined a credible "anticommunist credential" with an image of restraint. Having played his cards brilliantly, he had only to hold to his "middle of the road" position at home and abroad.

Although the events of 1956 reflected both the isolation of veteran critics such as Flynn and the weakness of Buckley and his associates, in the long run it was neither Flynn nor the Buckley group who emerged with the greatest loss of intellectual independence during the Eisenhower era, but rather critics such as Rossiter, who in supporting the "vital center" emerged as custodians of Eisenhower's definition of the situation. To examine Rossiter's vocabulary is to confront an analytical confusion peculiarly illustrative of the mid-1950s. In postulating a postwar "revival of conservatism in American politics and culture," Rossiter listed Eisenhower along with Hoover and Taft as the three "most distinguished figures" among modern American "conservatives." After having thus reified both "conservatism" and "conservatives," Rossiter went on to say, "As to specific policies, which one must forbear to think of as inherently conservative or liberal, most new conservatives can be counted on for the present to support the long-range policies, if not all the short-range maneuvers, of President Eisenhower."[29]

Rossiter's declaring the labels inapplicable to specific policies while still relying on them to categorize people was only one aspect of his confusion. Equally dangerous was his unquestioning acceptance of Eisenhower as a "conservative," for apart from reifying both "conservatism" and "conservatives," Rossiter's approach was a classic example of transforming the political categories of the political arena into the analytical categories of social science. Although Buckley had similarly reified the labels, he had done so as an open and acknowledged partisan. Rossiter's vocabulary, however, brought scholarship itself into a custodial relationship with the president's views.

Rossiter's utilization of the linear spectrum ultimately emerges as the most serious aspect of his custodianship. His denouncing the "demagogue of the Right" as "every bit as distasteful and dangerous as the demagogue of the Left" was a specific way of distancing himself from McCarthy supporters such as the Buckley group. Yet, the broader impact of this symmetrical denunciation of the "extremes" was

29. Rossiter, *Conservatism in America*, pp. 2–3, 203, 294.

precisely the same as that of Eisenhower's adoption of the "middle of the road" metaphor. In both cases the result was to narrow the boundaries of acceptable political debate to illegitimate anyone who still attacked the New Deal. Once again the professor reinforced the president.

Of all the political effects American social science scholarship had in the 1950s, this reinforcement of Eisenhower's definition of the situation was the most significant. Indeed, Rossiter was but one of several scholars who lent their talents and prestige to the assault on the "extremes." This group also included Columbia University sociologists Daniel Bell and Seymour Martin Lipset and historian Richard Hofstadter. In 1955, the same year in which Rossiter's book *Conservatism in America* first appeared, Bell brought together essays by Hofstadter, Lipset, and others with an introductory essay of his own, and published them under the title *The New American Right.* The anthology quickly became a standard reference work for students of contemporary American politics.

Like Rossiter's volume, *The New American Right* is notable not only for its explicit political content but for the political perspectives implicit in the vocabularies of its contributors. An examination of their use of language reveals a custodianship at once more subtle and more direct than that of Rossiter. The subtlety lies in their introduction of what was at the time an innovative analytical concept; namely, "status politics."

The social turbulence of "mid-century America," Bell argued in his introductory essay, had been "born not of depression, but of prosperity." Far from having eliminated "all social problems," prosperity had brought "new social groups, new social strains and new social anxieties" such as those of "prosperity-created 'status groups' which, in their drive for recognition and respectability, [had] sought to impose older conformities on the American body politic." The purpose of the anthology was to shed light on "the role of status groups as a major entity in American life and status resentments as a real force in politics."[30]

Subtlety in political analysis lies not in what is explicitly stated but in what is left implicit and assumed, and thereby rendered beyond

30. Daniel Bell, ed., *The New American Right* (New York: Criterion Books, 1955), pp. 4, 16.

argument. By juxtaposing "prosperity" and "status anxieties," Bell and his colleagues not only assumed (without ever stating or proving) a general American prosperity but implicitly illegitimated the very anxieties they were analyzing by denying them any connection with genuine political or economic grievances. The term "status" itself lent an aura of irrationality to those accused of being preoccupied with it. In addition, by superimposing the vocabulary of "status politics" on the traditional linear spectrum, the contributors linked the assumption of irrationality to a direct and devastating attack on Eisenhower's self-styled conservative critics.

Like Rossiter, Bell and his colleagues viewed McCarthy as a secondary target, a mere catalyst. The primary target in both cases was that diverse yet vocal group of Americans who, in Lipset's words, stood "opposed to the social and economic reforms of the last twenty years, and to the internationalist foreign policy pursued by the successive Administrations in that period." This group Lipset dubbed the "radical right" because it sought "to make far-reaching changes in American institutions" and "eliminate from American political life those persons and institutions which threaten either its values, or its economic interests."

Accepting Rossiter's analytical categories, Lipset noted that "conservative elements" in America were divided into "the moderate conservatives and the radical right." The two groups could be "differentiated by their attitude toward the New Deal era." The "moderates" were generally willing to accept the "Roosevelt reforms" and the labor movement as well as "the policies of Roosevelt in the last war." They also believed in "constitutional processes, civil liberties, and due process."

The "radical right," on the other hand, refused "to accept the recent past," and was "radical in the quixotic sense that it rejects the status quo." Irrationally threatened by the developments of the last twenty years, and unable to find a rational justification for its fears, the "radical right" sought to "explain" the "calamitous errors" of those years in terms of "the penetration of the government and the agencies of opinion formation by the Communist movement." It was the "radical right," with its irrational fixation upon "communism," that provided the backbone of the new "status politics."[31]

31. Ibid., pp. 166, 189–190.

Whereas Lipset used the terms "radical right," "extreme right," and "extreme conservatives" interchangeably, Hofstadter chose a different approach. Although he labeled the "new dissent" both "extreme" and "right-wing," he denied that it was either "radical" or "conservative." Instead he borrowed a term from Theodore Adorno's *The Authoritarian Personality* and described it as "pseudo-conservative" because "its exponents, although they believe themselves to be conservatives and usually employ the rhetoric of conservatism, show signs of a serious and restless dissatisfaction with American life, traditions, and institutions." Hofstadter described the distinguishing characteristics of "pseudo-conservatives" in this way: "They have little in common with the temperate and compromising spirit of true conservatism in the classical sense of the word, and they are far from pleased with the dominant practical conservatism of the moment as it is represented by the Eisenhower administration. Their political reactions express rather a profound if largely unconscious hatred of our society and its ways—a hatred which one would hesitate to impute to them if one did not have suggestive evidence both from clinical techniques and from their own modes of expression." As the term "status" imputed irrationality to Eisenhower's critics, so the introduction of "clinical techniques" into Hofstadter's discussion was a particularly powerful form of attack, for it suggested something medically unsound about the "pseudo-conservative" mind. Hofstadter noted that on the basis of "clinical interviews and thematic apperception tests," the Adorno study had established that "pseudo-conservatives" showed "conventionality and authoritarian submissiveness" in their conscious thinking and "violence, anarchic impulses, and chaotic destructiveness in the unconscious sphere." Hofstadter quoted Adorno: "The pseudo-conservative is a man who, in the name of upholding traditional American values and institutions and defending them against more or less fictitious dangers, consciously or unconsciously aims at their abolition."

Hofstadter admitted to having some difficulty identifying adherents to "pseudo-conservative" ideology because such individuals could not be identified by social class, although the appeal of the "pseudo-conservative impulse" was largely to "the less-educated members of the middle classes." Similarly, the "ideology of pseudo-conservatism" could be "characterized but not defined, because the pseudo-conservative tends to be more than ordinarily incoherent about politics."

After thus rescuing himself from the difficulty of defining what he was attacking, Hofstadter offered a list of "representative" examples of the "pseudo-conservative" mentality. These included "the most ardent supporters of the Bricker Amendment," "many of the most zealous followers of Senator McCarthy," and a woman who had "stalked out of the Hilton Hotel" in Chicago after Eisenhower's nomination, exclaiming, "This means eight more years of socialism." In addition, Hofstadter identified the "pseudo-conservative" as one who "is opposed to almost everything that has happened in American politics in the past twenty years" and who "hates the very thought of Franklin D. Roosevelt."

Deriding the "pseudo-conservative" as one "who does not think much about the world outside and does not want to have to do so," Hofstadter declared: "It will be the fate of those in power for a long time to come to have to conduct the delicate diplomacy of the cold peace without the sympathy or understanding of a large part of their own people." From "bitter experience," he added, "Eisenhower and Dulles are learning today what Truman and Acheson learned yesterday."[32]

In supporting Eisenhower's "practical conservatism" and denying his critics their claim to the conservative label, Hofstadter was being even more explicitly custodial of Eisenhower's position than Lipset. Yet, Hofstadter shared Lipset's fundamental reliance on the linear spectrum, for he continued to locate Eisenhower's critics on its "extreme right wing."

For all their apparent preoccupation with one "wing" of the spectrum, however, the contributors to *The New American Right* were at one with Rossiter and Eisenhower in launching a symmetrical assault on both "extremes." As Rossiter found the "demagogues" of the "left" and "right" equally distasteful and dangerous, so Bell and his colleagues argued that "communists" on the "left" shared responsibility with the "radical right" for the current American malaise. Lipset specifically stressed the "contribution of the Communist Party to current coercive measures" in America: "The presence of a foreign controlled conspiracy which has always operated partially underground, and which engages in espionage has helped undermine the basis of civil liberties. Democratic procedure assumes that all groups will play

32. Ibid., pp. 35–37, 53.

the game, and any actor who consistently breaks the rules endangers the continuation of the system. In a real sense, extremists of the right and left aid each other, for each helps to destroy the underlying base of a democratic social order."

Bell agreed. "As a conspiracy," he wrote, "rather than as a legitimate dissenting group, the Communist movement is a threat to any democratic society. And, within the definition of 'clear and present danger' a democratic society may have to act against that conspiracy." Yet, he added, the "tendency to use the Communist issue as a political club against other parties or groups (i.e. to provide an ideological guilt by association), or the tendency to convert questions of law into issues of morality (and thus shift the source of sanctions from courts and legitimate authority to private individuals), imposes a great strain on democratic society."[33]

There was irony in both the logic and vocabulary of the argument, for the similar and complementary illegitimacy of McCarthy supporters and "communists" (the "extremists of the right and left," as Lipset put it) not only promoted precisely the kind of "ideological guilt by association" that Bell condemned but illegitimated in the name of "democracy" any definition of "democratic society" other than that of the "vital center." In addition, by using the "communist conspiracy" theme to undercut the "radical right," Lipset and Bell again demonstrated the value of anticommunist rhetoric to supporters rather than critics of the administration.

Lipset recognized the political weakness of Eisenhower's critics in this respect. The "radical right," he wrote, "has not succeeded in building even one organization of any political significance." This failure was "not accidental, or a result of inept leadership," but stemmed from the fact that "the only *political* issue which unites the various supporters of radical right politicians is anti-Communism." It was hard to build an organization around a negative self-definition. Lipset also recognized that turning the opposition's anticommunist rhetoric against them would leave them devoid of not only organization but their main negative issue. It was therefore not accidental that the symmetrical use of the linear spectrum emerged as the final "punch line" of Lipset's own article.[34]

33. Ibid., pp. 233, 29.
34. Ibid., pp. 214, 233 (italics in original).

Despite the common assault on the "extremes," *The New American Right* did contain an unresolved disagreement between Hofstadter and Lipset with respect to the use of the conservative label. Bell did not resolve it. Preoccupied with "status politics," he used the conservative label only three times in his entire introductory essay. Far from being a limitation on the custodial function of the anthology, however, this unresolved linguistic conflict neatly mirrored and reinforced Eisenhower's own position.

For all his efforts to redefine conservatism, Eisenhower never needed to deprive his critics of all connection with the label in order to turn back their challenge. All he needed was to secure acceptance of his own "conservative credential." In fact, to accept the Rossiter-Lipset dichotomy between "moderate and extreme conservatives" was to accept Eisenhower's definition of the situation because it allowed one to "be a conservative" while accepting the New Deal. At the same time, the term "extreme" put critics beyond the pale of respectability, and in so doing nicely complemented the simultaneous inclusivity and exclusivity of Eisenhower's "middle of the road" metaphor.

There was a paradox in the situation. If Buckley sought to reaffirm the Rooseveltian categories while altering popular responses to those categories, Eisenhower sought to modify the categories in order to solidify the Rooseveltian political boundaries. The "two conservatives" dichotomy served Eisenhower's purpose very well, and thus a tactical reshaping of the conservative label had the ultimate strategic effect of reinforcing the broader Rooseveltian perspective.

Years later, Eisenhower noted in his memoirs that although the Republicans had "failed to regain control of either House of Congress" in the 1956 election, the "national ticket" had "swamped the Democratic nominees" and thus demonstrated that the nation had "approved the administration's policies and the performance of the past four years." Eisenhower could afford to be pleased. Approval of his policies was far more important than having a Republican-controlled Congress.

The 1956 election was more than a personal victory, however. It was a warning to congressional Republicans in all but the safest localities that they would survive politically only by accepting what Eisenhower referred to on election night as "Modern Republicanism," meaning his "middle of the road" approach. By 1957 he would be defining his conservatism as fighting only against "needless" expansion of federal power, and on this basis called for a "unity based on . . . essentially conservative principles applied to 20th century conditions."[35]

In the circumstances it is understandable why some contemporary analysts saw the events of the late 1950s as heralding an end to any meaningful ideological debate in America. By reifying the linear spectrum and its cognates, and accepting Eisenhower's own subsequent claim that his policies won support from "the vital and massive American Center," one can indeed extrapolate a generalized "exhaustion of ideology" in the late Eisenhower era. When one moves from reification to critical examination of political vocabulary itself, however, another picture emerges.[36]

Political labels and the apparent end of ideology

Few serious minds believe any longer that one can set down "blueprints" and through "social engineering" bring about a new utopia of social harmony. At the same time, the older "counter-beliefs" have lost their intellectual force as well. Few "classic" liberals insist that the State should play no role in the economy, and few serious conservatives, at least in England and on the Continent, believe that the Welfare State is "the road to serfdom." In the Western world, therefore, there is today a rough consensus among intellectuals on political issues: the acceptance of a Welfare State; the desirability of decentralized power; a system of mixed economy and of political pluralism. In that sense, too, the ideological age has ended.

Daniel Bell, 1960

In social science as in politics, the wish is often parent to the belief. To assert a consensus on "political issues" provided a reassuring outcome, particularly after Bell's earlier warning that the "conversion of questions of law into issues of morality" was dangerous to democratic society. As he had put it in 1955, "The tendency to convert issues into

35. Dwight D. Eisenhower, *The White House Years: Waging Peace, 1956–1961* (Garden City, N.Y.: Doubleday, 1965), p. 19; memo of conversation with Hauge, February 13, 1956, Box 5, DDE Diary MS.; Eisenhower to Alcorn, August 30, 1957, Box 15, DDE Diary MS.

36. Eisenhower, *Waging Peace*, p. 154; on the "end of ideology" debate, see below.

ideologies, to invest them with moral color and high emotional charge, invites conflicts which can only damage a society." By contrast, "pluralism"—or, in Bell's words, the acceptance of "a plurality of norms and standards, rather than the exclusive and monopolistic social controls of a single dominant group"—was both a stabilizing and a healing phenomenon. The triumph of "pluralism" over "McCarthyism" signified the survival of a healthy balance between consensus and diversity in American society. In this sense the "end of ideology" was not to be mourned but celebrated.[37]

Political scientist Michael Paul Rogin has since suggested that the "pluralist" analysis contained in *The New American Right* and other writings of the time was itself based on a broad distrust of "the masses" and an instinctive sympathy for "elites." Rogin notes that because of their own preoccupation with "irrational mass movements" Hofstadter, Lipset, and the others mistakenly traced the origins of McCarthy's support to an earlier "agrarian radicalism." Rogin argues that the political purpose of "pluralist" analysis was to undermine "mass politics" and restore confidence in "responsible elites." He concludes that "pluralism may best be judged not as the product of science but as a liberal American venture into conservative political theory."[38]

Like the terms "radical," "liberal," "conservative," "McCarthyism," and so on, the terms "pluralist" and "pluralism" are political labels to which no "correct" definitions can be ascribed. To the extent that Rogin assumes such definitions, his analysis emerges as an exercise in reification and misses the historical effects the language itself had on the situation he is analyzing. Within these limits, however, he provides a fundamental and powerful insight into the political content of the writings he has discussed. These writings were designed to illegitimate both whatever political behavior their authors defined as radical and "ideology" itself for being, as Bell put it, "morally colored" and "emotionally charged."

Illegitimization of "mass politics" and "ideology" went hand in hand because it was "the masses" who were notoriously susceptible to the

37. Daniel Bell, *The End of Ideology: On the Exhaustion of Political Ideas in the Fifties* (Glencoe, Ill.: Free Press, 1960), pp. 373, 29; Bell, ed., *New American Right*, p. 27.

38. Michael Paul Rogin, *The Intellectuals and McCarthy: The Radical Specter* (Cambridge: M.I.T. Press, 1967), pp. 27, 44, 282.

irrational appeals of "ideologized" rhetoric, whereas "elites" were more rational and less prone to "convert issues into ideologies." As Rogin's analysis suggests, there was an irony in the "end of ideology" argument, for in reifying such labels as "the Welfare State," "pluralism," "the radical Right," and so on, Bell's "serious minds" were accepting a vocabulary as value laden, morally colored, and emotionally charged as the "ideological" vocabulary they condemned. Roosevelt's success in the political use of language had been such that the evocative impact of his political categories had come to be generally taken for granted. Furthermore, the struggle by the Buckley group to reshape popular responses to those categories indicated their ongoing political significance. The academic vocabulary of the 1950s was equally political.

In fact, because it was based on reification of both the linear spectrum and the Rooseveltian categories, the "end of ideology" argument was not a statement of intellectual independence but an act of custodianship which indicated an inability to transcend the intellectual limits of Roosevelt's vocabulary. Far from demonstrating an "exhaustion of political ideas" within society as a whole, the argument was a projection of the hopes, fears, and intellectual limitations of its adherents.

In political terms, the main result of the "end of ideology" argument would be to leave its adherents unprepared for the social upheavals of the 1960s. Those upheavals would not only expose the superficiality of the consensus of the previous decade but the intellectual limits and political implications of the linear spectrum itself as well. Indeed, in the late Eisenhower era there was already emerging an American political phenomenon that both challenged and transcended traditional political categories. That phenomenon was the struggle for racial equality led in the first instance by Dr. Martin Luther King, Jr. and his associates.

In a world of continuing social violence, the moral stature of Dr. King's abiding faith in nonviolent action stands out ever more clearly with the passing years. At the same time, linguistic analysis highlights the equally significant fact that Dr. King himself never identified with any of the popular political labels, whether of the linear spectrum or its cognates. Nor were his contemporaries able to assign him such a label. To label him would have been to demean and limit the moral and political implications of nonviolence itself. Finally, and for the same reason, historical analysis has failed to find convincing traditional categories through which to integrate Dr. King and nonviolent action into a traditional interpretation of American politics.[39]

This is not to say that Dr. King and nonviolent action defy explanation; on the contrary, they require it. The point is that the very task of providing such an explanation forces one to transcend traditional categories and confront the relationship between political language and political action.

That Dr. King himself never used traditional labels was not accidental. If Eisenhower as a head of government sought an ecumenical appeal by being a man for *all* labels, Dr. King as a private citizen relying on moral suasion sought an even higher ecumenical level by being a man *above* labels. The reason for the difference is clear. For Eisenhower, political action meant utilizing the machinery of government and a vocabulary that would legitimize and secure his control of that machinery. For Dr. King, political action meant direct nonviolent voluntary action by private citizens, so he used a vocabulary that would have the broadest possible appeal to conscience.

For Dr. King, language was more than a means to voluntary action, however. It was a means of promoting direct nonviolent confrontation with the government itself. Herein the significance of his approach emerges most clearly. In the confrontation with unjust laws, nonviolent direct action became nonviolent civil disobedience, the object of which was to redefine social problems as arising from the presence of government rather than its absence. Nonviolent civil disobedience pointed not toward the augmentation of laws but their diminution.

What Dr. King and his associates thus did was to resurrect Hamlin Garland's insight about the need for "fewer laws and juster interpretation thereof." Although this in itself was a development of tremendous political importance, by adopting the technique of nonviolent civil disobedience they were going far beyond what Garland and earlier, like-minded critics had proposed. Dr. King was not merely moving outside the legal boundaries of the system itself, but challenging the

39. It is of course difficult to prove a negative, but no writer of whom I am aware has attempted to classify Dr. King as "liberal" or "conservative" or to assign him a place on the linear spectrum. Alonzo L. Hamby, *Liberalism and Its Challengers: F.D.R. to Reagan* (New York: Oxford University Press, 1985), pp. 139–182, devotes an entire chapter to him, enlarging at length on his popularity with "white liberals" but without ever applying the liberal label to Dr. King himself.

very moral and rational foundations of that system in a most powerful fashion.

Here one specifically confronts the relationship between nonviolent direct action and the social science assault on "mass politics" in the late Eisenhower era. For critics such as Bell, the danger of "mass politics" lay precisely in its reliance upon irrational, "morally colored" and "emotionally charged" rhetoric. To study the rhetoric of Dr. King and his associates in the late 1950s is to confront a vocabulary as morally colored and as emotionally charged as any in American history. It was, after all, primarily a religious rhetoric, specifically meant to mobilize masses of people. To label it irrational, however, is to make a political and arbitrary judgment.

Nor did nonviolent direct action, even when it took the form of civil disobedience, "shift the source of sanctions from courts and legitimate authority to private individuals." The point of nonviolent civil disobedience was not to ignore, evade, or flout the law but to subject oneself to its consequences and thereby force the government and citizenry alike to confront the moral and rational basis of the law itself. Because its impact depended not on coercion but on an appeal to conscience, civil disobedience had to be used with great discrimination in order to be politically effective. In short, nonviolent direct action combined a moral and emotional rhetoric to mobilize masses of people in a manner that put the onus of immorality and irrationality not on the masses but on the government.[40]

Under the circumstances, it is understandable that critics of "mass politics" did not attempt to apply their thesis to the struggle for racial equality. To do so would have had devastating consequences for the thesis itself. Yet, so long as Dr. King and his associates confined their activities to challenging the more visible segregation laws, those activities could still be labeled in a way that evaded the larger relationship between nonviolent direct action and the American political system.

The label used, of course, was "civil rights," a Reconstruction-era phrase that implied a category of political action separate from larger issues of economic and social structure. In the 1960s, as Dr. King and other leaders broadened their activities, they would burst the bonds of such labeling. During the 1950s, however, it was still politically

40. See, for example, the discussion of nonviolence, ibid., pp. 152–154.

possible to segregate antisegregation activities from their larger political context, so that "serious minds" could applaud the "civil rights movement" and still believe in the "end of ideology."[41]

Not surprisingly, Eisenhower himself described the struggle in terms of traditional labels. His own position on school desegregation, he noted early in 1956, was that of a "moderate." Being consistent in his "middle of the road" rhetoric, he later wrote that his administration's approach that year had been one of steering "a difficult course between extremist firebrands and extremist diehards." In a specific reference to racial issues he afterward described his policies as having won support from "the vital and massive American Center." Eisenhower also noted that his approach had encountered initial obstruction from several Democratic senators "who normally proclaimed themselves champions of 'liberalism,' and the 'little people.'" These "liberals," he wrote, had "joined conservative southerners" in attempting to delay consideration of his 1957 "civil rights legislation."[42]

The jibe says much about how Eisenhower and many of his contemporaries defined the situation. By using quotation marks he was at once distancing himself from the liberal label and challenging the Rooseveltian equivalence between liberalism and federal intervention. Yet in linking opposition to such intervention with conservatism he was disregarding his own reshaping of the latter label while reinforcing the Rooseveltian definition of that term.

However inconsistent Eisenhower was with respect to his usage of labels, he was in this case underlining two important points: first, he insisted, even in retrospect, on controlling verbal politics (consistency was less important than mastery); second, his language reflected "standard" usage among those who defined political action as federal intervention and described themselves as "liberal" or "conservative" depending on whether they supported or opposed such intervention.[43] In short, Eisenhower's thinking reflects the imposition of the Rooseveltian categories on the struggle for racial equality,

41. There were two Civil Rights Acts passed during Reconstruction, in 1866 and 1875. See George Brown Tindall, *America: A Narrative History* (New York: Norton, 1984), pp. 682, 721. Also see Bell's brief comments on "civil rights" and the "Negro community" in his 1962 essay "The Dispossessed," in Daniel Bell, ed., *The Radical Right* (New York: Anchor Books, 1964), pp. 23, 42. This was an updated and expanded edition of the original *New American Right* anthology.

42. Eisenhower, *Waging Peace*, pp. 152, 154–156.

43. Ibid., pp. 155–156.

though Dr. King and other participants in nonviolent direct action did not define the situation in such terms.

Here, however, language reflected and reinforced a contradiction within the situation itself. The target of nonviolent direct action was what Dr. King called "unjust laws," chiefly on the state level. Insofar as he and his associates initially sought federal intervention, they did so for the purpose of dismantling these state laws, as in their federal suit against segregated buses in Montgomery, Alabama. In this sense even their request for federal intervention pointed toward "fewer laws and juster interpretation thereof," whereas the phrase "civil rights legislation" implied a countervailing power in the form of additional new legislation. Thus while nonviolence itself pointed toward a diminution of governmental power, the dominant rhetoric of the political arena pointed in the opposite direction.

Considering the racial situation in the late 1950s, the emergence of the contradiction is understandable. Mass nonviolent direct action was a new and relatively unfamiliar phenomenon to most Americans. For those not involved in such action and skeptical of its potential, countervailing federal power seemed at least a necessary complement. Perhaps because of the high visibility of state-level segregation laws, it was also easy to view state and federal power as wholly antagonistic on this issue. The only apparent danger of increased federal power was that it might be insufficiently applied, that is, "watered down."

Nor could the leaders of nonviolent direct action themselves be expected to refrain from utilizing the momentum created by apparently "friendly" federal legislation. Passage of the Civil Rights Act of 1957 was quickly followed by an announcement that Dr. King's newly created Southern Christian Leadership Conference (SCLC) would attempt to register two million new black voters. Eventually, the limits and dangers of increased federal involvement would become apparent. For the balance of the Eisenhower era, however, the tendencies toward nonviolent direct action and countervailing federal power continued to develop side by side.[44]

Although the struggle for racial equality posed the most immediate challenge to traditional thought and action, it was not the only such challenge to emerge during the era. Midway through Eisenhower's

44. Tindall, *America*, p. 1244.

second term, a new challenge began to develop, in ways reciprocal to the first. Where the racial struggle was primarily domestic with international implications, the new challenge initially centered on foreign policy and had domestic implications. Where the racial struggle at first ignored traditional vocabulary and thus threatened to transcend it, the foreign policy challenge began thoroughly immersed in traditional labels and thus threatened, albeit inadvertently, to lay bare fundamental contradictions within those labels.

The new foreign policy critics shared certain common ground with Eisenhower's self-styled conservative opponents. Both groups stressed the continuities in policy of the Roosevelt, Truman, and Eisenhower administrations, and both used the term "liberal" as a pejorative. In all other important respects, however, the new critics were as far removed from the anti-Eisenhower "conservative" perspective as from the perspective of Eisenhower himself.

The new critique was based neither on a commitment to "anticommunist" crusading nor a perception of the New Deal as "communist." It stressed instead that twentieth-century American foreign policy had been continuously formulated in terms of a corporate-government alliance. Defining that alliance as "capitalist" and seeing no possibility of breaking the alliance short of an abandonment of "capitalism," the new critics tended to describe themselves as "socialist." To distinguish themselves from the prewar and wartime "old left," which had largely disappeared with the postwar "anticommunist" crusade, the new critics labeled themselves "new left." By 1959 they had launched a journal, *Studies on the Left*, which featured historical articles critical of American "imperialism."

That the new critics described themselves as "left" and wrote critically about "liberals" provides an important clue to their later strengths and weaknesses. The "left" label implied both diagnosis and prescription and would render them attractive to some and anathema to others. The pejorative use of the word "liberal," intended as a rejection of Wilsonian and Rooseveltian policies, would also have a mixed political impact.

Most important, however, was the effect of the new critics' vocabulary in limiting their own understanding of both the evolution of policy and the potential for ideological realignment. Their "left" label notwithstanding, what the new critics were actually doing was reviving many of the concerns of Roosevelt's self-styled liberal critics, especially their opposition to "militarism" and an "American Century" approach to foreign policy. Under the influence of such teachers as William Appleman Williams of the University of Wisconsin, self-styled "new left" students began reexamining the careers of such earlier critics as La Follette, Borah, Hoover, and Taft. Early in 1959, Williams published *The Tragedy of American Diplomacy,* which called on Americans to abandon "open door economic expansion" in favor of an "open door for revolutions."[45]

The self-styled "new left" remained very much a fledgling movement in the late Eisenhower era, insufficient in numbers or influence to attract much attention from the administration. There was one group, however, that immediately noticed the new critics, and reacted in deeply hostile fashion. This was the Buckley group, which saw in the new critics' rejection of the "anticommunist" crusade a direct challenge to the position taken by *National Review.* That journal's review of Williams' book set the tone for future confrontations between the two groups.

M. Stanton Evans began his review by stating that the current "struggle for direction of America's foreign policy" was "the century's most important controversy." Basing himself on the linear spectrum, Evans declared that those "on the left" were frightened of nuclear war, whereas those "on the right" feared the continued successes of Soviet intrigue, but neither group was focusing on the most dangerous menace of all, the internal one. Life's "greatest terror, to a sane man," wrote Evans, "must always be the possibility of losing his sanity. If he cannot exert some reasonable control over his own system of responses, there is no external force so negligible that it might not prove his undoing." The Williams book, Evans suggested, showed that "America is now confronted with a danger of just this sort; namely, that its reasoning class—the segment of the population that deals professionally in ideas—has given over the orderly employment of reason." In short, Williams was insane.

Evans noted that because Williams' book united "relativism's imprisoning fakery with a blunt defiance of most known truth concerning its subject," it was one of the most frightening he had ever read: "Its

45. William Appleman Williams, *The Tragedy of American Diplomacy* (Cleveland: World, 1959), pp. 204, 212. All other references are to the 1972 Delta Books edition, unless otherwise indicated.

theme is that the United States, since it is verbally committed to libertarian forms of government, is guilty of something called 'open-door imperialism,' which now seeks to thwart the interests—implied to be legitimate—of the Soviet Union." Ignoring the fact that Taft and other critics had attacked American "imperialism" in the late 1940s and had explicitly conceded (without morally approving) a Soviet sphere of influence in Eastern Europe, Evans instead concentrated on Williams' call for an "open door for revolutions." "This kind of analysis," he concluded, "offered as sober counsel on foreign relations by an American professor, sends more chills through me than any vision of atomic holocaust, or the lurking menace of Soviet power. Other dangers may promise death in the future; this is death here and now."[46]

The vehemence of Evans' reaction was an unintended if prophetic compliment on the importance of Williams' analysis. Within a few years *The Tragedy of American Diplomacy* would emerge as the seminal critique of American foreign policy for an entire generation of teachers and students. Of equal significance was the fact that Evans did not explicitly attack Williams as "left." Nor did the book itself call on Americans to take a "leftist" position on domestic or international matters. Williams' very omission of the label marked his analysis as being equally compatible with old anti–New Deal "liberal" and "new left" premises—common premises that the label of the new critics would ironically obscure. These shared premises also made Evans' rejection of Williams a corollary to Buckley's earlier break with Flynn.

The common denominator linking Flynn and Williams was of course their rejection of the "anticommunist" crusade abroad, and this was the reason for *National Review*'s rejection of both of them. By the mid-1960s, the reassessment of anticommunist rhetoric would become the most important issue in American foreign policy and provide a potential meeting ground for critics who identified with both ends of the linear spectrum. Although Williams himself did not confront the politics of language, his book would nonetheless help set the stage for subsequent inquiry into the ideological content and political implications of the linear spectrum itself. By the mid-1960s, that inquiry would be well under way.

For the balance of the Eisenhower era, however, the new critique

46. *National Review*, April 25, 1959, pp. 23–25.

of foreign policy was confined to a relatively small number of icono-clastic academics. The rhetoric of "civil rights" continued to dominate public discussion of racial issues and anticommunist rhetoric of foreign policy. In the 1960 election campaign, Democrat John F. Kennedy neatly combined an emphasis on his party's domestic Rooseveltian heritage with an attack on Eisenhower's "anticommunist" record abroad. Buoyed by the Rooseveltian legacy and a growing popular frustration over the presence of a "communist" government "ninety miles from home," Kennedy narrowly defeated Nixon. As in 1948, a combination of liberal and anticommunist rhetoric carried the day. [47]

Years later, in an oftquoted postpresidential valedictory, Eisen-hower wrote:

If the nation should turn decisively . . . toward sound fiscal procedures in government, toward less intrusion into the business and individual lives of the nation, toward depending more, in pursuit of national objectives, upon the initiative and ambitions of its millions of citizens and localities and toward methods calculated to prevent further erosion in the value of our currency, then the future would hold encomiums for my administration as the first great break with the political philosophy of the decades beginning in 1933. . . .

On the other hand, if the citizenry should adopt and the federal govern-ment should intensify its practice of the theories of recent Democratic admin-istrations, then the growth of paternalism to the point of virtual regimentation would so condition the attitude of future historians that our time in office would be represented as only a slight impediment to the trend begun in 1933 under the New Deal.

The statement is often taken as proof that Eisenhower was not a "New Dealer" at heart. Such an interpretation, though accurate on his ideological preferences, nonetheless misses the point with respect to the impact of his years in office. Faced with the responsibilities of power, he consciously determined not to let personal predilection override political judgment. For all his antipathy to what he called "New Deal stuff," he reiterated time and again the political impos-sibility of "turning the clock back." [48]

47. For texts of various Kennedy campaign speeches, see "Senate File" and "1960 Campaign File," esp. Boxes 910–916, 995, Pre-Presidential Papers, John F. Kennedy Manuscripts, John F. Kennedy Library, Boston, Mass. (hereafter JFK MS.)

48. Eisenhower, *Waging Peace*, p. 654. See the interpretation in William Leuchten-burg, *In the Shadow of FDR: From Harry Truman to Ronald Reagan* (Ithaca: Cornell University Press, 1983), pp. 53, 61.

One is inevitably led back to the definition of the situation which Eisenhower espoused while in office; that is, his ecumenical use of labels and "middle of the road" metaphor. That metaphor in particular stands out as his most important contribution to the evolution of American politics, for not only did it define a political style, but served to dispatch recalcitrants within his own party, cement the Rooseveltian boundaries, and co-opt supposedly critical scholars into a custodial relationship to his views.

Most important of all, the "middle of the road" metaphor not only helped to reify the linear spectrum, but allowed adherents to define themselves in opposition to the "extremes." Such self-definition could have only one result, for defining oneself as "anti-extreme" meant defining one's policies as "safe." Thinking one has found the "middle of the road" precludes perceiving one's enthusiasms as having potentially "extreme" consequences. When reinforced by the "end of ideology" argument, Eisenhower's "middle of the road" metaphor would leave Americans intellectually and emotionally unprepared for the conflicts and upheavals, domestic and international, that were to follow. The middle of the road would prove a dangerous place to live.

8

The Era of Negative
Self-Definition

The decline of the Rooseveltian vocabulary

A people who have been real to themselves because they were *for* something cannot continue to be real to themselves when they find they are merely *against* something.

Archibald MacLeish, 1949

Liberalism . . . seeks not only the negative challenges of Communism and survival, but the far more searching challenge of our own ideals.

John F. Kennedy, 1960

I confess that I know who is a conservative less surely than I know who is a liberal.

William F. Buckley, Jr., 1970

LIBERAL. 1. Noun. One who dreams of a golden future built on the previous decade's failed ideas. 2. Adjective. Of, relating to, or characteristic of a school of thought which holds that it is better to spend than to tax, but better to tax than to do nothing at all.

CONSERVATISM. A philosophical vacuum whose time has come.

Russell Baker, 1976

Albert Einstein once remarked that the splitting of the atom had "changed everything save our mode of thinking and thus we drift toward unparalleled catastrophe." There are times in human history when the avoidance of catastrophe is contingent on a change in "modes of thinking." Such change requires more than the recognition of scientific and technological advance; it requires recognizing that old intellectual categories no longer work and that a new vocabulary is needed.

Americans developed no new vocabulary in the years after Eisenhower despite the vast changes in the nation and in the world at large. The Rooseveltian vocabulary, modified and assimilated into Eisenhower's "middle of the road" metaphor, continued to dominate political thinking, and Americans still classified political leaders and their programs as "liberal" or "conservative." If columnist Russell Baker's demolition of the labels indicated the degree to which they had lost intellectual respectability since Roosevelt's death, it also indicated that no new intellectual categories had arisen to replace them. In short, Baker's "definitions" were a commentary on the intellectual bankruptcy of American politics. As Roosevelt had initially inherited the "good" labels by default, so almost half a century later the Rooseveltian vocabulary itself persisted by default.[1]

Baker's demolition was at once masterful and timely. Fifteen years after Eisenhower's retirement, American politics was in a state of ideological paralysis. During the 1960 campaign, John F. Kennedy could still talk of "liberalism" as seeking out the "searching challenge of our own ideals," and four years later his running mate and successor could still climb atop an automobile and exclaim enthusiastically, "We're in favor of a lot of things and we're against mighty few," thereby defining his own "liberalism" in positive terms as ever-greater governmental generosity. Even so, the massive federal programs of the sixties produced no lasting solutions to social problems, and a decade later, as Baker suggested, the term "liberal" evoked for many people an image of frantic spending on the part of politicians anxious to avoid the appearance of inaction.

Similarly, during the same 1960 campaign, Richard Nixon could tell interviewer David Susskind, "I'm conservative, may I say, because I want progress, not because I'm against it." By the end of yet another decade in opposition, however, self-styled "conservative" pundit William Buckley was confessing to knowing more surely who were his enemies than his friends, and within two years of Nixon's own resigna-

1. Archibald MacLeish, "The Conquest of America," *Atlantic Monthly*, 184, 2 (August 1949); Kennedy address to New York Liberal party, September 14, 1960, Senate File, PPP, Box 911, JFK MS.; William F. Buckley, Jr., ed., *American Conservative Thought in the Twentieth Century* (New York: Bobbs-Merrill, 1970), p. xviii; and *New York Times*, June 1, 1976.

tion as president, the term "conservative" tended to evoke, in Roosevelt's words, the image of an opposition "doing nothing—waiting for the other fellow to put his foot in it." At this level of generality, neither of the two major labels explained much or commanded much respect. In such circumstances, it was understandable that by the mid-1970s, rising politicians such as Jerry Brown and Jimmy Carter were carefully equivocating on both labels, not wishing to be too closely identified with either one.

As Baker's commentary also suggested, however, the Rooseveltian labels were by no means obsolete. In the absence of a newer, more compelling vocabulary, they retained evocative power with particular audiences in particular situations. Thus on the eve of the 1976 election, in his famous *Playboy* interview, Carter described the Democratic platform as "very liberal, very socially motivated." And two years later, Brown capped his successful campaign for reelection to the governorship of California by resurrecting Eisenhower's old ecumenical approach, arguing in favor of a "middle path" and claiming to be both "liberal" and "conservative."[2]

Such utterances were highly revealing of American politics in the post-Eisenhower years. Considering the domestic frustrations and the foreign policy disasters of the sixties, the seventies should have been a time of reassessment. Instead, like another postwar decade fifty years earlier, the seventies became yet one more instance of lost opportunity, of retreat from a confrontation with failure. A peculiar irony of the retreat was the rise of the prefix "neo." To talk of "neo-liberals" or "neo-conservatives" was to suggest new perspectives on old ideas; yet the innovative content of these labels was minimal and their usage merely a further indication of the intellectual bankruptcy of the era.

There was, however, an important difference between the two postwar experiences. Apart from the disinclination to confront failure too closely, what had kept the rhetoric of progressivism and liberalism alive in the 1920s was a still widespread faith in governmental activity, a

2. Lyndon Johnson's 1964 campaign remark is quoted in William L. O'Neill, *Coming Apart: An Informal History of America in the 1960s* (Chicago: Quadrangle, 1971), p. 119; Nixon's comment to Susskind, made on the "Open End" interview show, May 15, 1960, is quoted in "What Nixon Said," a compilation of Nixon quotations, p. 624, in 1960 Campaign File, PPP, Box 1023, JFK MS. Carter's *Playboy* interview is quoted in William Leuchtenburg, *In the Shadow of FDR: From Harry Truman to Ronald Reagan* (Ithaca: Cornell University Press, 1983), p. 315 n. 16; and Brown is quoted in the Vancouver (B.C.) *Sun*, October 25, 1978.

sense of unfinished business with respect to the prewar era. By the 1970s, that faith was badly eroded, despite the efforts of such people as Brown and Carter to sustain and rekindle it. What remained for many Americans was not so much faith in government as a fear of change and of the consequences of admitting a loss of faith; hence their continued susceptibility to a familiar vocabulary and perspective.

In such circumstances there was also a powerful temptation to search for scapegoats rather than alternatives. Retention of an old vocabulary and an old perspective allowed Americans to do the former rather than the latter. If old verities were valid, then the only thing wrong was the failure of one's opponents to abide by them. Thus Carter's description of Democratic promises as "liberal" and "socially motivated" was an implied accusation that Republicans lacked generosity and social conscience. The charge nicely complemented his explicit suggestion that whatever Americans found wrong in Washington, they should "blame on" his incumbent opponent Gerald Ford. Ironically, four years later Carter's challenger and successor would turn the same trick on him.[3]

Although Baker's commentary skillfully spotlighted the devaluation of the liberal and conservative labels, it nonetheless lacked one crucial aspect: it ignored what became in the post-Eisenhower era the most powerful political label of all; namely, the anticommunist label. As early as 1949, poet Archibald MacLeish had warned of the consequences of defining American politics negatively, in opposition to Soviet actions. Postwar American foreign policy, he noted, had already become "a mirror image of Russian foreign policy." Whatever the Russians did, Americans did in reverse. By the same token, "American domestic politics were [being] conducted under a kind of upside-down Russian veto: no man could be elected to public office unless he was on record as detesting the Russians, and no proposal could be enacted . . . unless it could be demonstrated that the Russians wouldn't like it." Postwar America, MacLeish charged, "gave up its independent mind, contracted its national will to the dry negation of the will of others, and threw away the historic initiative which, in the lives of nations as in the lives of men, is the key to greatness." The result could only be a growing sense of unreality in America's image of

3. Carter's invitation to voters to blame Ford is quoted in George Brown Tindall, *America: A Narrative History* (New York: Norton, 1984), p. 1330.

itself. Having "been real to themselves because they were *for* something," Americans could not "continue to be real to themselves [should] they find they are merely *against* something."[4]

Barely a quarter of a century later, Baker had caught with unerring accuracy the growing unreality of the Rooseveltian vocabulary. Neither the term "liberal" nor the term "conservative" commanded general respect as a positive self-designation. But what Baker failed to make clear was the connection between America's negative, "anticommunist" self-image and the decline of the traditionally positive labels.

One of the chief "failed ideas" of the 1960s had been the very notion that America could use governmental generosity to buy insurance against "communism," "radicalism," and social upheaval at home and abroad. Both Kennedy and Johnson had sincerely espoused the word "liberal" as a positive self-designation; yet both had ultimately built their political and economic policies upon a negative, "anticommunist" presumption. As a candidate for the presidency, Kennedy could contrast the "negative challenge of Communism" with the positive challenge of America's "own ideals." Once in office, he found it increasingly difficult to distinguish between the two. From his insistence on defending "democratic liberal leaders" in Latin America against "Castroite influence" to his fear of international embarrassment over racial violence resulting from "civil rights" demonstrations, Kennedy always seemed preoccupied with a "cold war" policy context.

Similarly, when Johnson first announced his Great Society program in 1964, he did so without reference to the Russians; yet he, too, was ultimately unable to separate his own generous impulses from his fear of "communist" advance. Promising "both guns and butter" at home as well as abroad (a "TVA on the Mekong") was his way of fusing the two in the most positive way possible. Even so, as his own "anticommunist" presumption led him deeper into war, he slowly saw his policies, however sincerely couched in positive terms, becoming increasingly negative and defensive in practice. By 1967, American troops patrolled the streets of both Saigon and Detroit.

Meanwhile, self-styled conservatives fared no better. They were accustomed to trying to make "anticommunist" rhetoric work for them

4. MacLeish, "The Conquest of America, pp. 17–22.

politically, and many hoped the election of Richard Nixon in 1968 would at last usher in an era in which "genuine anticommunism" replaced "liberalism" as the mainspring of federal policy. By the mid-1970s, what Baker called the "philosophical vacuum" of "conservatism" reflected the confusions and frustrations of self-styled conservatives angered by Nixon's apparent capitulation to "the liberals."[5]

Although Baker's "definitions" neatly captured the intellectual *outcome* of these events, they did not explain the gradual, almost imperceptible *process* by which a positive vocabulary had come to symbolize a negative or confused outlook. Baker did not specifically explain the impact of "middle of the road" imagery and thinking on post-Eisenhower America.

By establishing his "middle of the road" framework in both domestic and foreign policy, Eisenhower had neatly defined his own approach as "antiextreme" and "safe," but had blunted public sensitivity to the potentially dangerous consequences of his policies, especially his "anticommunist" policies. The result was that his successors proceeded to build an ever more militant "anticommunist" policy framework, secure in the belief that their increasing militance was well within the bounds of a "middle of the road" approach. The most dramatic result of this approach was the Vietnam quagmire.

The war in Vietnam exposed and deepened the most fundamental contradictions in American life and thought. Precisely because the war evolved as a "middle of the road" or "moderate" approach to fighting "communism," it drew broad support from self-styled liberals and conservatives alike. And because it developed slowly and gradu-

5. Kennedy's comment on "democratic liberal leaders" in Latin America is in his news conference of April 12, 1961, *Public Papers of the Presidents of the United States: John F. Kennedy, 1961* (Washington: Government Printing Office, 1962), p. 259; for his attempt to call off a "civil rights" demonstration in Montgomery because of the "potential for embarrassment in Europe," see Herbert S. Parmet, *JFK: The Presidency of John F. Kennedy* (New York: Dial Press, 1983), p. 255. For Johnson's views on the Great Society program, see Lyndon B. Johnson, *The Vantage Point: Perspectives of the Presidency, 1963–1969* (New York: Popular Library, 1971), pp. 104, 326. The text of his University of Michigan Address, May 22, 1964, announcing the program, is in *Public Papers of the Presidents of the United States: Lyndon B. Johnson, 1963–1964* (Washington: Government Printing Office, 1965).

For attacks by self-styled "conservatives" on Nixon's adoption of "liberal" policies, see William F. Buckley, Jr., "Is Mr. Nixon One of Us?", *New York Times Magazine*, August 13, 1971, and *New York Times*, January 11, 1972. A critique written from a different perspective is William Shannon, "The Missing Conservative," *Newsweek*, June 4, 1973, p. 11.

ally, each "escalation" was accompanied by the most careful ideological justification. As a result, by the time the war had reached its truly massive proportions, its supporters were ideologically trapped, unable to see their way out or appreciate the vehemence of domestic antiwar protests.

To antiwar activists of the 1960s, the contradictions exposed by the war were inescapable. Coercion and confiscation at home were not producing freedom and generosity abroad. Nor was there a "middle of the road" or "moderate" way to die in battle. Yet even when the war became visibly unwinnable, and antiwar protests became too widespread to ignore or explain away, the same "middle of the road" thinking that had produced gradual escalation made anything other than gradual de-escalation impossible. Thus the process of extrication took as long as the process of entanglement.

Most important, because the war "wound down" on a gradual, "middle of the road" basis, there was no shock of defeat, no inescapable moment of truth. Americans did not experience anything comparable to what the Germans or the Japanese had experienced in 1945. Consequently the Vietnam War produced no stimulus to reassessment, no confrontation with the language that had been used to justify the war in the first place. All that emerged was a deep psychological need to put the war in the past and to reassert American power and self-respect by other means. The contradictions within the language remained unaddressed.

In particular, the end of the war brought no reassessment of anticommunist rhetoric. The anticommunist label itself incorporated a contradiction because it legitimized, in the name of "free enterprise," massive governmental control over America's own economy precisely to combat the "communist" enemy. The war had shown "anticommunism" to be a highly expensive proposition, and for this reason alone anticommunist rhetoric merited reassessment. Yet American self-respect had been defined for so long in terms of "standing up to the communists" that the legacy of frustration in Vietnam was a heightened preoccupation with "communism" elsewhere. Post-Vietnam military expenditures went up, not down.[6]

---

6. For a comment on Secretary of State Henry Kissinger's advice to the American people to "put Vietnam behind them," see Walter LaFeber, *America, Russia, and the Cold War* (New York: John Wiley, 1980), p. 288. For early post-Vietnam military

But retention of anticommunist rhetoric served another purpose—
the search for scapegoats. By legitimizing high levels of military expenditures, such rhetoric diverted growing taxpayer resentment away
from the military and toward social service programs, thereby making
the poor politically responsible for burgeoning inflation. Ironically, by
focusing on the poor as the supposed chief beneficiaries of government spending, postwar anticommunist rhetoric also helped reinforce
the equating of "liberalism" with governmental generosity just as
events of the preceding decade were calling that equation into
question.

While the post-Vietnam years were not marked by any return to the
language or tactics of the McCarthy era, the late 1970s did witness an
upsurge in the popularity and influence of several religious movements that seemed bent on a militant fusing of "anticommunism" and
Christianity. By 1980 these movements had gained considerable footing within the mass media. They accepted the traditional Rooseveltian
labels, identified as "conservatives," and eschewed "liberals." The
beneficiary of their political influence was Ronald Reagan.

If an ability to confuse scholars, journalists, and rival politicians
were a mark of greatness, Reagan would have to rank high in the
presidential pantheon. He was the logical outcome of the politics of
language: an actor who transformed his acting ability into political
reality. He spoke the words, he portrayed the character, he got the
part. In politics the only truly indispensable ingredient is the existence of the linguistic process itself, for the purpose of the process has
always been to confuse opponents. That Reagan so easily confused
critics and rivals indicated only that they failed to recognize or confront the process itself.

During the 1980 campaign and afterward, many observers such as
academics, professional political analysts, and Democratic party officials were at once baffled and angered that Reagan frequently quoted,
of all people, Franklin Roosevelt. The idea that a "conservative" like
Reagan should exploit the "liberal" Roosevelt "for conservative ends"
was anathema because the contrast between the two men could not
have been clearer. Most baffling of all was that Reagan's obvious
enthusiasm for Roosevelt undercut the charge of hypocrisy. As histo-

---

expenditures, see *New York Times*, January 4, 1976, sec. 3, p. 28, and January 24,
1978, p. 17.

rian William Leuchtenburg put it, Reagan's attempt to appear as a
"latter-day Franklin Roosevelt" was so "contrary . . . to reality that
one might register it as the greatest sleight-of-hand of modern American politics, save for one thing. No one believed it more sincerely than
Ronald Reagan."[7]

So long as one remained trapped in Roosevelt's vocabulary, Reagan's behavior was indeed baffling. But that was the whole point.
Reagan's references to Roosevelt were not designed to clarify but to
confuse. Like Carter in 1976, Reagan recognized the danger of undue
reliance on one label or image—hence his strategy of keeping people
guessing about his true beliefs while he concentrated his fire on Carter's shortcomings. Quoting Roosevelt was Reagan's way of sounding
as broadly ecumenical as possible even as he was launching his partisan attack on his opponent.

But Reagan also recognized what his critics missed. The public's
disinclination to confront difficult, basic questions about America's
role in a post-Vietnam world meant that in the immediate situation
style was far more important than substance. Americans craved reassurance and Roosevelt's image suited the situation perfectly. As another historian concluded after interviewing him, the new president
saw Roosevelt as "his 'kind of guy'—confident, cheerful, theatrical,
larger than life." Praising Roosevelt also gave Reagan a two-edged
sword. It allowed him to criticize "New Deal panaceas" even as he
was linking himself with Roosevelt as one who wished "not . . . to
destroy what is best in our system of humane, free government" but
"to save it." In an atmosphere of growing disillusionment with governmental generosity, Reagan's approach also had the effect of putting
critics on the defensive, forcing them to justify a definition of "liberalism" that had long since lost its lustre.[8]

There was yet another, even more important reason for Reagan's
use of Roosevelt, however. Keeping alive the debate about "liberalism" versus "conservatism" was a distraction that effectively diverted attention from the fact that Reagan's most important political label
was not "conservative" but "anticommunist."

Despite their historic and intellectual connection, the two labels

7. Leuchtenburg, *In the Shadow of FDR*, p. 232.
8. David McCullough, "The Legacy: The President They Can't Forget," *Parade*,
January 31, 1982, pp. 4–6; Leuchtenburg, *In the Shadow of FDR*, p. 230.

were not equivalent as political weapons. Although Baker had not spelled out their implicit common content, his "definition" of conservatism had correctly spotlighted the fact that by itself the conservative label stood for nothing. It symbolized no program of action, only opposition. Had Reagan relied solely or even primarily upon it, he would have been lost. Anticommunist rhetoric, in contrast, still pointed toward government action, and also scapegoated the Russians, the Democrats, and the poor while justifying the ever-expanding military expenditures that were the mainstay of every postwar administration's efforts to prevent economic collapse. By 1983, Reagan was talking of extending the arms race to outer space, in what commentators disbelievingly dubbed his "Star Wars" plan. Such talk was possible only in an atmosphere of carefully maintained fear of "the communists."

Still, because Reagan's "anticommunist" approach was so expensive and fraught with the potential for unprecedented military confrontation, the Reagan-Roosevelt sideshow remained an important diversion. By drawing the fire of academics and journalists alike it diverted attention from the more dangerous aspects of Reagan's "anticommunist" program and from what columnist Philip Geyelin called "the strong suspicion that Ronald Reagan has attracted to his strategic councils a collection of certifiable Dr. Strangeloves." Thus anticommunist rhetoric and the "liberal-conservative" debate neatly complemented each other by allowing Reagan to proceed while fundamental contradictions in American political language remained unaddressed.[9]

Again, there was irony in the situation. By keeping the debate over the Rooseveltian labels alive long after they had ceased to have an emotional impact on most voters, Reagan had actually provided critics with an important opportunity. As Baker's earlier commentary had suggested, the labels themselves retained currency only by default. What Reagan was now demonstrating was that in operative political terms, the "liberal-conservative" polarity might actually be in the

9. See Robert Scheer, *With Enough Shovels: Reagan, Bush, and Nuclear War* (New York: Vintage Books, 1983), pp. xix, 283–297. Geyelin's comment is included on the back cover. For Reagan's reliance on "anticommunist" rhetoric with respect to his Central American policy, see Luis Maira, "Reagan and Central America," in Martin Diskin, ed., *Trouble in Our Backyard: Central America and the United States in the Eighties* (New York: Pantheon Books, 1983), pp. 36–73, and Walter LaFeber, *Inevitable Revolutions* (New York: Norton, 1984), pp. 271–278. Also note Herblock's cartoon "Damn Russians," *Washington Post*, May 11, 1984.

process of being superseded by the "anticommunist" versus "communist" polarity.

In short, an important juncture in American politics was at hand. Without in any way intending to, Ronald Reagan had provided yet another opportunity for reconsidering the politics of language itself. Before critics could avail themselves of that opportunity, however, they would first have to transcend their custodianship of the Rooseveltian labels. As events of the post-Eisenhower era indicated, this would be no easy task.

Labels as barriers

Whether or not Americans will choose to be free is the transcendent political question. . . . If Americans choose freedom, there can be no totalitarian America, and without a totalitarian America, there can be no American empire.

This central question is not clarified, it is obscured, by our common political categories of left, right, and center. . . . The socialist radical, the corporatist conservative, and the welfare-state liberal are all equally capable of leading us forward into the totalized society.

Carl Oglesby, 1967

Hindsight has its uses. What is of far greater historical importance, however, is the challenge that is issued at the time, in the midst of momentous events. When Carl Oglesby, president of Students for a Democratic Society, questioned the utility of the "political categories of left, right, and center" for understanding America's predicament at the height of the Vietnam War, he was issuing a challenge fundamental to political reconstruction. He was asking critics and public alike to transcend the linear spectrum and its cognates, and thereby the contradictions and intellectual limitations inherent in those cognates.

As events indicated, however, the intellectual hold of the spectrum remained too strong, not only with the public but among the critics themselves. The very labels Oglesby identified remained barriers to communication among those who in many respects shared common fundamental insights into the "pathology of social institutions" in America. Like Truman in 1948, the administrations of the post-

Eisenhower era profited from and indeed survived politically because of a fragmented opposition.[10]

During the summer of 1964, while Lyndon Johnson was reaffirming his own definition of "liberalism" as government doing "a lot of things" for people, there appeared in an obscure journal called *Continuum* an article titled "The Transformation of the American Right." Its author, economist Murray Rothbard, had written several articles for Buckley's *National Review* in the 1950s but had eventually broken with Buckley over the latter's "anticommunist" crusading.

Rothbard's 1964 article was an account of how Roosevelt's prewar self-styled "liberal" opposition, which Rothbard dubbed "the old Right," had gradually been transformed during the postwar era into a militantly "anticommunist," self-styled "conservative" opposition, which Rothbard called "the new Right." The "prevailing trend, certainly among the intellectuals of the old Right," wrote Rothbard, "was a principled and trenchant opposition to war and to its concomitant destruction of life and liberty and of all human values." Slowly but steadily, "old right" leaders had either died out or been co-opted, at least in part, into a worldwide "anticommunist" crusade. By the mid-1950s, the "new right," no longer based on the "libertarian" values of the "old right" but on the "authoritarian" ones of the state itself, had almost entirely taken over the leadership of the American "right wing."[11]

For a small but active group of academic writers, Rothbard's article quickly became a milestone in critical analysis. His portrayal of such "old right" figures as Taft, Nebraska congressman Howard Buffett, and journalist Frank Chodorov struck a responsive chord with them. Of equal importance were his categories of antiwar "old right" versus prowar "new right" which appealed to critics who opposed war yet could not identify with the labels "left" or "socialist." At the same time, the Rothbard article was an invitation to self-styled "new left" critics to reach across the intellectual barriers of the linear spectrum and join hands in a broadly based antiwar movement. Shortly after the appearance of the *Continuum* article, Rothbard joined with historian Leonard Liggio and H. George Resch in founding a new journal titled

10. Carl Oglesby and Richard Shaull, *Containment and Change* (New York: Macmillan, 1967), pp. 163–164.

11. Murray Rothbard, "The Transformation of the American Right" *Continuum* 2 (Summer 1964):221.

Left and Right: A Journal of Libertarian Thought. Early issues of the journal concentrated on such themes as the relationship between the "old right" and "new left" as well as the political and intellectual shortcomings of the "new right."[12]

As the war in Vietnam continued to escalate, an alliance began to develop between self-styled "old right" and "new left" supporters. In an article titled "Left and Right Meet," published in 1966 (of all places) in Herbert Croly's old journal, *New Republic*, historian Ronald Hamowy welcomed the "New Left" as an "emotional heir" to the "intellectual background of the American Right." Praising the antiwar stance of the "New Left," Hamowy also noted with approval its growing skepticism regarding governmental generosity. "The New Left," he wrote, "is beginning to realize . . . that increasing the power of government rarely operates to the benefit of the poor, who are ritualistically invoked to justify government action." In reality, he noted, government intervention benefited "the plutocrats (capitalists who use the government rather than the market to attain their ends), trade union officials and other dignitaries . . . who know how to apply leverage on the sources of power."

Hard on the heels of Hamowy's analysis came Oglesby's article in 1967 which was the first attempt to transcend the labels themselves. Linking the contemporary "Negro freedom movement" with the "student movement against Great Society-Free World imperialism," Oglesby wrote: "That these movements are called leftist means nothing. They are of the grain of American humanist individualism and voluntaristic associational action; and it is only through them that the libertarian tradition is activated and kept alive. In a strong sense, the Old Right and the New Left are morally and politically coordinate." At the same time, Oglesby added a prophetic caution. The "intersection" of "Old Right" and "New Left," he warned, could be missed. "Their potentially redemptive union can go unattempted and unmade. On both sides, vision can be cut off by habituated responses to passé labels."[13]

Oglesby's warning proved prescient. Despite a common revulsion to the war, the two groups did not coalesce. Although a tactical intel-

12. See *Left and Right*, Winter 1966:3–7, 8–13, 19–35; Spring 1966:39–57; and Spring-Summer 1967:22–42.

13. Ronald Hamowy, "Left and Right Meet," *New Republic*, March 12, 1966, pp. 15–16; Oglesby and Shaull, *Containment and Change*, pp. 166–167.

lectual alliance continued to develop, it did not eventuate in a unified ideological analysis of American society. When the war finally ended, there remained a still fragmented opposition. Most important, there was no challenge to the politics of language or its implications.

There were many reasons for this outcome. One was the continuing attractiveness of governmental action to many self-styled "new left" adherents. Like certain of their critical counterparts in an earlier era, they continued to believe that government could solve "the enigma of the world" if only the coercive machinery were put in the "right" hands; that is, the "left" hands. As Hamowy put it, there were still many in the "new left" who remained susceptible to the "State-oriented ideology of the Liberal Establishment," and he cited the supporters of John Kenneth Galbraith's concept of "a wicked, egoistic 'private' sector *vs.* a virtuous, altruistic, but impoverished 'public' sector." What these "young radicals" overlooked was that the "private sector" was "precisely the area of relative individual self-determination and autonomy and of voluntary interaction among people" while the "public sector" was actually "the sector of force or the threat of force, ultimately exercised, behind whatever high cause is invoked, by the government's bureaucracy and, in the last analysis, by its police." Hamowy's comments were apt. Even as self-styled "new left" adherents continued to document the links between government and corporate power, even as they angrily rejected what they called "corporate liberalism," they retained faith in the coercive machinery of the state itself.

The result was a movement that did not explore "the potentialities of free enterprise and free markets for the realization of their voluntarist aims" but instead remained limited by its own "left" label and "socialist" rhetoric. Thus most self-styled "new left" critics never got past calling for a vague and ill-defined "socialism," a call that completely glossed over the paramount problems of coercion and confiscation. Such a call could hardly be expected to allay the traditional fears of "socialism" and "communism" that had produced public support for the Vietnam War in the first place. Within a few years of the war's end the "new left" had passed into history, whereas public susceptibility to anticommunist rhetoric remained as strong as ever.[14]

Self-styled "old right" critics meanwhile carried a double burden,

14. Hamowy, "Left and Right Meet," *New Republic*, March 12, 1966, p. 16.

one part of which consisted of having to confront the same public fear of "communism" that had so weakened the "new left." Although their "old right" label protected them from being "red-baited," or accused of "procommunist" sympathies, it did not protect them from a revived denigrative usage of the old "isolationist" label. In the 1960s, the term "neo-isolationist" became an effective pejorative in the hands of pro-war groups anxious to undercut the impact of the "old right" critique. The second part of the burden consisted of having to confront the fear, shared by the "new left" critics and public alike, that without strong government the entire economy would collapse. Like their prewar forerunners, the "old right" critics of the 1960s faced the fear that in the absence of a powerful "public sector" either unchecked corporate power, depression, or both would result. The ghost of Herbert Hoover or, more precisely, of Roosevelt's image of Hoover, hovered over them.

Briefly stated, the self-styled "old right" critics did not succeed in discharging either burden. No more than their self-styled "new left" counterparts were they able to lay to rest the anticommunist rhetoric on which American foreign policy still depended. Nor were they able, despite the declining public respect for the notion of governmental generosity, to persuade many people that there was a viable, "libertarian" alternative. Just as the term "new left" lost currency within a short time after the war ended, so did the term "old right." Scholars in both groups continued to produce carefully documented historical critiques, but their impact on contemporary policy making remained slight.[15]

The failure of the self-styled "new left" and "old right" critics alike to press home their respective viewpoints reflected their common failure to heed Oglesby's warning. Despite their tactical antiwar alliance, they themselves remained trapped in their own labels; they remained "left" and "right" in their own minds. They did not develop a unified ideological perspective or engage the American public in a

15. For a brief and unsuccessful attempt by Walter Lippmann to turn the term "neo-isolationist" into a positive self-designation, see Ronald Steel, *Walter Lippmann and the American Century* (Boston: Little, Brown, 1980), p. 586. A party calling itself the Libertarian party did manage to poll some 920,000 votes in the 1980 presidential election, but this was only 1.1 percent of the total, or less than one-sixth the number of votes polled by Independent candidate John Anderson. See Mary Beth Norton et al., *A People and a Nation* (Boston: Houghton, Mifflin, 1982), p. A–21.

reconsideration of how the labels were being used politically. This was because they themselves did not analyze either their own vocabulary or that of the government and its supporters. In short, they allowed the labels to remain conceptual barriers and political weapons.

Some "old right" critics did give the matter of labels some consideration. In a moving obituary for Frank Chodorov in December 1966, Rothbard noted that even at the height of the McCarthy-era hysteria, Chodorov had done his best to "stem the . . . rush of the right-wing to adopt the label of 'conservative.'"

Frank knew his intellectual history; he was and always would be an "individualist," and he recognized "conservatism" to be the embodiment of the creed of the ancient Statist enemy. Writing to protest the designation of himself as a "conservative" in the pages of *National Review*, Frank retorted: "anyone who calls me a conservative gets a punch in the nose." His *cri de coeur*, alas, went unheeded; and a lot of deserving folk remain unpunched to this day.

Recognizing the fight that Taft and others had made during the prewar era to prevent Roosevelt from appropriating the liberal label, Rothbard also attempted to revive that earlier struggle. In an article published in 1968 titled "Confessions of a Right-Wing Liberal," he stated his own claim to the label and pointed out the incongruity of the American labeling system itself. Twenty years ago he had been "an extreme right-wing Republican" who believed that "Senator Taft had sold out to the socialists." Today he was "most likely to be called an extreme leftist, since I favor immediate withdrawal from Vietnam, denounce U.S. imperialism, advocate Black Power and have just joined the new Peace and Freedom Party." And yet, Rothbard wrote, "my basic political views have not changed by a single iota in these two decades!"

Perceptive as Rothbard's comments were, he nonetheless fell into the same trap as his prewar predecessors. Reclaiming the individualist and liberal labels was still an exercise in counter-reification and linguistic competition. By the late 1960s such an approach stood even less chance of success than in the 1920s and 1930s: it was simply impossible to rescue the old labels. Although Rothbard had accurately noted the incongruity of his being relabeled from "right" to "left," he did not carry through his own de-reification of the linear spectrum, and failed to address the problem of how the labels themselves were being used for political purposes.[16]

Even so, Rothbard's reference to "black power" spotlighted yet another issue that "new left" and "old right" critics alike had neglected. In the 1950s, Dr. King and others had developed nonviolence as a form of direct political action that could not be subsumed under ordinary categories. Throughout the late 1950s and early 1960s, nonviolence and the demand for countervailing federal power had developed conjointly. By the mid-1960s, the limits of governmental intervention had become clear. The slogan "black power" was a reassertion of independent black political action, but as Rothbard's comment indicated, "black power" was in fact being labeled "left," even "radical" and "violent."

This labeling of black political action was both a danger and an opportunity. The danger was that many blacks, particularly among the young, were becoming impatient with nonviolent civil disobedience and opting for a slogan that made them vulnerable to being labeled and treated as "illegitimate." The opportunity was that the phrase "black power" itself challenged "sincere whites," in the words of Malcolm X, to "go and teach nonviolence to white people."[17]

Few whites took up the challenge, however. Neither "new left" nor "old right" critiques of the war had resulted in any organized, mass civil disobedience comparable to what blacks had organized to fight segregation laws. Draft resistance remained sporadic and isolated and was thus easily labeled "left." Hastily passed federal laws outlawing "advocacy" or "counseling" of draft resistance succeeded in intimidating critics and preventing the emergence of a mass nonviolent movement among the white majority. The result was that not only did the war drag on far longer than it otherwise would have, but the transformation of a predominantly black phenomenon into a generalized form of political action was left "unattempted and unmade," although it was

16. *Left and Right*, Winter 1967 p. 5; Murray Rothbard, "Confessions of a Right-Wing Liberal" *Ramparts*, August 15, 1968, pp. 48–52.

17. See editorial, "The Cry for Power: Black, White, and 'Polish'" *Left and Right*, Autumn 1966, pp. 11–14; and Malcolm X, *The Autobiography of Malcolm X* (New York: Ballantine Books, 1973), p. 377. For Dr. King's fear that even his own Southern Christian Leadership Conference might be labeled "left," see King to Jack H. O'Dell, July 3, 1963, in "Martin Luther King File," Box 8, Burke Marshall Manuscripts, John F. Kennedy Library, Boston, Mass.

the one form of mass action that might have forced a reconsideration of traditional categories of political thought.

The failures of the critics of the 1960s to reexamine either the traditional vocabulary or the broader possibilities of nonviolent direct action were mutually reinforcing. The retention of the traditional labels allowed blacks themselves to be labeled and thereby isolated. Left to themselves, blacks understandably hesitated to extend nonviolent civil disobedience to the war, even though blacks were being drafted in disproportionate numbers. Adopting civil disobedience in opposition to state-level segregation laws, where the federal government was bound to support them, was one thing; turning the same tactic against the federal government itself was quite another.

As nonviolent direct action faded away in the face of war, black political action became increasingly traditional. By the time the war ended, blacks had become in essence one more "pressure group" seeking governmental generosity through "affirmative action," and the stimulus that mass nonviolent direct action among whites might have given to a reconsideration of traditional political categories was lost. By the mid-1980s, nonviolence as a form of political action lay dormant, and a reconsideration of traditional American "modes of thinking" was no closer.

Starting at the verbal end

> One ought to recognize that the present political chaos is connected with the decay of language, and that one can very probably bring about some improvement by starting at the verbal end. Political language—and with variations this is true of all political parties, from Conservatives to Anarchists—is designed to make lies sound truthful and murder respectable, and to give an appearance of solidity to pure wind.
>
> George Orwell, 1946

There is a story that when Tolstoy and his brother were children, they formed a club. To qualify for membership, one had to be able to stand in a corner and not think of a white bear. By the mid-1980s, to ask Americans to conceptualize politics without relying on the linear spectrum or any of its cognates was much like asking them not to think of a white bear. Yet there was a difference. To start "at the verbal end," in Orwell's phrase, did not mean banishing the linear spectrum from one's mind, but rather transforming that spectrum and its cognate labels from *analytical* categories into *political* data and reexamining the *political* role such vocabulary had played in the evolution of American politics. In short, it meant moving from custodianship to the critical analysis of language. [18]

One could say many things about the evolution of American political vocabulary from the 1880s to the 1980s. To begin with, the progression from the individualist label to the anticommunist label represented an unmistakable progression from positive to negative self-definition. To adopt a negative label as one's primary self-identification was to define oneself in opposition to somebody else's idea. Defining oneself in opposition to an idea was not merely a negative act but, in MacLeish's words, "a declaration of political bankruptcy."[19]

In addition, all of the major American self-identifying labels from individualist to conservative to progressive to liberal to anticommunist had evolved so as to camouflage contradictions: nature versus artifice; tradition versus innovation; forward movement versus stability; coercion versus freedom as well as confiscation versus generosity; and finally, free market economics versus ever-growing governmental control. Indeed, the progression of labels itself showed a distinct pattern. As the rhetoric became more antigovernment, the policies became more controlling. Massive governmental interference in the name of anticommunism was the ultimate contradiction in a supposed "free enterprise" system. If Ronald Reagan was the logical outcome of the politics of language, so was his anticommunist label—the ultimately contradictory politician wedded to the ultimately contradictory label.

Reagan, to be sure, did not stand alone: the system had produced him; he was the culmination of a century of linguistic and political evolution. And that was the point. If Reagan could only be understood in terms of the evolution of American political vocabulary, that vocabulary would provide clues on how to deal with him.

In this as in other things, Reagan himself provided the opportunity. Baffled though reporters had been by his constant quoting of Roose-

18. George Orwell, "Politics and the English Language," in Carlyle King, ed., *A Book of Essays* (Toronto: Macmillan, 1973), p. 98.
19. MacLeish, "The Conquest of America," p. 21.

velt, they figured out within a few months of his inauguration that, as Leuchtenburg put it, "whenever Reagan cited FDR, an action contrary to the spirit of the New Deal was sure to ensue." Inadvertently as usual, Reagan himself had sensitized political analysts to the process of contradiction and opened the door to a critical analysis of language.[20]

The task was not to turn the analysis on one man, but rather to focus it on the political arena as a whole. Unless the very process of camouflaging contradiction was itself confronted and exposed, it would only be a matter of time until someone else not only succeeded Reagan but perhaps even replaced the anticommunist label itself with a new political term that stretched the boundaries of contradiction ever further. In short, a general process of reconstruction was in order.

Reagan himself provided the starting point. As his military expenditures mounted ever higher and the national debt passed the one-trillion-dollar mark, he announced that government was "not the solution but the problem." Cutting down the power of government was indeed the task, but one had to look very carefully at Reagan's own approach to it.

Here the key label, espoused by Reagan as by his immediate predecessor, was "deregulation." The term had emerged in the late 1970s partly as a demand for increased industrial "efficiency" and partly from a growing public understanding that what was called governmental "regulation" of corporate power often functioned as a means of protecting or promoting that same power. Americans of the late 1970s were beginning to learn the verbal lessons of the pre–World War I era. The term "deregulation" reflected not merely a demand for efficiency but also a genuine grass-roots demand for a weakening of the ties between government and corporate power.

The lessons of the earlier period required careful study, however. If they showed that what was labeled "regulation" often functioned as a form of "promotion," they also showed that these two supposedly distinct phenomena were indeed linked in a complex web of legislation that included both restrictions and subsidies. To remove the restrictions without also removing the subsidies would not necessarily encourage competition in the long run. On the contrary, such one-sided action might become a way of unleashing the strongest. Under

20. Leuchtenburg, *In the Shadow of FDR*, p. 231.

the circumstances, to accept the term "deregulation" uncritically was to set up the possibility of another camouflaging of contradiction, hence another transformation of mass arousal into mass quiescence.[21]

Again, the point was not simply to focus on specific examples but to analyze the politics of language itself and act on that analysis. By the mid-1980s, it was clear that Hamlin Garland's insight really had been a "once and future" insight. Americans wanted "less protection of the rapacious demands of the few, and more freedom of action on the part of the many." In order to restore that freedom of action an ongoing process had to be set in motion which would involve several things: institutionalizing de-reification, or studying the political vocabulary of both the past and present to recognize specific contradictions and their political consequences; exposing those contradictions and organizing to act on such exposure; and finally, avoiding the trap of counter-reification and competition over labels. In short, the process involved recognizing, confronting, and transcending the politics of language.

As a first step, Americans faced the task of freeing themselves from the emotional bondage that had allowed their current self-identifying label its political power. This meant relieving themselves of the burden of negative self-definition that had led to organizing their society and their lives around the fear of someone else's idea. Common sense, and even the most casual look at the state of the world in the mid-1980s, would be an ally in this task. During his 1984 reelection campaign, one of Reagan's most effective television commercials began with the ominous words, "There's a bear walking the forest. . . ." In actuality, if the Russians could not even control Afghanistan, it was hardly likely that they could run the world. In the closing decade and a half of the century, there was no longer any excuse for mortgaging the American future to anticommunist rhetoric.

De-reifying the anticommunist label did not mean "isolating" America economically or politically; nor did it mean total or unilateral disarmament. It did mean recognizing and giving up what Flynn had called "the need for enemies," and creating instead what he had called

21. Ibid., p. 231. For varying approaches to "deregulation," see David P. Calleo, *The Imperious Economy* (Cambridge: Harvard University Press, 1982), pp. 186–190; Roger G. Noll and Bruce M. Owen, *The Political Economy of Deregulation: Interest Groups in the Regulatory Process* (Washington: American Enterprise Institute for Public Policy Research, 1983); and John R. Meyer and Clinton V. Oster, Jr., *Deregulation and the New Airline Entrepreneurs* (Cambridge: M.I.T. Press, 1984).

"an economic equivalent for armaments." Most important, it meant recognizing the need for what MacLeish had called "affirmative re-commitment," specifically commitment to build a public political con-sciousness that transcended superficial, government induced arousal and quiescence.[22]

As America moved beyond Orwell's apocalyptic year and into its third century of constitutional government, all signs seemed to point toward starting at the verbal end.

22. MacLeish, "The Conquest of America", p. 22.

Index

Library of Congress Cataloging-in-Publication Data

Green, David, 1942–
    [Shaping political consciousness]
    The language of politics in America : shaping political consciousness
from McKinley to Reagan / David Green.
        p.   cm.
    Originally published: Shaping political consciousness. Ithaca, N.Y. :
Cornell University Press. 1987. With a new preface.
    Includes bibliographical references and index.
    ISBN 0-8014-8054-X (pbk.)
    1. Political oratory—United States. 2. English language—Political
aspects—United States. 3. United States—Politics and government. 4.
Politicians—United States—Language. I. Title.
PN4193.P6G67   1992
815'.0109358—dc20   91-46982